PRISON POST
from Lock-up to Lock-down
A Sentence
in Letters

TOM THORESBY

DEDICATION

For my dearest, long-suffering wife Sara and son 'Harry' who gave me the best possible reasons to survive. And for the many kind and concerned family and friends (especially John and Maggie, to whom these letters were addressed) who visited, sent cards and books and so regularly wrote to me.

Finally, a word of appreciation for all my former 'prison mates'. If you recognise yourselves in these pages, I hope you will not take offence. You were amongst the most original, entertaining and warm-hearted people I have ever known and your wit, wisdom and good cheer helped keep a smile on my face. We may never meet again, but good luck to you all, wherever you are now!

CONTENTS

FOREWORD
Into the Inferno - A Divine Comedy

For the best part of seventy years, I gave prisons very little thought. I watched the occasional 'fly on the wall' television documentary filmed in some Dickensian 'nick', and shuddered. British prisons were, it seemed, a cause of national shame. They were overcrowded and rat-infested, characterised by drug-fuelled violence and intimidation. And starved of cash, compounded by out-of-date thinking and often ineffectual management. Staff were leaving in droves. How could anyone survive in such places, least of all someone like me?

Then the unthinkable happened. I found myself standing trial for alleged crimes of which I was entirely innocent. Despite inconsistent and wholly uncorroborated 'evidence', I was convicted by the majority verdicts of a perverse jury. Had they even been listening? Almost everyone in court gasped in astonished incomprehension at such a blatant and gross miscarriage of justice. I was in total shock. I could hardly believe my ears as the foreman read out guilty verdicts on all charges. I looked round at my wife. That bottle of champagne she had hidden in her bag to celebrate my acquittal would have to wait for a future occasion. A month later, I returned to court to be sentenced to spend something over two years 'inside' – if I managed to survive that long!

I arrived in prison in a blizzard, the start of the 'beast from the east' of 2018. In that respect, things could only get better. And they did, slowly. Within days, letters and cards started to arrive from family, friends and neighbours, even a tongue-in-cheek 'Welcome to your New Home' card from my big brother. Once I was able to make telephone calls I spoke every day to my wife and weekly to my son who visited as often as they could, often bringing along friends and supporters. I felt buoyed up by their love and support and, with no Internet access, began a handwritten correspondence with so many people that by the time of my release I had received (and also written) over 700 letters. John and Maggie, friends since university days and both now retired lawyers, wrote weekly and, unbidden by me, kept all 64 of the fortnightly letters I wrote to them that now appear in this book. In them I record the downs and ups of prison life, with all its strange routines and often bizarre incidents, and describe the idiosyncrasies of some of my new associates.

Everyone's experience of prison is different and I soon discovered that prison life for most people, most of the time, is far more nuanced and even bearable than its grim portrayal in the media might suggest. Yes, loss of liberty and separation from home and family are acutely painful. The prison system is out of date, under enormous pressures politically and financially, and often incompetently managed. There were times when I felt miserable and angry, such as when a governor turned away my 99-year old father-in-law from a visit because his name was not on the list, an administrative error entirely the prison's fault, as the Governor later begrudgingly admitted. I never saw him again as he died the following year, shortly before my release. But I never felt intimidated, threatened or in danger. I found most fellow prisoners (and officers too) to be supportive, often kind and likeable characters with more than their fair allocation of odd-balls and eccentrics. I shared many times of companionship and comedy with my 'prison mates' who were some of the most entertaining and interesting people I have ever met.

The letters that follow are lightly edited versions of the original correspondence though I have changed most names to protect identities and spare some blushes. I wrote the first forty letters under the restrictive regime of a 'B-Category local' prison; the remainder from the freer environment of a D-Category 'open' prison – which became markedly less free and open with the creeping imposition of Covid restrictions in 2020.

SECTION ONE
A Divine Comedy – *Purgatorio*

---

1. Wednesday 28 February 2018

Dear John and Maggie,

Wednesday 28 February 2018

What a day to begin a prison sentence! Prison vans are laughably known as 'sweatboxes' to their passengers, as I now know. But it would be hard to think of a more inappropriate name when whatever minimal heating they possess is rendered totally powerless by the Arctic blasts of the 'Beast from the East'. Iceboxes would be more accurate. I did not enjoy a comfy ride here.

You've probably seen these boxy Serco vans, white with blacked-out windows. Inside they are divided into several little cells about the size of airline lavatory cubicles (a similar smell too) and with the doors firmly bolted, but only from the outside, of course. Each compartment contains nothing but a single rigid plastic seat with a vertical back, as uncomfortable as a Victorian posture chair, and little knee room even for a shortish convict like myself. No seat belts. The window was deeply tinted and the decoration confined to the solitary word "WANKERS" scratched at eye level across the partition. Lest any of us should try to break free, the ensemble was supervised by a plump and unsmiling female officer seated at a little desk behind the driver's cabin, equipped with telephone, control panel with an array of coloured lights and no doubt alarms to trigger in the event of a holdup or breakout. The long-forecast heavy snow arrived soon after we set off at about 5.30 pm, and by the time we had turned off the dual carriageway a full blizzard was blowing outside, snow ploughs and gritters were at work, lights flashing like a macabre funfair, and ridges of compacted snow were beginning to build at the roadside.

Many thanks for your 'good luck' card which arrived at home on my final morning of freedom – I shall need it. Sara will have told

3

you of my fate. 28 months! Not as bad as it might have been, but worse than we had all hoped. Poor Sara, and Harry who had travelled up from London for the day, looked mightily dispirited. Stephen (who managed to appear remarkably crestfallen for a barrister – or is this just part of the act?) feels that an appeal against the verdict and sentence would be pointless unless new evidence comes to light, so I must anticipate 869 days inside…. The first few will be the worst, he said, so I must just bite the bullet stoically and hope it will get better.

On arrival at HMP, we were handcuffed, name-checked and led across to Reception to be 'processed' in a number of stages. Mercifully I was spared a strip search and was handed a bundle of prison clothing to change into – everything except the socks and pants I came in with was exchanged for regulation sky-blue prison T-shirt, fleece top and pocketless 'joggers' in sad shades of grey (well-worn, slightly frayed but not uncomfortable). My own clothes (e.g. court suit) were consigned to my 'prop box' to await release in 2020. Lest you are wondering, the T-shirt is not patterned with arrow symbols like the ones they sell at Primark. Next I was mouth-swabbed (for DNA), finger-printed and photographed next to a measuring rod for a hastily laminated ID card that I must always carry with me. In my non-existent pockets? No, tucked into a sock! The card bears my (grim) photo, name and new prison number that will from now on be my principal identifier, engraved in my brain if not on my arm and to be quoted on all correspondence (see header).

From there I was seen by the prison (male) nurse, mainly on account of the month's supply of pills I'd brought in. All of these were confiscated to be issued morning or night as required, subject to the decision of the yet-to-be-seen prison doctor. I'd more or less given up last night when someone came and poked a Zopiclone through a sort of screw-out peephole in the cell door. Later on I had a really bad acid attack and had to make myself sick to stop it (pretty effective treatment). Unfortunately the pill probably went away with the rest, though I did manage about six hours sleep, better than I feared.

Back to the next stage of my 'processing' by two other guys who went through all my belongings. Just my rotten luck to have followed the online list to the letter, only to be told that many of the recommended items are not allowed in this 'nick'. Some, perhaps most, of my clothing may be returned to me after 14 days but the bad news is that I can't keep the radio. Only radios purchased through the prison catalogue are allowed. And no headphones (said to be a 'must' in the online info.) Nor was I allowed to keep my washbag, so no face flannel, hairbrush, razor or electric beard trimmer. Not my sheets or towels or even my cosy new dressing gown (after all that effort to get a warm one from M&S!) The strangest and saddest prohibition is that I have not been allowed to keep my photos of Harry, not even the most recent, as both the officers said they thought he looked under 18. I explained that he's my son, 26, music producer in London, gave his birthday, etc., but nothing would sway them. Don't tell Harry who would be mortified. As am I. I should realise from my court experience that I am now trapped in a parallel universe where nothing I say is to be believed. My word is my bondage.

Then followed a long series of rather hostile questions, like the interrogation on arrival at an American airport but even more intrusive. Had I ever been a drug dealer? Did I have any drugs about my person? (In this context, 'person' is a euphemism for bum!) Was I ever involved in sex work? (In my case it would not have been a profitable career option!) Had I been a victim of domestic violence? Did I hold racist or homophobic views? Had I been 'radicalised'?! (I didn't confess my membership of the Labour Party in the 1970s. It wasn't the moment). Was I or had I ever been a member of a gang? Thinking it over later, I may have concealed a guilty secret here. At school, aged about ten, I was briefly a member of Grogan's Gang. Grogan was a farmer's son and a bully who did unspeakable things to frogs, so I got out asap and found kinder friends instead, though to this day I can never look a frog in the eye without thinking of him. I believe Grogan went on be a major in the army. Pity the poor frogs! Other questions on the checklist followed a no doubt familiar litany of box-ticking – disabilities, mental health issues, sexuality, learning difficulties, allergies or food intolerances and so forth. For religion I suggested Anglican, adding 'communicant' for emphasis. 'That's not on the list,' objected the officer, looking puzzled. 'C of E?' I suggested.

'Fine. That's what most of 'em say.' He gave the box a reassuring tick. It is good to know that I will have something in common with my new companions!

And so, eventually, I was brought here to C Wing, which is reserved for VPs (Vulnerable Prisoners), a category which apparently covers a multitude of sinners from police informants to sex offenders (known hereabouts as 'nonces' – acronym for Not On Normal Courtyard Exercise) and almost anyone over the age of fifty or so. By now it was about 9.30pm and the landings were in near darkness and eerily silent apart from the muffled crackles and booms from a hundred television sets behind cell doors. I was very insistent about wanting to be alone, but single cells are few in number and much in demand. Eventually I was allocated this empty double with single occupancy (for now, as explained above). I am on the topmost of three landings, cell number 24 – C3-24 for short. Before he left, the accompanying officer pointed to a button on the wall next to the light switch. 'That,' he said, 'is the emergency bell. It is **NOT EVER** to be used except in a **GENUINE** emergency. Ringing the bell unnecessarily is a punishable offence.' With which he waltzed out of the cell, clanging the heavy metal door firmly behind him, then, for an encore, flipping open a little external flap to peer at me briefly through a narrow glazed slit. I expected to be 'banged-up', but not to become the object of a peep show.

My residence here may only last for a day or two until the upper bunk is needed for some other hapless new arrival. An officer in Reception said that I was entitled to an initial 'phone call home on my first night, but for some unexplained reason this was denied and I was then told that I could call Sara early this morning instead. It hasn't happened yet, so I wait in hope. The good news is that I'm allowed a 'reception visit' from S, bookable online or via a telephone booking line. I have been warned that rules are not always followed and may change on a whim or at a moment's notice.

As I write, it is now 10.30 am and a note from Duty Governor Edwards has just been poked under the door. 'Due to today's severe weather conditions there will be a <u>limited regime</u>. The main priorities are your food and medication... I apologise for any inconvenience caused.' I guess the heavy snow has prevented some staff getting in. This probably means that the next stage of my induction will be postponed. I'm feeling reasonably stable and otherwise OK, but hope they will bring the rest of my pills before long.

The biggest issue I have so far (and not HMP's fault) is with the as yet unseen bloke in the next cell who had his TV on loud until the early hours last night and switched it on again at 5am this morning. The walls must be very thin as the sound carries. My foam earplugs were in the disallowed wash bag, so I tried to improvise with moistened prison-issue toilet paper. It didn't work well, so I have only had one short doze since then. Loo paper, of which there's an abundant supply, has proved more effective at limiting the draughts coming in from the iron-barred windows. Heat in the cell comes from a wide diameter pipe running round the end wall. It is fighting a losing battle against the draughts coming through the windows from the arctic conditions outside. I have squeezed and poked loo paper into the gaps but water from the melting snow outside bubbles up and blows in, dribbling across the sill and down onto the hot pipe below where it fizzes like spit on an iron before running across the floor to disappear under the bed.

The bunk bed is made of cream-painted tubular steel, like an old-fashioned hospital bed but bolted tightly to the wall and floor. I guess beds are knocked up by inmates at some other 'nick' using ¾ inch iron water pipes and plumbers' fittings. With only sheets, a couple of loosely woven orange cellular blankets looking like giant waffles and a stained bottle-green bed cover, I had to sleep fully clothed last night. Even then, I was not warm enough. Nor was there a pillow, though I was able to stuff surplus clothing into the long thin pillowcase I had been given. No doubt in due course I will discover a technique for making up the bed. I always find it a chore but it is doubly so with an immoveable bed frame plus livid green sheets ripped at the edges and barely wide enough to tuck in. Needless to say, the mattress is firm and thin, a couple of inches at the edges but dented to almost zero in the middle. I can feel the ridges of the iron straps of the bed base in the small of my back. The mattress is made of foam rubber encased in slippery blue vinyl and resembles an Indian train mattress, but unrelieved by that gentle jolting motion and clackety-clack of the rails to ease one into sleep with the promise of adventure ahead. Amazingly I didn't get painful legs, as I usually do on hard beds, and felt quite snug thanks to a man-shaped dip in the middle. Victorian workhouse beds, constructed to a similar pattern, don't seem so punitive after all.

My cell is approx. 10' x 8' and, in addition to the bunk bed has a wash basin, and WC which would be discreetly curtained except that most of the curtain hooks are broken. There's an open shelf unit with a Formica top for a small kettle and in-cell rations (tea, coffee, mini carton of milk, breakfast cereal, etc.) but no chair or table. So I'm writing this sitting on my lower bunk. There's also a wall cupboard with a small TV with clear plastic case on the shelf. So last night I was able to watch another documentary about the Queen, just imagining I was cuddled up on our big sofa with S, my queen... The window looks out across a wide-open area towards the original 1880s prison block. Now, of course, all is entombed in deep snow and as I write two blokes are leaning into the blizzard attempting to shovel and sweep a pathway through the snow. I wonder how S is coping at home and if she's been able to visit her father? I fear that if/when I get to make that promised 2-minute initial 'phone call I will merely hear the answer phone and lose the chance to speak. It may be a few days before the process is cleared for me to make regular out-going calls. I think they have to check out the numbers by calling them to verify the identity of those I want to call. I can understand why, but it will be a pain if every time they call home they hear my voice on the recorded message!

One little thing I already miss is a clock, despite its being on the 'recommended' list. Apparently, like radios, they are only allowed here if bought through the prison. I queried the reason for this and was told that I might be able to use it as bomb-making equipment. I can see their point, of course. Had I been radicalised, I might have bartered it with some would-be ISIS sympathiser. So my little red clock is left ticking to its lonely self somewhere in the bowels of the prison stores. Will the batteries will last another 869 days?

I'd better stop here in case there's a chance to post this at lunchtime, whenever that may be. I have not been given a timetable

8

or even the most basic information about the whos, whats, whys and wherefores of prison life. But I am coping, just.

Much love,

Tom

2. Thursday 1 March, 2018

Oh misery! The arctic blizzard still blows relentlessly outside, where the view is a study in grey and white, of wired-off yards that in normal life could almost be tennis courts but here are separated by razor wire. Beyond them are the fortress-like structures of the old Victorian prison with its rows of tiny windows and heavy slate roof topped by massive long-cold 'Tudorbethan' chimneys. The wind has not abated but seems to have grown even stronger this afternoon, wolf-whistling at me through gaps round my rusting window frame. I take some comfort from the thought that the weather, at least, can only get better! As for everything else, I must wait and see.

So many staff are off that we were all locked in our cells yesterday, only let out briefly to collect food. Another letter came under the door this morning, this time from Governor Jeeves (very Wodehousian) saying 'Thank you all for your patience today. We will attempt to offer a <u>limited regime</u> tomorrow dependent on weather conditions. I apologise… etc. etc.' Since I still don't know what an <u>un</u>limited one would be like, I am little the wiser. I trust it will be based on liberal values of compassion and respect. I'm guessing that staffing levels are reduced because of the weather and we inmates are consequently locked up all day rather than… whatever. It begins to feel like solitary confinement, which is not entirely unwelcome as I need some space to collect my thoughts and readjust to this strange environment. I just wish the guy in the next cell didn't have his TV blaring out all day long.

Unfortunately, my 'meds' (usual prison term) failed to arrive yesterday. Instead, the nurse came to my cell at 10pm, unscrewed the emergency hosepipe hole in the door and fed through it a single Zopiclone wrapped in a twist of paper. Am I too dangerous for normal civilities? Today I feel more optimistic as a duty officer tells me that I will be able to collect a whole month's supply later this afternoon. Not only that buy, for the first time, I have experienced genuine concern, even kindness. But I really am feeling the effects of having my regular anti-depressants suddenly stopped and have been quite shaky. With luck it will soon be sorted and I'm looking forward to a better night's sleep.

This will depend on my neighbour's TV – he had it on loud all last night. Since 5 am I've heard everything from an OU programme on cathedral organs (!) to kids' cartoons and, currently, 'property porn'. Perhaps I should have raised this issue when I spoke to the officer, but it seems too early in my detention to start complaining. I don't want to earn a reputation as a troublemaker. Others, however, have complained to the staff and, very vocally, to the man concerned. I can't repeat what was being said lest it attracts the censor's ire, but you can imagine. Not content with blasting the wing with his top-volume TV, my neighbour contrived this morning to flood his cell until water ran out onto the landing and dripped onto the floor beneath. An officer appeared, turned off the water supply (there's a stop tap for every cell so I guess this may be a common occurrence) and remonstrated with the occupant mocking him and calling him every sort of name. A little group of braying onlookers gathered round, cheering on the young officer then shrinking back as the man appeared in his doorway. He was utterly dishevelled, filthy, smelly and wild-eyed and clearly had no business being locked up here when he should be in a secure psychiatric unit. He was handed a bucket and mop before the door was banged shut again. Compassion may be in short supply here.

Cells were unlocked for a couple of hours this morning so I got to raise various issues with staff and have been given my PIN number which I must enter in order to use a telephone (there are two on each landing serving about fifty men each). But not anytime soon! Apparently 'PIN Services' must check all the telephone numbers I applied for, which may take several days, before I can be issued with a PIN to allow any calls at all. Why didn't they say? I'm just a clueless ingénue in this strange world. Oh Kafka, how your spirit lives on! I wonder if S has been able to book my initial 'reception visit' yet? There is some urgency about this as it must be booked within the first seven days. There seems to be a rule or a protocol about everything and the devil is in the detail. Also, I was not on the list for lunch today, ending up with a belated offering of four cold sausages and a penguin biscuit (appropriate for the Arctic conditions outside my window). This diet may help me lose an inch or two round the middle if it continues for my remaining 866 days 'inside'. Of more concern just now is the lack of medication as my pills have yet again failed to arrive. Anyway, I had a word with the amiable officer who eventually let me out to collect my sausages, and he assured me that the nurse will come round to see me later. He also took my first letters to post. What a good job they allowed me to keep the stationery and stamps I brought in.

Things are looking up – I had a brief visit this morning from the Anglican chaplain, a jovial black guy who looks like a younger version of our friend Jackson. He will book me in to attend chapel on Sunday, though I suspect the form of service will be at the 'low' end of the ecclesiastical spectrum. I may also give Bible Study (Mondays, 1.45 – 4 pm) a go. All major faiths are catered for, so I could possibly try the Hindu, Sikh or Buddhist (meditation) sessions too. There is a Pagan service on Tuesdays, which intrigues me. No, I think I'll stick to C of E for now. During today's 'association' time out of cells, I had a long and helpful chat with another chapel-goer of the 'born again' variety who was a little pushy, but genuinely kind, which I appreciated.

I have been looking at the photos I was allowed to keep, e.g. me with S in front of the Taj Mahal, and my big picture of the watermill with daffodils and willows appropriately weeping. These two I have stuck on the cell pin board in the recommended fashion using prison-issue toothpaste – I wasn't allowed to keep the tube I came in with lest I had impregnated it with illegal substances. Prison toothpaste comes in plain white tubes and in consistency and colour resembles ready-mix Polyfilla, so maybe it's good for cavities too. It certainly works as an adhesive, but I wonder what it will do to my poor old teeth? I have still not been able to telephone S or H, which is very frustrating (and contrary to regulations). Apparently some prisons have in-cell phones (but not cell-phones, which are strictly banned). If only! I hope she is coping, and that her Dad has not been too upset by my surprise conviction and imprisonment. He's 98 and not in the best of health so I fear I may never see him again. That is very hard.

P.S. Soon after lunch my neighbour was taken away, protesting, by a couple of officers. I hope he gets the help he so clearly needs, but at least I should have an undisturbed night.

3. Saturday 10 March, 2018

Thank you so much for your letters. They certainly help cheer me up! Bizarrely, I was handed ten letters yesterday evening, five from Sara and five from others. There seems to be no accounting for how long mail takes in either direction, though it seems to be least a couple of days before outgoing letters reach the GPO. As you probably realise, we have to hand mail in open so that everything can be checked before letters are sealed for posting. Likewise, all incoming mail is opened (and may be read), for obvious reasons. But what a tedious job for some underling in the prison post room; I just hope he/she gets a kick out of being privy to so many men's secrets! Sara must have told you my prison number which should appear with my name on the envelope; look carefully and you will see that I also have to write it at the top of outgoing letters and under the envelope flap. In these parts I am known mainly by my number! On a positive note, I finally got to speak to Sara and Harry mid-week when a compassionate lady officer telephoned them from the office and handed me the phone for a short chat. Just yesterday, armed with my 8-digit PIN number and some credit, I was at last able to call them myself from the landing pay phone. Good things come to those who wait!

After ten days I am only just beginning to learn my way round the system. At first no one seemed able or willing to communicate much apart from a degree of sympathy coupled with surprise at this being my 'first time inside' despite my visibly advanced stage of life. At 68 I am not the oldest lag on the wing (see below), but the average age must be forty-ish and the youngest inmates are still in their late teens (18+) and known as "Yos" (Young Offenders, mostly on remand). On day two, when let out to collect my lunch, I tentatively approached an officer saying, 'May I ask you a question?' 'Yes,' he said, 'As long as you don't expect an answer.'

And reply came there none! Fellow-prisoners are generally more forthcoming, but when I ask the same question of two people I often get three different replies; some exaggerate the awfulness of life as if to scare the crap out of me, others make light of the ordeals ahead. So it's like normal life, really. I must keep reminding myself that while my body is captive, my mind remains free.

On day three the Induction Orderly – a presentable young man of about thirty called Darren with finger nails so hard bitten they have all but disappeared – invited me into his cell. I perched on his bed a little nervously at first, but soon decided that he was a good egg, and safe. His cell, unlike mine, is almost obsessively tidy with an air of ordered domesticity including a faux-oriental rug on the floor and a pair of bedroom slippers neatly toed under the desk. I counted 21 pink bottles of Vosene shampoo lined up on his shelf in three rows of seven. He's demonstrably an orderly Orderly. Darren rattled through a long tick list of rules and procedures covering everything from mental health to money, telephone usage (if lucky) and laundry arrangements (somewhat hit and miss). And haircutting. Darren is the wing barber, a service paid for in Vosene, available, he explained, on the canteen sheet at £1 a throw. (I shall soon be in need of his professional ministrations.) There was so much to digest that I wished I had taken along a note pad and pen, not least because it might have shown Darren that I can, in fact, both read and write. He was most insistent that I should not be embarrassed to say if I need help with English or Maths as Level 1 courses are from time to time offered in both. I politely declined. I still know my times tables (to 12, not 10 as nowadays!) though my recollections of algebra and geometry (or 'gum tree' as we called it) are decidedly vague. Darren tells me there is a charity-run scheme providing help with basic literacy and also a 'Listener' scheme organised by the Samaritans with prisoners trained to support any fellow inmates who may be distressed or suicidal. I came away feeling reassured, if confused by so much information, but clutching a blotchily-printed Welcome Pack. I forgot to ask Darren if he charges extra for a beard trim.

Truly, for the first time in my adult life, I see some benefit from my boarding school education. What an excellent preparation for life behind bars! It's odd being back in an almost all-male environment

– almost because about half the officers are women. Most inmates address them as 'Miss', primary school style, but to me this sounds rather demeaning. I guess it's a generational hang-up on my part. Even the food is reminiscent of 1960s school refectory fare, though prison meals win by a morsel, mainly because there is some element of choice via a weekly advance menu sheet. I'm not sure how they manage to feed us on the government allocation of £1.85 per head per day. However, porridge does not feature in 'Porridge', if you see what I mean. 'Rice Krispy' would be nearer the mark. Breakfast comes in small goody bags, handed out with the previous night's meal, and consists of a little bag of cereal (usually Corn Flakes or Rice Krispies), a carton of milk, tea bags and paper fingers of sugar. This week I have been able to order (and pay over the odds for) a jar of coffee to provide some variety. 'Regulation' tea is of the dark and dusty brown variety swept up from the floors of Indian tea factories. Its taste tends to hang around like herpes, and I fear how it may stain my stomach lining. Prisoners who are truly desperate for a fag (smoking was finally banned here as recently as January this year) are said to smoke roll-ups made from tea bags, though I'm not sure how they get a light. Vaping is popular, but expensive.

Arriving here at the start of the 'big freeze' was not a good strategy. For most of last week the prison was in virtual lockdown with so many staff unable (or unwilling) to report for work that 'normal regime' was suspended. Initially I was locked in a double cell on the top landing (known as 'the threes') and for a couple of days it was almost like solitary confinement, just let out to collect food, take it back to the cell, then 'banged up' again. It wasn't as bad as you may think; it gave me some thinking time to come to terms with my predicament and my stark new surroundings. But it was a pretty Spartan existence up there, not only very cold but lacking in basic amenities such as the chair, desk and window blinds that Darren the Orderly said should be part of standard equipment. Oh dear!

Thanks again for writing so soon!

4. Thursday 15 March 2018

Good news at last. On Friday evening, I was given five minutes to throw my meagre possessions into a bin bag and escorted down to the ground floor (known as 'the ones') to a shared cell. It's a better environment down here and at least it gets me away from the guy in the next cell up top who kept his TV on loud all day and most of the night too. Down here my cellmate is a tall eighty-year old West Indian guy originally from St Lucia called Mr Samuel Samuel (true!). Sam (or Sam-Sam?) is the polar opposite of me in just about every respect, but he is considerate, genuinely friendly, and doesn't want to watch TV beyond about 9pm (when he takes out his teeth and puts in his ear plugs). So we get on just fine, not least because he's been in prison long enough (18 months) to know the system and is pretty reassuring about most issues. But he is turning out to be very garrulous and sometimes I crave a little P & Q. With his Thatcherite and pro-Brexit views we don't exactly see eye-to-eye on many things. I'm surprised the Tories won't accede to EU/human rights requests for UK prisoners to be given the vote as they would have a clear majority here. On the plus side, Sam and I manage to share some laughs – a very necessary tonic – and we both have a healthy disillusionment with the workings of the English judicial system born of bitter experience. His is one long horror story.

Sharing a room with a complete stranger is a new experience. Wish me luck!

It was such a treat to receive a bundle of letters yesterday that I began to feel just a little connected with the outside world. More arrived this morning including the inevitable one saying that my state pension has been stopped and I must reapply when I'm released (July 2020). Apparently, once all my details have been processed, I will get a retirement allowance of about £8 per week from my pension to add to the weekly 'spends' I can draw down from my 'private account' – i.e. the £100 cash I brought in with me. I'm just starting to get my head round the 'canteen' system whereby I can spend a certain amount each week on items from a tick list. This includes snacks, drinks (but no G & T), toiletries, stationery etc. and even such necessaries as rosary beads or white Muslim robes. All, or most, religious persuasions are catered for, even Paganism (note capital P) led by the female Pagan chaplain. I've filled in forms for C of E services and Buddhist meditation.

My cell faces NNE, so I won't be seeing much sunshine. However, now the snow has cleared it reveals a patch of grass outside the window with a couple of stumpy palm-like trees. It resembles the set of *Waiting for Godot*, and is equally grim. Despite, or perhaps because of, my daily requests, it has not yet proved possible to find me a prison-issue fleece coat. (Darren tells me there is a room full of them upstairs, but maybe they have lost the key.) So I have only been outside for one very chilly exercise session looking like a bag lady padded up with layer upon layer of insulating fleeces and jerseys (I haven't yet been issued with a coat). Exercise = tramping anti-clockwise round a tarmac yard, just like in old movies or Van Gogh's famously depressing painting of prisoners exercising in, I think, Newgate Prison. I could, of course, sign up for twice-weekly gym sessions. Can you imagine that? No, I can't either. I'm sure the gym instructor is a thoroughly nice guy, but one look at his tight-hitched shorts, rippling biceps and unnaturally tanned legs (and Acme Thunderer patent whistle on a lanyard round his neck) brought me out a cold sweat reminiscent of school PE. Thank God for music lessons! I wasn't much cop at the piano, but arranging lessons to coincide with PE kept me safely out of the gym for years. For sanity, I'm attempting to read Yuval Harari's *Homo Deus*. It's brilliant, witty but too intense for prison reading. I find concentration so hard as Sam (who is 'functionally illiterate') wants to watch telly all day long and I daren't deprive him of his one form of solace. He does keep the volume down for me, despite his creeping deafness in both ears.

Sorry about the handwriting. We have just one chair and a narrow desk space shared between us. I started off at the desk this morning, but now it's Sam's turn so I'm squatting on my (top) bunk with the writing pad balanced on my knee.

5. Tuesday 20 March, 2018

Many thanks for your second letter and also for keeping in touch with Sara by email. It is comforting to know that you care. So many people have sent letters and cards that I have been very busy with 'snail mail' replies. How I miss my computer! Sara and Harry have now both mastered the prison email system that turns round a message and reply within 3 – 4 days. They have both sent photo attachments, though the printout comes in fifty shades of grainy grey so needs interpreting with some imagination.

I hope that you received my first reply without too long a delay. Don't expect nuggets of exciting news – one day here merges into the next slowly, very slowly (yawn...). However, since my last letter Sara has been in for a visit and our previous vicar also came for a 'pastoral visit' for which we were allocated a (very cold and bare) room upstairs in the Visitor Centre. This Saturday, all being well (I'm learning never to count on anything until it happens) Sara and Harry are both coming. I hope it won't be too daunting an experience for Harry, who seems to have taken everything in his stride so far. He now has an agent who is finding him plenty of work, and he's also busy setting up a new studio (shared with a musician friend) in Hackney. So I don't think he has the time, let alone the inclination, to sit around fretting about his poor old Dad! But I know how angry he felt about the wholly unexpected outcome of the trial. Paul recommended that I should read Trollope during my incarceration so Sara is looking out a copy of *Barchester Towers* to bring in for me. This is not as straightforward a process as you might imagine. To obtain the necessary authorisation, I must submit a formal application (an 'App') in triplicate (white top copy plus carbons in yellow and pink). I was warned that Apps are quite routinely ignored, but also that some prisoners submit Apps almost daily with completely trivial requests 'just to keep the officers on their toes', so perhaps I was lucky my request for a Trollope (so to speak) did, in fact, elicit a response. Which was that it will be 'at the discretion of Visitor Centre staff on the day' whether or not I am allowed to receive said book – so I hope they are 'discreet'.

I am now officially what Victorians called a 'devil dodger' having registered myself (by App, as above) for Buddhist as well as C of E ministrations. Strictly speaking this is contrary to regulations that lay down that prisoners may only be of one faith at a time and must submit an official 'Change of Religion' form before they can attend other denominations. If challenged, my argument will be that one may attend Buddhist *meditation* (as I have often done 'on the out', as they say) without actually formally *becoming* a Buddhist. The Buddhist chaplain has an unpronounceable name that I cannot quite remember but is otherwise called Rupert, which probably was (or is) his name for official purposes. He visited me today, having received my App, and I greatly liked him. We will start weekly meditation sessions when he returns from retreat at the end of the month.

The Anglican chaplain, who is Nigerian with an unpronounceable name, presumed Evangelical, visited me soon after my arrival and told me I would be 'on the list' for Sunday services. Since then he and his ministrations have proved rather elusive. Three Sundays have now passed and I have yet to be called. The first week I just let it go (I was still in a haze); the second week I protested and was told in future to listen out around 10 am and then press the (emergency) cell bell button if nobody came to unlock me. Last Sunday I did as told. Eventually an officer did show up and asked me, through the crack in the door frame, what the matter was. By this time the (noisy) chapel party had long since gone, but I was treated instead to a lecture on why I should *never*, ever press the bell unless there was a genuine and dire emergency e.g. fire, flood, heart attack, assault or attempted suicide by cellmate. I have now submitted yet another App. I wondered about approaching the Catholics, if only to discover how they come to have a *female* chaplain.

Last Sunday, to compensate for missing chapel, I watched *Songs of Praise*, now broadcast around lunchtime (choice of roast pork or chicken followed by gloopy rice pudding) and definitely not the programme it once was. I remember the rigorous rehearsals when it was broadcast from our church. I enjoyed singing along with the hymns in the cell, of which Sam, my cellmate, was tolerant but utterly bemused by my blatant eccentricity. He knew some of the tunes but his minimal reading skills could not keep pace with the rolling subtext so he was unable to participate. Still, it helped redress the balance for all the horse racing and motor sports I have been obliged to watch with him. Sharing at such close quarters with someone so different takes some adjusting to and I often crave a little silence. But on balance, it's better to have company when the days drag so slowly, though the 'old lags' assure me 2020 will come soon enough – they envy me my 'short' sentence!

A letter has arrived from the Governor (or 'a governor' – there seem to be lots of them though I've yet to clap eyes on a single one – 'governing' is an office-bound job, it seems) saying that I will be moved to a 'C-cat' prison (lower security) elsewhere in due course. I had always imagined, in my ignorance of penal procedures, that prisoners were sent to a convenient 'nick', ideally near their home and family, where they stayed until their release however many years hence. Not a bit of it! General practice seems to be to move people on at frequent intervals. Sam, who has been 'inside' less than two years, has already been HM's guest at four prisons – Bedford, Peterborough, Isle of Wight and now here – and expects another call at any moment. (Also, for no good reason, he is optimistic of being released early. I fully expect he will have to slog out his term, if he lives that long. He will be well into his nineties.) When I get moved to a 'C-cat', the regime will, from what old lags tell me, be much more relaxed than here ('B-cat Local'). But I am anxious about the impact on Sara if it is much further from home, especially as she is currently spending so much time caring for her father (who is now 98). With luck I may get a day's notice of the move, but it may be only 15 minutes, the statutory minimum, just long enough to throw my few possessions into bin bags for the journey. Watch this space!

Tomorrow, being Sunday, may be chapel – or may not, depending on whether the chaplain has got round to adding my name to the list. I'll report back next time. There are just a few signs of religious observance here on the wing such as a mark on the ceiling outside the food servery showing the direction of Mecca for our Muslim brethren. Not a proper Mihrab, just a painted arrow. One or two rather unlikely characters sport strings of tawdry plastic rosary beads round their necks. These are available for purchase via the canteen sheet and make a cheap substitute for a necklace but rarely serve any devotional purpose.

The weather is now more clement and regular outdoor exercise periods have been reinstated. It may be no more than shambling round a tarmac yard surrounded by high fences topped with razor wire, but it is liberating to move the muscles and feel a ray or two of sunlight on the face. On Wednesday I had a health check with the nurse practitioner who has prescribed Vitamin D supplements.

6. Saturday 24 March

I'm writing this sitting on my top bunk with *You've Been Framed* (rather apt, in a legal context!) playing in the background. I know, it's an awful trial, but I'm learning to shut it out. I'm not sure how those in 'solitary' coped with the silence and isolation of prison life in generations past, but it is an option Sam is unwilling to explore. Anyway, we survive, and have not come to blows, yet. (Were we to do so, I would almost certainly come off worse. For all his nearly eighty years of age, Sam is not only healthy but physically fit, as he demonstrates with press-ups on the cell floor and his attendance at the voluntary twice-weekly gym sessions where he works out on the running machine.)

It is very kind of you to send s.a.e. It's really not necessary, but if you'd like to enclose just a few surplus stamps at some point I won't object. Sara set me up with several books of stamps when I came in. Mercifully I was allowed to keep them, and am still working steadily through them.

Great joy today!

1) A selection of my own clothes was returned to me from the stores – including my new and super-snug M & S dressing gown, navy blue with white piping. It is of the traditional hoodless design (quite hard to find these days) as hooded ones are banned. So much for Cameron's 'hug a hoodie'! I also now have two pairs of my own jeans, but no belt. An officer tells me this may be because the buckle is too big. I'm looking into that one but meanwhile have borrowed a yard's length of string from the guy next door. I'm not sure why I wasn't allowed to keep these items on arrival, which would have been much simpler, unless they needed to de-louse them and check for big buckles and other illegal substances. Sensibly, my suit (sober navy blue for court appearances, though in the circumstances a hoodie might have helped win over the jury) was not delivered. This reminds me that when playwright William Douglas-Home was sent to prison his older brother (and later PM) Alec advised him to pack his dinner jacket as 'surely you will be invited to dinner with the Governor'. I have still not glimpsed the elusive Governor here, let alone been invited to dinner. However,

it feels truly liberating to be able to bag up most of my prison-issue clothes and shove them out of sight and mind amongst the fluff balls and dust under the bed. Anyway, the grey 'trackie bottoms' were way too loose round the waist. Though I've put on an inch or so since I've been here, there is still some way to go before I get an authentic prisoners' paunch, which appears to be a badge of honour amongst over-fifties, and many younger inmates too. Also, the legs were at least six inches too long so I had to stuff them into my socks, along with my ID card (kept there for want of pockets). I used to give talks about workhouses and described the indignity of wearing the workhouse uniform... well, you can complete the sentence...

2) S and Harry came in together for a visit. Seeing H was a real tonic. He made it here from London in the nick (unintended pun!) of time and took the entry process with its searches and sniffer dogs completely in his stride. He said that he was relieved to find me so chatty, so I hope I'm not picking up bad habits from Sam. Sam's unending monologues are very wearing at times, not least because he has a loud voice (he is quite deaf) and talks such nonsense most of the time. "It's a funny old world," as he so often says. S, now on her second visit, is finding visits quite daunting, not just all the waiting around and intrusive entry procedures but also the public forum of the busy Visitor Centre. Once in, it's not so bad. They have done their best to make the surroundings bright and cheery with comfortable seating, though we aren't allowed to sit together but must face each other across a heavy low table. Discreet holding of hands and kisses of greeting are allowed as long as not too protracted. Strictly no fond fumbles!

Our former vicar has also visited, but for this we were allocated a private room upstairs. He has since written to say that when leaving he found himself trapped in a stair well where he was let in at the upper level, the door locked behind, but no-one appeared to unlock the door at the bottom. Only after ten minutes vigorous banging on doors (something agitated inmates are also prone to!) did another officer come to release him, begrudgingly and without apology. Perhaps he mistook the clerical collar for a cunning disguise?

3) We won the Boat Race! I watched Oxford's trouncing on our little TV with Sam who had never seen it before and couldn't understand what all the fuss was about. Glad as I am to see Oxford lose by three lengths, I will try not to gloat too fulsomely when I write to my bro – I don't want him to stop writing as his letters are so funny, though he does ask an awful lot of questions. I guess prisons have the fascination of the unknown for most people (lucky them).

Yes, Sara brought *Barchester Towers* on her visit and showed it (as instructed) to the officer on duty who immediately confiscated it – only temporarily, I hope, while they check it for subversive content. She's coming again in ten days' time and expects to visit at least twice a month for as long as I'm here. Sara, bless her, even wrote to the elusive Governor to ask for me to be moved somewhere near home as, with such a huge commitment to caring for her Dad, she would find it almost impossible to go much further afield. He did reply, non-committedly.

Now the weather is milder, regular outdoor exercise periods have been restored. Sharing a 10ft x 8ft cell c. 21 hours a day can become claustrophobic, so the daily forty minutes or so of fresh air and exercise are very much needed. At least, I find it so, though there are some who never venture out. Also, while in the exercise yard yesterday, I spotted a new arrival who looked lost and scared and stood apart from the rest and we enjoyed the first intelligent conversation since I came here. Sorry, I know that sounds snotty, it's just that I haven't yet found any other 'kindred spirits'. J is our age, worked for a mental health charity and faces the triple blows of incarceration, divorce and loss of home, so has huge anxieties about his future. He is, like a couple of our local friends, a Quaker. A Friend indeed! We vigorously chatted away while ambling round the perimeter of the yard, so engrossed that the high fence and razor wire (not to mention a couple of bored-looking officers on supervision duty) seemed to melt from view.

I am now grappling with the 'canteen' system. This has nothing to do with meals (which are pre-selected from a separate weekly menu sheet) but is the HM Prisons-wide procedure for purchasing from a list the little extras that make life bearable. Money for purchases is taken from my 'spends account' which may be topped up by 1) earnings from prison work (which I do not do, see below); 2) an 'in-cell allowance' of about £8 per week, notionally funded from my (now suspended) state pension; and 3) drawn down from my 'private account'. The latter is the £100 cash I brought in on arrival or, in future, money that S will send in. There is no millionaires' row here as amounts are drawn down automatically (subject to availability) and restricted to £15.50 per week for a standard-level prisoner. However, for the first few weeks I am on 'Basic' (£10.50) and if I'm a good boy I may ultimately be 'Enhanced' and able to draw £25.50 per week. Simple, eh?

Top of my weekly canteen shopping list come telephone credits. Prison telephones are outrageously expensive to use, a frequent cause of complaint, though we are assured that the service is provided 'at cost'. So much for HMPS's declared intention to encourage prisoners to maintain contact with their families! (My cellmate calls his son every Saturday after the football results. It is his only, and precious, contact with the outside world.) Be that as it may, I now spend an average of £8 per week on telephone credits which funds no more that a daily call to Sara and once a week to Harry. The remaining credit is displayed on the phone and drops so rapidly that I have taken to listing in advance topics to discuss and my habitually circumlocutionary forms of speech have become decidedly terse. The phones are very public with much noise from the servery queue and the table tennis table plus a degree of general noisy 'arsing around' in the background. We must enter an 8-digit PIN to get connected and all calls may be monitored (not just those by prisoners with 'harassment issues'). Also, they are time-limited to a few minutes per call, and can only be made during brief intervals around meal times and during the evening 'association' time when cells are unlocked. There is often a queue by the payphones, but we are lucky to have three phones on this landing as against two on the others. Just one of the reasons I am very glad now to be located on the ground floor rather than the landings above.

Life has improved in a few other small ways as I have been able to use my 'spends' allowance to purchase non-essential but desirable extras. Sam tells me to keep a careful record of canteen expenditure as otherwise 'the bastards' are sure to cheat me. I still cling to a naïve belief in human goodness, even of prison officers, but will take his advice re. accounts. My initial purchases have been confined to essentials such as a proper toothbrush. The free issue one was shedding all its bristles in the gaps between my teeth. Prison razors in cheery orange and white are issued free but, like our plastic cutlery, are blunt by design and easily broken, better at scouring chins than actually chopping off bristles. So I have invested in a six-pack of disposables (£1) to banish my hirsute appearance, and a tiny toenail clipper (£1.01). This is too blunt to cut anything, least of all fingernails, and was probably chosen as harmless enough to sell to potentially dangerous prisoners. I have also bought cod liver oil tablets, sweeteners and coffee (very expensive at £2.49, but necessary as only tea is issued free, and not much of that), washing-up liquid, soap box and Vosene shampoo (for myself and to pay the barber). Also a writing pad and envelopes, BIC pen, orange squash and a McVitie's ginger cake for a treat. You get the drift. I'm now saving up for a big splurge at the end of the month by when I hope to have accumulated enough 'spends' to buy a real pillow (£9.99 – fireproof) and pillowcase (£2.99). Prison pillows/headrests are firm sausages of some black rubbery substance covered in the same tacky blue vinyl as the mattresses. They are horrible and about as useless at inducing sleep as a pair of old boots or one of those wooden neck props provided for Tutankhamun's afterlife.

S has been telling me about our garden as it begins to emerge from the recent winter battering. Yet another task she must take on for the duration. Here, there are gardens and even greenhouses – I spotted a tub of pink camellias as I walked to the exercise yard recently. They were in a sheltered spot in the lee of a greenhouse, but even so were hanging their heads dolefully, just like us prisoners in fact! Near the Visitor Centre a few daffodils are bursting into bloom. I so wanted to crouch down and sniff them – or, even better, pick some for the cell! – but I was (maybe unduly) sensitive about being labelled a 'wuss', so desisted. Imprisonment, in theory, is defined as deprivation of liberty, but of course it's much more than that. Is this Magdalene Man becoming a maudlin man? No matter. I'm trying to remain positive, and largely succeeding.

Tomorrow, being Sunday, may at last be chapel – or may not, depending on whether the chaplain has finally added my name to the list. Is God listening? I came across a quip by the Cato Conspirators, 'May God, if he exists, save my soul, if I have one.' I'm beginning to wonder. One of the most fervent chapel attendees is working hard to save my soul during my period of involuntary exclusion from worship. He sends me little scribbled notes with suggested Bible readings, like those listed in the front of the dusty Gideons Bibles once found in bedside cabinets of cheap hotels. So born-again is this kind gentleman that he has recently changed his surname to something more descriptive of his fundamentalist faith, so I shall refer to him henceforth as Mr Fundament (not his real or even his assumed name, of course).

7. Easter Saturday 30 March, 2018

Many thanks for your letters and Easter wishes. You are such true friends – not something I ever doubted – and am most touched by the regularity of your communications. My mail, in both directions, must be keeping the prison post room busy not least because (so I am told) they are obliged to keep a record of all correspondence. Today I received five letters and a couple of emails prompting the landing officer who delivered them to ask if it is my birthday. That, of course, is next month, the same date as Tony Blair's!

In answer to your concerns about my comfort, yes, my little cell is reasonably warm now the 'big freeze' has passed, and not just from all the hot air expelled by my cellmate Sam. A six-inch diameter pipe runs along the wall under the window and provides background heat which is quite adequate now that I have installed improvised draught excluder (loo paper) round the opening windows. The pipe is also ideal for drying hand-washed socks and 'smalls'. (Larger items such as prison-issue shirts and sheets are exchanged weekly and disappear into a communal wash.) The heating has been turned off twice so far on mild days, only to be restored as soon as the weather deteriorated again. I definitely feel the cold much more than most Brits and often wonder if I was an Indian in a previous incarnation. If so, it could explain why I always feel so very much at home in that beloved land! In here it's a macho-image status thing to wear as little as decency allows, even out of doors, not that I would ever feel pressured into following suit. The string singlet, that most hideous and embarrassing of garments (male equivalent of fishnet tights?), seems to be making a comeback. I find I need a woollen jersey when Sam, despite his West Indian origins, makes do with a cotton vest. I go out for exercise whenever I deem it warm enough and crave the touch of sun on my face, not least because a clutch of tests of blood (routinely extracted from all new prisoners) reveal a Vitamin D deficiency for which I now take supplements. Comparing notes, I find that almost everyone here over a certain age takes Vit. D pills.

I have now had a significant haircut that makes my laminated prison ID card image look positively hippie by comparison. The wing barber, as previously described, doubles as Darren the Induction Orderly whose other name, serendipitously, just happens to be Trimmer. Mercifully he bears little obvious resemblance to Sweeney Todd – who would probably not have been placed on C Wing – and in any case scissors and cut-throat razors are, like all sharp implements, banned. (Prison plastic cutlery knives are blunt by design so it's just as well we don't get steaks for dinner.) The only sharp(ish) items are tiny Chinese-made nail clippers that break on first use. The entire haircutting operation is therefore performed with an electric clipper, much as I experienced years ago in the seedy salons of Dar es Salaam. I've never understood numerical barbering so took Darren's advice and opted for a number 8 on top and a 5 down the sides, despite which I now look like a real convict – seriously shorn, though not quite as severe as numbers 1 or 2. I am reminded of Harry Stubbs, the lovely old shepherd on Hawerby Home Farm in the fifties. Harry used his sheep shears to barber the farm workers and their families (my occasional childhood playmates), though I think he used graded pudding basins rather than clippers to demarcate the numbers.

<u>Note to self</u>: I must order an electric hair trimmer of my own. I can't keep troubling Darren at £1 a throw. I'm told trimmers are obtainable via a catalogue zealously guarded by the Argos orderly. This may take some serious saving but is an essential bit of kit if I am to stop my beard bushing out and my moustache becoming a food trap or harbour for meldrops.

Now for the good news, or should that be 'Good News'? Which is that I finally made it to chapel in the nick of time for Holy Week and Easter! (The chaplain explained that I had been overlooked on previous Sundays as my name had been 'wrongly assigned to the bottom of the list', a lame excuse if ever there was one.) The prison regime has bowed to the customs of our once-Christian country and I received the Calling to attend on Palm Sunday and again for Good Friday and (I trust) Easter Sunday. The route from C-Wing to Chapel involves an obstacle course of no fewer than twelve doors (fourteen from the upper landings) to be unlocked and relocked with much key clanking as we pass through, accompanied by a couple of reluctant officers. (All officers have heavy rings with multiple keys of different weights, sizes and shapes and chained to their belts.) First the cell door, of course, then a gate and door to get from the wing to an assembly area known as 'the bubble' followed by a further three to reach the outside. There are two gates to pass through a high-fenced yard, then a further two to get into the back of the original Victorian cell block (now disused), plus gates at the foot and top of the stairs to reach the old first landing, and finally the appropriately arched oak doorway into the chapel itself.

My first impressions of the chapel are positive. It's a rather austere bare redbrick structure with rounded windows, a genuflexion perhaps towards the Norman origins of its predecessor, Norwich Castle. It seems to have been tacked as an afterthought onto one side of the original Victorian prison wing. But efforts have been made to humanise it with carpeted floor, colourfully padded individual seats and a kitchen, lavatory and chaplains' office constructed internally at the back. It has an air of breezy non-conformity about it. There are tables with a range of free-to-take Bibles and reading materials e.g. *The Universe*, *Watchtower* (for JWs) and *C of E Newspaper* (that's the Evangelical one), a sort of discussion area with low seats, coffee tables and TV screen, and a rather handsome electronic organ with two manuals, lots of stops and pedals. This, though, remains silent as there is no-one to play it and anyway the chaplain has forgotten where the key is kept, so singing is accompanied (?) by a sort of juke box sound system featuring pre-recorded hymns and songs from *Mission Praise*. It's all slightly incongruous.

It is, of course, an inter-denominational space, so as well as standard C or E style altar table, lectern, paschal candle, etc. there are small modern carved wood Stations of the Cross, crucifix and red sanctuary lamp (electric) for the Catholics. The most striking items are a pair of elaborate castellated brass candlesticks plus altar cross, all set with (apparently) semi-precious stones. They are grand enough to have been designed for the Palace of Westminster by Pugin himself, and I am surprised that no inmate with a taste for High Victorian Gothic has so far legged it with them in a (large) swag bag. I must admit, it's tempting. During the week I met the 'managing chaplain' who is an Orthodox priest, though I'm not sure whether of the Greek, Russian (or Coptic) variety, and his surname contains no clues. He is also an organist – but chooses not to play for services here – and tells me that he once gave a recital at my old school (but was very scathing about the organ!) He has kindly arranged another pastoral visit from our former vicar – these are in addition to the regular visit allowance as long, he says, as I don't have 'too many' (undefined).

Palm Sunday was celebrated with a fairly traditional service of Holy Communion (modern rite), which left some of the dozen or so occasional worshippers visibly bemused. All were 'our lads' from C-Wing – we neither mingle nor meet with our brethren from other wings who have their own earlier service. It was a back-to-back service-a-thon for the Chaplain, but at least he could rehash his earlier sermon, though it was so lengthy and impenetrable that I was not the only one to wish he hadn't bothered. I read from the Old Testament and little Mick, aka 'Mr Fundament' the self-appointed would-be leader of the C-Wing God Squad, declaimed the Gospel with great gusto while the old lags sniggered and the officers at the back dozed, eschewing any sign of participation. In line with broad-church practice, palm crosses were handed out and twiddled with. Most of our congregants didn't know where to put them, though some impolite suggestions were just audibly whispered. But that other great Anglican tradition of holding an outdoor Palm Sunday procession led by a donkey was, obviously, not followed here (besides, there is a run on donkeys at this time and some parishes use a Shetland pony as a stand-in.)

Communion was a novel experience – instead of administering the bread and wine separately, the Reverend dips the wafer in the chalice (held at the ready by Mr Fundament) before placing it rather soggily in our outstretched palms with the words, 'The body <u>and</u> blood of Christ.' I asked him about this afterwards and he explained that it is to prevent communicants from seizing the chalice and quaffing the entire contents! (Which reminds that 18th century communicants were charged for the wine and took a good swig to get their money's worth, hence those tall silver flagons nowadays relegated to ecclesiastical treasury displays.) Here it's a sensible precaution, I'm sure, in this officially teetotal setting. After the service the Chapel Orderly offered tea or coffee from the kitchen, apologising for the lack of sugar sachets and biscuits, all of which had been nicked by the B-Wingers at the earlier service. He gamely made the drinks anyway, though just as they were produced the officers announced that we had overrun and it was time to return to the wing where dinner was about to be served, so our coffees were left undrunk. A reduced-length sermon would have been preferable.

The Good Friday service, for which we had to sign up in advance, was an ecumenical affair led jointly and slightly awkwardly by the C of E and RC chaplains, the latter being a timid Irish lady with a burning bush of bright red hair. It was held, as is customary, mid-afternoon and was surprisingly well-attended, a fact accounted for by, a) there was no work, it being a bank holiday (for staff); b) it provided an opportunity for prisoners to get out of their cells; and c) word had been put around that PG tea and hot cross buns would be served afterwards, which they were. The service included some of the usual gloomy and penitential hymns played on the 'karaoke' machine, and a long Passion reading part of which I was asked to deliver. I tried to make it sound as compelling as possible for the benefit of those who did not already know how the story ended. (I was complimented afterwards by a friendly lady officer who said she'd enjoyed listening to an 'educated voice'!)   Then came Veneration of the Cross. A large though less than life-sized wooden cross, probably knocked up in some prison workshop, had been carted in from the office in an incongruous and obviously unrehearsed procession at the start of the service. Now, our flame-headed Catholic lady produced a smaller crucifix which she invited the faithful to come out and venerate with a genuflexion or a kiss. At this point everyone became extremely still and silent, glancing anxiously around to see who would make the first move. The lady chaplain herself started the ball rolling, so to speak, and kissed the feet of the Lord. One or two others bravely followed suit until someone went up, kept his pursed lips to himself (very sensible in these surroundings, I think) and solemnly bowed before retiring to his seat. This rather set the trend from then on and there were no other kissers. Mr Fundament, having no truck with such blatant Popery, remained rigidly in his seat.

Happy Easter!

8. Sunday 15 April, 2018

Well, Easter has been and gone and I much enjoyed Maggie's amusing account of your colourfully protracted religious frolics in Greece. The Orthodox chaplain here is a rather rotund but dour sort of chap and I doubt if he would sanction such dramatic additions to the Liturgy. We had no chocolate eggs, nor any Easter egg hunt round the wing – it might have been fun, though I guess some of my 'colleagues' would not wish the contents of their cells to come under close scrutiny from egg-hunters, especially those with blue uniforms, clip-on ties, body-cams and fistfuls of jangling keys. In a very slight nod towards tradition, we were treated to a special Easter Sunday 'tea' with hard-boiled eggs and salad. I thought of decorating my egg and hiding it in the cell for Joe to find, but the novelty of being given a whole egg got the better of me so I ate it instead.

Rumour has it that this establishment tops the prison league tables for the quality of its food, or so some of the 'regulars' who have been widely shunted around the 'prison estate' tell me. In that case, the other establishments must be pretty dire, though I concede that our food is generally decently tasty and prodigious in quantity. I must be very restrained to avoid the prisoner's paunch, but I do so with difficulty. The servery workers (it counts as a job for which they are paid about £12 a week) seem to compete to see who can heap the most food onto a 9-inch plastic plate. I plead lamely and ineffectually for small portions but was rudely put in my place with 'You'll get what you're given, mate.' Sort of Oliver Twist in reverse. So I end up dumping solid matter in the bin and flushing softer comestibles down the loo. I note your Aunt Margaret's observation that the young 'don't know how to chew'. HMP foods require little chewing being over-cooked to a degree, probably just as well as our thin white plastic cutlery could hardly cope with a firm pie crust let alone a rare steak (dream on!) Aunt M's comment belongs in *The Oldie* magazine, which I know you take. I was always a bit sniffy about it until my bro Michael, who kept banging on about its delights, seduced me with a year's subscription as a Christmas present and now I'm hooked. Sara forwarded it to me here and happily it was allowed, the censors having failed to find anything subversive (they must have missed Wilfred De'Ath's column).

Today being Sunday I have again been to chapel. Despite my name's repeat appearance on the list, it is still touch and go whether anyone comes along to unlock my cell so I can join the other attendees. As soon as there are sounds of movement outside I stand by the door squinting to see what is afoot. Today I had to resort to kicking and banging on the door and shouting through the crack to attract the attention of a passer-by who alerted the officer to my presence. I was let out in the nick of time. Last Sunday was Low Sunday, apt as the service was indeed very 'low', just a hymn sandwich or mingle-mangle of hymns/songs interspersed with readings, brief prayers and – of course – the sserrmonnnn. The shorter the rest of the service, the longer the sermon. Groan! The pattern is Communion on the first Sunday of the month and major feasts and this simple service every other week. Strictly speaking this may be contrary to church rules, but I guess St Mark's Chapel (the official title of the prison church) falls outside normal regulations. Is it a 'Royal Peculiar', like Westminster Abbey, or just plain peculiar? Today we sang John Newton's 'Amazing Grace' – "He loosed my chains, he set me free..." with more fervour than credible anticipation.

Thanks to your generosity with stamps, and a regular stamp supply from Sara, I don't need to spend my precious 'canteen' allowance on postage. This would be a real hardship as I have letters to reply to most days. I am truly humbled by the great many friends, neighbours and family who have written or sent cards – my brother Michael came up trumps with a 'Welcome to your New Home' card (featuring thrush on nest) hoping I will 'hunker down and settle in quickly'. Hum! For outgoing mail, the prison will only fund ONE second class letter per week – to use this facility we must write W/L (weekly letter) where the stamp goes. Try putting more than one letter through per week and it will not be sent (they keep a tally).

Since my last letter I have also been to healthcare (in a separate relatively modern building) for a check-up. I liked the doctor. He had a mild manner and a sense of humour and was in no rush to see me out of the door. We agreed some minor changes (i.e. reduction) to my pill regime and that, broadly speaking, I am not yet going senile and am no more loopy than most people here. What I did not like was having to wait around all morning with a dozen or more loud-mouthed know-it-alls squeezed into a tiny, cold and scruffy room with hard slatted seating and not even enough of that. There was a basic seatless WC, with no ventilation, no paper and an unlockable door which swung loose on its hinges out into the sitting area. The word 'decency' gets bandied around as a prison service aim – I'm told our cells are subjected to occasional 'decency checks' – but I saw no sign of it in there.

Showering facilities may also come under the 'decency' heading and are, anecdotally, widely viewed with trepidation. The old joke about Scots prisoners Ben Doon and Phil McCavity still has currency, along with the warning 'Don't drop the soap'. I doubt if, at my age, I'd have much to fear. But I've always been rather coy about public nakedness and nothing would induce me to join the steamy morass of limbs and torsos in our showers, likened by one wit to a seal colony on the Essex mud flats. Four showers are lined close together along one wall, without partitions, and showering is only possible during the brief interlude of association between the guys' return from work and the serving of tea (dinner), hence the inevitable crush of bodies. On an officer's recommendation, I have tried nipping in for a quick one once most have left, but this means running the gauntlet of everyone in the servery queue outside the window, and then perhaps missing my meal! So I prefer an 'all-over' wash in the cell while Sam is out. This requires a face flannel.

'What flannel?' you ask, suspecting (rightly) that the new ones I brought in may have been impounded along with the rest of my wash bag contents. So my first 'canteen' order included a flannel (99p), a paltry thing of minimal absorbency about the size and consistency of a lady's evening dress hanky. But at least it's better than the free-issue J-cloth I had been using until now, which left my cheeks, neck and privates liberally stippled with pink fluff.

9. Friday 4 May, 2018

Thanks, as ever, for both your letters and for bringing me up to speed with your news. I continue to hear from many people including our mutual friend Paul. He is a member of some august church committee who are very exercised at the unauthorised removal of Victorian furnishings from one of the smaller northern cathedrals. Should I draw his attention to the disappearance of almost all the original chapel fittings here? I guess the Justice Secretary and his minions have more urgent priorities in the prison system, so it would probably be a fruitless complaint.

I am at last learning to block out some of the background noise from Sam's TV (nominally a shared facility but he treats it as his prerogative) and focus instead on reading – or writing, as now, with an American 'soap' battering my right ear. I am resolved, once I leave prison, never again to watch daytime television. It's sad that Sam's reading level is too basic to cope with anything more taxing than the *Daily Mirror*, to which he subscribes on Saturdays for its racing news and TV guide for the week ahead. With anyone else I might be concerned that he would read my letters, but I am confident that he is totally incapable of deciphering my handwriting, let alone yours! Whenever forced to write anything (e.g. an 'App') Sam does so entirely in BLOCK CAPITALS and tells me that he never learned joined-up writing at school in St Lucia. He now gets me to write Apps on his behalf. News of my ability and willingness to perform this service is spreading and I now get regular requests from others too. Being useful feels good! I am looking into joining the charity-run Shannon Trust scheme that recruits literate prisoners to help their less-learned companions develop basic reading and writing skills. The orderly (in more senses than one) Darren told me about this and I have noticed a few cells with 'Shannon Trust Mentor' emblazoned on their T-shirts and door cards.

My service to Sam also runs to reading his occasional correspondence and trying to explain it to him. It can be a thankless task, especially when (as with almost all official letters) he really does not want to know their contents. His last such legal letter threatened repossession of his house and seizure of contents if he failed to take certain actions. 'Give it here,' he demanded, snatching it out of my hands. 'I'll show you what I think of those bastards.' With which he screwed the letter into a tight ball and lobbed it into the bin. I wish I had his audacity.

A propos of letter writing, my nephew Anthony tells me that when his wife Sally worked on horseracing for Channel Four they frequently received handwritten letters from prisoners. Apparently prisoners are almost the only people who still write 'real' letters to TV companies rather than sending texts or emails.

Yesterday I had a receipt from the prison censor to say that a book had arrived for me. He has approved it, so I hope he awards it an official *nihil obstat* stamp, like some of our Catholic school books. What he fails to reveal is the name of the donor of this unexpected (birthday?) gift. Surely someone with a black sense of humour as the title of this joyous manual is *The Sun Does Shine. How I found life and freedom on Death Row* by Anthony Hinton. (There's a further irony here: my cell faces north, so is not touched by winter sunlight.) The book will be delivered to me on Saturday and I await it eagerly as I am getting low on reading matter. I have not yet found how to access the 'library', a small cubbyhole somewhere upstairs that opens briefly once a week at the precise time when 'tea' (i.e. dinner) is served down here.

Thank you for offering to visit and it would indeed be a wonderful tonic to see you both. Before this can be booked, I shall need your full names and dates of birth as they appear on the photo ID you must present on arrival (passports, driving licences or whatever). I can then fill out a 'PNOMIS Electronic Visitor List' application form so that you can be approved (or otherwise) prior to making a booking. Please liaise through S (my Manager in this respect) as she knows the drill. I am entitled to two visits per month plus a discretionary one for 'good behaviour', an incentive to curb any aggressive instincts and watch my Ps and Qs in the vicinity of my superiors. When – or if – I get moved to a lower category establishment (which could happen at any time with only fifteen minutes' notice) I assume that such lists will carry forward, though of course the location may be even less convenient for you. It's such a boon to have S only a short drive away that I'm happy to forego the freer, less-regimented conditions of a C-Category prison – not that I will be given any choice in the matter! It is curiously liberating for once not to have to make any decisions for myself, though I guess this could be problematic for long-term prisoners when finally released into a changed and confusing world.

Yesterday I was called to Healthcare again, this time for a so-called 'Age-Sensitive Assessment' by the (female, this time) nurse. Mercifully there were fewer bodies in the horrid little waiting room and, now being wise to its exigencies, I took an extra jersey to sit on, a book to read and a fistful of toilet paper 'just in case'. (Happily, I didn't need it.) I'm not sure what was 'sensitive' about the assessment, nor indeed if I passed. However I was weighed, had blood-pressure taken, stood on one foot to check my balance (I didn't topple over), had medication reviewed (again) and so forth. I was then asked if I was OK with reading and writing. Did I know the date? Could I tell her approximately what time it was (without referring to my watch)? Could I mention a significant recent event? (I mentioned Amber Rudd's resignation as Home Secretary over the Windrush Deportation Scandal – was this significant enough?) Next question, did I know the Prime Minister? Was the nurse merely asking for Mrs May's name, or was she concerned lest I was a spy planted in their midst? 'Not personally,' I replied. She did not display any obvious relief, so I assume the former. 'That's what they all say,' she said. Could I name a famous person? Well, I had to think hard about that one before naming Jeremy Corbyn. I hope this choice didn't adversely affect my score. Come to think of it, I wonder if Jezza has taken an 'age-related assessment'? He's only twenty days younger than me! A minor embarrassment was that I was quite incapable of producing a 'sample' having had a pee just before leaving the cell (always a wise precaution at 69). There's a little phial on the shelf in front of me as I write, waiting to be filled for next time. The authorities have subjected me to so many tests over the past couple of months that they are clearly determined to keep me alive whilst in their care. Or, failing that, they are making sure they have plenty of plausible excuses should I expire sooner than my sentence. Given the choice, I'd rather be let out to take my chance in the big bad world beyond these walls.

I cannot imagine how you came to receive two letters from me on consecutive days. Very strange. My supply of envelopes is almost exhausted so I ordered four packs of ten @ 45p on last week's canteen sheet. When the delivery arrived this morning I had received just four envelopes at a cost of £1.80. Anyone would think they were on hand-marbled paper and ordered from Harrods. The money has now been refunded – at least, an officer gave me a signed chit to say it will be, in due course – but I'm told there is an envelope famine in the Prison Service. So if correspondence from me inexplicably dries up, you'll know why. (And don't even think of sending some – that's not allowed in case they are impregnated with 'illegal substances' for me to sniff.) A local friend has however discovered that it is possible to send books to prisoners via Amazon and last week one of Patrick O'Brian's tales of low life on the high seas duly turned up. It will make a refreshing antidote to *Barchester Towers*. My reading speed, never the best, is hampered by the constant TV noise and that of my cellmate who has been chattering away in the background while I've been writing this. I just ignore him. He doesn't seem to mind, but I so look forward to 9pm when he takes his teeth out and retires to bed. I can see the teeth now, grinning at me from a mug on the shelf above the sink. (Standard prison-issue mugs are sky blue, leave a rancid after-taste of cheap plastic and are best avoided by the coffee connoisseur.)

Teeth are not the only body parts I'd rather not see. A young man from another cell (to keep the censor guessing, I shall not name him) came in for a chat the other day and, without so much as a 'by your leave' or a 'with your leave' suddenly unzipped his jeans and flapped his tackle in my face. I cannot imagine why he thought I might be interested (nor was it an especially impressive display). I promptly showed him the door at which he flounced out with a withering smile. Strange. Until that point I had thought him borderline-normal, as far as prisoners go.

The weather here has been very miserable for the past couple of weeks, sunless, windy and bitterly cold so outdoor exercise has been cancelled most days. I miss the warm touch of the sun and also the chance of an intelligent conversation with one or other of the older gents from the landings above. On wet days we get 'indoor association' instead of outdoor exercise. All cell doors are left unlocked for a time so we can chat, play snooker, cards or table tennis. Access between landings is however closed, which means that I can't meet up with my outdoor companions or other 'kindred spirits' who mostly live on the twos and threes. Did I mention that I have at last been given a regulation grey outdoor jacket (with distinctive orange shoulder patches), a cross between a fleece and a hoodless 'parka' (hoods banned, as previously mentioned re. dressing gowns)? The jacket is thick but huge, perhaps following the contours of its previous wearers, so it reaches almost down to my knees (not complaining about that) with sleeves so long I can pull them down in lieu of gloves. Also it is dotted with random burn marks, so must have been worn by an absent-minded smoker when cigarettes – known as 'burn' – were still permitted. I don't mind the above as it is at least warm. Someone has kindly loaned me a woolly hat, just long enough to pull over my ears, as both the hats I brought in are still trapped in my 'prop box' somewhere in stores. No doubt they will be liberated as and when I am. Roll on 2020!

10. Thursday 17 May, 2018

Thanks for your latest with its description of your Lakeland adventures including your visit to Coniston (my favourite) and Ruskin's house. Envy! My writing this has been interrupted by a discussion with my <u>new</u> cell-mate who used the word 'pulchritude' in connection with Ruskin's (lack of) amorous affairs. Yes, the intellectual temperature of Cell C1-24 is set to rise. Last Saturday I took delivery of a little radio and headphones (ordered from the Argos catalogue) thinking, hurray, at last I will be able to blank out some of Sam's inane chatter, effing and blinding and TV babble. I was just settling down to a blast of Classic FM when an amiable orderly appeared at the door to say that Sam had been re-allocated to a single cell on the landing above. So, no more rants from that proud St Lucian about the shiftiness of 'Jam-Eye-Cans', no more monochrome fifties cowboy films, and no more stertorous breathing and sonorous farts (sorry!) in the middle of the night. Despite the above, and a lot more besides, I valued Sam's fleeting but warm friendship and shall miss him. He had a raw deal in life culminating in the tragedy of prison, the death of his wife in custody and the refusal of the authorities to allow him even to attend her funeral, in recounting which he broke down in tears. He and I may have been chalk and cheese, but we got on well – and he never punched me, as he had a previous 'pad-mate'. Cell-sharing must be one of the most punitive aspects of prison life. I have already heard some horror stories!

Sam's successor is Nigel, mid-fifties, highly self-educated, encyclopaedic memory, compendious vocabulary, amateur artist (self-taught, obvs.) and one-time activist for some far right ethno-nationalist political pressure group that you and I might regard with the gravest suspicion. His attitudes and opinions on most topics veer between Mussolini and Mystic Meg but, as long as we keep off politics and religion (he's also a signed-up Pagan), I think we'll rub along fine. He even shares my musical tastes, as well as being generally mild-mannered, considerate, and he doesn't swear (swearing, by staff as well as inmates, is endemic hereabouts). Nigel (or Nige) is especially contemptuous of 'mumpties' (one of his favourite labels) who address each other as 'bruv' or 'mate' and speak in catch-phrases liberally larded with f-words. But hey, "Misery acquaints a man with strange bedfellows," as the Bard said, and how true that proves to be. As for 'bed-fellows', I find myself still on the top bunk. Nige served in the army is his earlier days, strayed into the sights of an IRA rifle, and now walks (rapidly) with an irregular lollop which earns him the soubriquet 'Hopalong'. To lever oneself up onto the top bunk requires agility, co-ordination, a steady sense of balance and precise timing, especially for the final lunge across the end bar and onto the mattress. None of this would be possible for Nige, so I have more-or-less graciously resigned myself to another spell on top leaving the lower bunk for Hopalong.

Now for the positives. Unlike under the Sam regime, the TV is now off all day and we negotiate our evening viewing equitably with the (his) proviso that at least one antipodean soap of his choice (featuring young female characters) is included. Also, and critically, Nige is young enough to be obliged to work, so goes off every morning to the sewing workshop where he earns about £12 a week to supplement what his brother (or 'bruv') sends in. This leaves the cell for my solo enjoyment until his return at tea time, by when I am more than ready for some company. The choice of jobs here is limited to stitching things, printing things or growing things (in the prison gardens and greenhouses) or (as previously mentioned) serving food or cleaning duties on the wing. Apart from a few smart guys with advanced IT skills who work in the print shop control room for extra pay, they are all wearyingly mundane tasks. Sometimes there isn't enough work to go round, so the order comes, 'Go slow, lads, just look busy'. It reminds me of an activity group at school called CALBO, said to stand for 'Keep All the Little Buggers Occupied'. Nigel would prefer a more creative task, but creativity is not encouraged in prison, perhaps for very good reasons. However, our cell walls provide an outlet for Nige's artistic endeavours, enough to cover the bare patches where the paint has long since peeled. He specialises in still life, some rather awkward-looking attempts at the human form (rear view, thankfully), and experiments with perspective. He despises post-modern or abstract art and is not aiming for the Royal Academy, sensibly in my view. Anyway, thank you for your offer to send more pictures, but, as well as Nige's *oeuvres*, I have already accumulated quite a circulating gallery of cards, photos and illustrations sent in by various people since I took up residence. 'Blu-tak' is not allowed (it can be used to block locks) so, as I may have mentioned previously, we must make do with prison toothpaste as an adhesive. I find that after a month or so it starts to burn through the paper turning it brown until it drops off the wall. Whatever does it do to teeth?

Nigel/Hopalong reports well of the C-cat prison where he resided for the best part of four years prior to a brief release before being recalled here, currently on remand. I think that's his story, but don't ask. I don't. One of the more useful skills he has acquired over the years is how to make up a prison bed (anchored, as you will recall, to both floor and wall). The shiny blue surface and thinness of the mattress quickly causes sheets to ruck up in the middle. The trick he has taught me is to take the sheet corners and knot them together <u>under</u> the mattress, thus holding them in place at the head and foot of the bed. I should say that this is often not possible as many/most bedsheets are too narrow, having long since had strips of sheeting torn off from their long edges. These can be plaited together into ropes to make improvised belts, washing lines or perhaps ropes to facilitate escape, or worse. So it is said – though I have learned to take everything with a generous dollop of salt.

Yes, I watched the first half of the recent TV programme on Strangeways, then started to find it depressingly familiar so went to bed. There are many similarities, but we no longer have three people to a cell, nor do we 'slop out'. It must have been a nightmare, and I'm not surprised tensions often ran high. All cells here (though not in all HMPs) now have WCs, the most efficient push-button flushers you'll find anywhere. Despite which, the atmosphere can get pretty noisome, especially when 'banged up' (i.e. most of the time) so there's no chance of a through draught. Air fresheners made of a sort of blobby pine-scented goo were available from 'canteen' until recently but have now been withdrawn. Why? Perhaps they induced a legal high? Febreze and hand wash are no substitute. Cell dimensions are still the same as Strangeways, but at least we can see out of the windows. Every few days an officer comes round to yank at the window bars (or, more accurately for the architecturally literate, mullions) to check that we have not loosened them. I wonder if one reason for the prodigious quantities of carbohydrate-laden prison food is to ensure that no-one can squeeze through the 12 cm gap between the bars.

M's letter arrived with a clutch of other mail this evening just as I was heading upstairs to 'Meds' to collect a weekly supply of pills from a small dispensary. I am lucky to be on 'weeklies' unlike the serious head-cases who must join (or barge into) this rag-tag queue twice a day so they can be given medication to take under supervision, washed down with a tiny paper cup of water. Many medications, particularly of the mind-bending type, have a potential currency in prison and can wreak havoc if they get into the wrong hands. The Meds queue lines up outside the part-glazed doors into B-Wing, our near neighbours-whom-we-must-never-meet. I begin to understand why, and not just because of the frequency of alarm sirens, riot shields and snarling dog patrols called to that establishment. Their reactions to seeing us mild-mannered C-Wingers outside their caged door indicates enemy territory within.

I note your comments on food waste. You would surely be horrified at the amount of food here that gets barely a lick or a look before being tipped in the black dustbins found on every landing or, if of the right consistency, down the loo. Unwanted tea bags for example (and no one with functioning taste buds would actually 'want' prison tea) often go straight in the bin as there are no collection points for surplus items. Decent tea bags (choice of Typhoo, PG or Yorkshire) are available at a price via the weekly 'canteen' sheet. I am also appalled at how much prison food is imported, e.g. chocolate bars (occasional treat) from France, tubs of yoghurt from Germany, milk from Ireland. My main issue with prison food is its prodigality, especially in the carbohydrates department, which are heaped high on our plastic plates whether we want them not. Basic sliced white bread is also available at lunchtime in seemingly limitless quantities and some guys regularly carry away half a loaf or more from the servery. 'Man shall not live by bread alone' the Bible says, but here it is consumed in such prodigious quantities as to leave scarcely any room for other victuals. Almost everyone over the age of about forty sports a protuberant prisoners' paunch. I have been trying to avoid comfort eating, but have already put on weight and – more visibly – girth. In line with school food (and centuries of Catholic practice), Friday is fish day when our evening meal is fish, chips and mushy peas (or baked beans). The fish is a battered (in both senses) greyish slab, but edible enough, though I think I may opt in future for the alternative of a jumbo sausage as it may have more flavour.

Food waste, of which there is an abundance, helps feed a burgeoning population of scavenging seagulls. These are mainly of the larger herring- and black-backed varieties, but with some obese-looking black-headed ones too. They maintain an almost constant chorus of squawks outside our windows as they wheel round the skies above, strut across the exercise yards or scrap among scraps pilfered from the bin-bags in the overflowing waste bins beyond the main wing entrance. When the gulls take a break, or head off for trips to the beach to menace holidaymakers and steal their chips, the pigeons take over. Some of them find their way inside the wing through open roof lights and swoop up and down between the landings, though the netting at first floor level stops them (but not their poo) reaching us down here. The disused original wing (next to the chapel) is a regular final resting place for the corpses of long-trapped pigeons. Sometimes we also see blackbirds and sparrows, recently-arrived house martins, and a pair of cheeky pied wagtails that live on the grassy patch outside the chapel. I think they must laugh at our confinement when their lives seem so free.

Like the food, some of the prisoners are also imported, including a thoroughly objectionable Lithuanian guy who at 7ft. tall stands a clear (and very large) head above everyone else and has to duck to get under the doors. How I wish he would sometimes forget. Large head, small brain — his chief amusement in the exercise yard is in flicking stones at the older residents, something that is observed by the officers but rarely acted upon. By and large, though, this is an Anglophone community (in line with the surrounding region). Currently, just a smattering of Arabic can be heard in the yard, there a couple of Poles, one Italian (understandably, he's very pissed off about the food) and I regularly exchange 'Hujambo' and 'Habari gani?' Swahili greetings with an agreeable young man whose parents were Ugandan Asian refugees from Idi Amin. Otherwise, the main language spoken by all prisoners is bullshit, or 'squit' as it's called in Norfolk. My new cellmate is a local lad, suspicious or hostile to foreigners, who talks like Alan Partridge and has a rich reservoir of local anecdotes, not always funny.

Did I thank you for the colourful birthday card of monkeys squatting on a Moghul tomb? It is still on display here along with many others, indeed more cards than for many years past. Some small compensation for being in prison. Memo to self: tear strip off sheet to make line for hanging card display. It turns out that it was nephew Anthony who sent *The Sun Does Shine*. I did what I very rarely do — I read the first few pages then skipped to the end. I'm pleased to say that, like a generously tipped masseuse, it comes with a happy ending. After thirty years on death row the author, Anthony Hinton, did indeed get his wrongful conviction for murder overturned, escaped the electric chair and found fame and freedom. Phew. BTW, the former 'long drop' execution suite still exists here, and was last used in 1951 when two young men were hanged for killing their pregnant girlfriends. It has now been converted into offices, said always to be icily cold, but maybe that's just a heating deficiency.

My birthday this year fell on a Sunday, and it was well worth skipping chapel so that S could visit on the day itself. From the canteen sheet I treated myself to a ginger cake (to share with Nige) and a carton of mango juice plus a hairbrush (present-to-self). I can't pretend that I greatly missed our Anglican ministrations in chapel, not least because I have now started attending Buddhist meditation on Tuesday afternoons and Quaker Meeting on Fridays. They both help to keep me sane.

N.B. I have now served one tenth of my sentence. Everyone says the first few weeks are the worst. Having survived so far there is a good chance that I will make it through to the end!

11. Friday 8 June, 2018

Your account of your Pembrokeshire holiday brought back happy memories of a stay near Tenby when S and I were first married. I remember the sloping nave at St David's, the monks of Caldey Island and Dylan Thomas's house at Laugharne. As you know, I always enjoy exchanging travellers' tales – but there's not much chance of that here. Few of my companions have ever had the means or inclination to travel outside England, nor can they understand why anyone would tolerate all the caboodle of incomprehensible languages, exotic foods and unfamiliar currencies let alone the wily ways of foreigners. Sam, for example, had made just one return to his native St Lucia, otherwise he had never been as far as Wales, the West Country or further north than Sheffield. Happiness was a mobile home at Hemsby.

I'll hear some travel tales tomorrow from friend Roger who is braving the entry procedures for a first visit. He should be used to suspicious and punitive regimes by now having recently returned from a mega-trip across China where (as here) he was under constant scrutiny, especially in the Muslim Uyghur region of Xinjiang province. He flew back from Osh (in Kyrgyzstan), which sounds monosyllabically mysterious, like Swat (Pakistan), where he's also been recently. He's spending a month at home in Cambridge before flying off on another trip, this time to Siberia. I'm not sure how he does it at 74, but he says if he doesn't do it now… A bit like me and prison, I suppose.

Just before I sat down to write this, Sam – former cell-mate – came over to say good-bye. He had been given the minimum fifteen minutes to bag up his belongings for a move, though the officers apparently had no idea (or were not allowed to say) where he was heading. I doubt if we shall ever meet again, but who knows? It's a funny old world, as Sam liked to say. I've heard no more about the likelihood of my own move, but I'm in no hurry. I feel that I've settled into the routine here and don't relish a change and having to start all over again with a different regime, even if it is one with more liberty. I've been told that this place is unusually restrictive for a 'local' prison and that, at my age, I should be entitled to far more time out of my cell. As it is, allowing for exercise, association, mealtimes, etc., I'm 'banged up' for at least 22 hours per day, much of it effectively in solitary confinement until Nigel (current pad-mate) returns from work at four-ish (everything here is 'ish'!) Am I really such a security risk?

Given an agreeable companion (I've been quite lucky so far), I've come round to the advantages of cell-sharing, though it is one of the complained-about aspects of prison life. Issues of personal hygiene loom large and regularly cause conflict. Obsessive cleanliness can be as much a problem as its lack. I was told of someone who banned his pad-mate from using the in-cell lavatory. Nor would he allow a curtain round it (as we have) claiming it would 'harbour germs'. His unfortunate companion responded by refusing to eat, i.e. went on hunger strike until he was found either a less fastidious companion or a single cell (which he was, after ten days.) I'd award both (so far) of my cell-mates 2:1 for cleanliness, but not firsts, which would surely be intolerable. To merit a single cell here you need to be one or more of the following – very old, very dangerous, very prejudiced, very dirty, very sycophantic or very trusty. I'm not 'very' anything much, so here I stay.

Quite apart from my books and the letters that continue to arrive most days, I don't lack reading material. I have already surpassed the twelve book limit (number allowed in cell) that Theresa May shamefully tried to impose on prisoners when she was Home Secretary. We can order daily newspapers (cost deducted from 'spends' account) that, if we're lucky, are delivered at lunchtime, but sometimes not until the following day. It all depends on which officer is on duty. Most are pretty good but some just can't be bothered. Currently only about eight people (out of 120 or so on the wing) take a 'daily'; rather more get weekly TV magazines (for programme listings and lurid tales of life in the 'soaps') or week-end papers with TV supplements. Sam used to take the *Sunday Mirror*, mainly for the racing (he was an avid follower) but Nigel is happy to share whatever I buy. Which is the '*i*' Mon-Fri, *The Times* on Saturdays and *Sunday Times* or *Observer* on Sundays. That is just affordable, about the same as many blokes spend on 'vapes'. I like to take the quick/short '*i*' and *Oldie* crosswords (I never could manage the cryptic ones!) out on exercise to share with some of the other older lads who prefer sitting out on the benches to any actual exercise. They also enjoy a chuckle over *Private Eye*, especially the cartoons and front covers.

Some approved magazines may be ordered through the prison (cost deducted from 'spends' account) or sent in direct from publishers, but not re-packaged and sent by family of friends in case they interleave or impregnate them with 'illegal substances' en route. Thus I receive *The Oldie* (sub from bro. Michael), CAM (free, re-directed), *National Geographic* (sub from niece Jezzie) and *Private Eye* (sub from friend Kate). The latter got past the censor, rather surprisingly as it is not on the officially approved list. He must have a sense of humour after all. A young 'screw' (officer) spotted my *Private Eye* and asked if it was a detective story magazine. I tried to explain, but don't think he understood the word 'satirical'.

The official list of permitted magazines is pinned on the wing notice board and makes strange reading. Maybe I can understand prisoners wishing to keep up with outside interests – e.g. (in no particular order), *Boxing News*, *Classic Car*, *Practical Boat Owner* (hurray!) and *French Property Magazine*. The list reads like an advertisement for the Prison Service diversity agenda and includes general lifestyle mags such as *Men's Health*, GQ, *Razzle* and *Gay Times*. However, a young man who applied to subscribe to the latter was told it was 'inappropriate'. Then why is it on the list? (A challenging task for the prison creative writing group, if we had one, which we don't, could be to write a story about a prisoner who subscribes to all the above.) Note: I had expected the walls of most prisoners' cells to be liberally plastered with revealing pin-ups from lad mags. Once again, the reality is rather different. I haven't seen a single tit (of the mammary variety) since I came here.

Don't worry about my health; I always walk a few laps round the perimeter fence in the track inexplicably marked 'out of bounds'. One of my regular 'exercise companions' is Ronald, who chooses to be known here as Steve (I guess he has his reasons), lives near us at home and, though we have never previously met, we have friends in common and have even attended some of the same parties and funerals! Quite recently, S took a photo of me at a classic car rally standing next to Ronald's 1930s Rolls Royce and trying to look proprietorial. I really coveted the Royce, hence the photo, but never anticipated the circumstances under which I would meet its actual owner. Unfortunately Ronald is quite deaf in both ears but too vain to consider a hearing aid, so our discussions (e.g. observations about 'screws' or other 'lads') are rarely confidential. We both enjoy the flower borders we pass on the way to the yard, now crowned by shoulder height hollyhocks in contrasting shades of papery pink. Meanwhile S has sent in photos of our home garden which is full of colour and none the worse for the lack of my ministrations apart from the bottom end where the convolvulus is winning.

Today is washday when the weekly prison laundry swings into action led by a landing laundry orderly. This service is only for prison-issue garments, sheets, cellular (two senses, being used in cells!) blankets and so forth, not for our personal property as we never get back the same items we send. So, do I risk sending in a fleece jumper or un-faded T-shirt that actually fits? It's risky, as I may up getting something gross back in return. In order to be issued with clean clothes we must tick a list, stating number and size of items required. I usually put down for prison T-shirts – Cambridge blue, appropriately – socks (grey tubes of pilled towelling fabric with no discernible heels) and grey fleecy sweatshirts. Size-wise, the latter are very hit and miss, often as broad as they are long, but with sleeves as shrunken as a fisherman's smock. Sometimes I wonder if the lads in Textiles, here or some other nick, make them up like this for a laugh. Strange but true, almost all prison clothing is labelled XL though the actual size is usually at least XXL round the chest. Perhaps there is method in this madness – many older (and some younger) prisoners are small in stature but great in girth. I guess we survive by keeping a secret cache of most-needed items, though the knock-on effect is inexplicable shortages for everyone else. Last week, for example, there were no clean sheets. Note: here we still live in a pre-duvet time warp.

Our own clothes, or anything we value enough to wish to preserve, we must hand wash in the cell hand basin. I have bought washing powder from 'canteen' and Nigel and I have improvised a clothes line out of knotted-together strips torn from free-issue J-cloths. This now stretches from the top bunk bed's tubular steel frame to a handy screw in the opposite wall and is now festooned with my damp but drying T-shirts and smalls; the cell is scented with the 'fresh garden' aroma of fabric conditioner rather than the sweaty sock aroma of my slippers. The alternative to hand washing is an industrial strength washing machine jealously guarded by the said laundry orderly (his services are notionally free, but a 'vape' or a bottle of Vosene may lubricate your way to the head of the queue). Unfortunately its reputation – and perhaps his too – is to pulverise anything small or delicate, so I don't risk it. I need my personal clothes to last another two years. Meanwhile, I have put in an App, more in hope than expectation, for the release of my belt from 'prop'. The pyjama cord that sustains my jeans is looking rather frayed.

12. Sunday 17 June, 2018

Today is Father's Day, but no card from H. I'll let him off as he's been away with five friends touring Romania and Bulgaria (for a music festival) in a locally hired campervan. I think he's due back today so I'll try calling him later, but he is due for his monthly visit next week-end. My impression is that there is no kudos among his friendship group in having a Dad 'doing time', but neither is there any real stigma. I've discovered that currently there is a (very presentable) young man on this wing who was at school with H and especially remembers him for his table-tennis prowess (county champion, etc.). He doesn't often play nowadays but I reckon he could thrash any of our inmates who monopolise the wing table tennis table during indoor association times. I've had a couple of games of snooker, but have trouble getting my (wonky) eye in and I never could play TT, or indeed anything that involved throwing, hitting or catching things. Nor am I much cop at cards, though I used to manage a hand of poker or pontoon. In the cell opposite mine is an ingenious and entertaining magician, entirely self-taught, who has had a long time (22 years) 'inside' to perfect his own brand of card magic. He tried several times to explain to me exactly how the card I picked out of (my) pack, despite much shuffling, then turned up inside *his* left shoe, but I still can't follow it. He hopes to make a career as a magician when he is eventually released.

This morning I attended chapel, Holy Communion, taken by a retired priest who covers for the chaplain when he's away (currently in Nigeria with his family). As we were only a small group of ten, he abandoned his scripted sermon and instead invited comments on the Epistle and Gospel readings. Inviting comments from prisoners sounds a trifle audacious, but his confidence in his congregation was repaid and a lively discussion ensued. I was able to contribute practical, rather than theological, observations on the differences between serrated sickles (referred to in the parable of the mustard seed), knife-edged reaping hooks and long-handled scythes. I never imagined that knowledge gleaned (note verb) from museum events would come in handy for Bible-study, least of all in prison. Better still, in chapel I usually sit with a Kurdish Christian whose Middle Eastern complexion, bushy beard, long straggly hair and beatific expression mean that he is known to everyone as Jesus.

This morning Jesus movingly described wielding a sickle as a boy to reap the wheat harvest on his father's fields. I was reminded of the bands of singing women out in the fields in Ethiopia stooping to sickle the precious harvest of 'tef' grain from which injera, their staple food, is made. It's another world out there.

Thinking back to my earlier museum incarnation, we often used to say how the Victorian workhouse robbed inmates of any practice in making decisions for themselves – even their tea was poured ready sugared. Prison may have a similar effect. However, weekends are a time for several small decisions that can impact on our quality of life. One such is how to spend our meagre funds on orders from the canteen sheets we hand in today (Sunday) for delivery on Friday. Telephone credits are a given, after which come the difficult choices. Should I get another squeezy jar of strawberry jam (to add piquancy to watery rice pudding)? Squeezy jam is far more expensive than jam in jars, but glass jam jars – or glass anythings – are not allowed as they could be dangerously weaponised. I also need more ketchup (also in squeezy dispenser), a useful alimentary lubricant for dry, over-cooked meat or veg. Can I make my box of tea bags last another week? Yes, I can, as Yorkshire bags are strong enough to recycle for a second brew (another hangover from Victorian times when the servants re-used the mistress's leaves). The contents of our four per day free-issue tea bags are also strong and dusky, but indelicately flavoured, like floor sweepings from the Ooty tea factory. Shall I top up my stock of envelopes or indulge myself with a chocolate bar? (Both!) There is no coffee allowance, so it's best to hide the (plastic) coffee jar from prying eyes as it is so often scrounged by people 'on the borrow', as they say. These loans are almost never repaid, and an unwritten rule drummed into me early on was never to 'lend' anything you can't afford to lose.

My App re. belt has come back, pink copy. Request denied. Belt buckle too big. Potentially it could be weaponised. I do wonder if anyone actually bothered to check. My recollection is that it is a very unremarkable and inoffensive Primark belt with a distinctly modest sized buckle. Actually, my waist continues to expand and I have less need of a belt now than on first arrival. Come to think of it, I never mentioned the saga of my clothing parcel. We are allowed to have a parcel of additional clothes sent in once we have been here for thirty days. My common-sense reading of this regulation was that we could receive a parcel <u>after</u> 30 days. I now know that it actually means <u>within</u> 30 days, so S didn't post it until after the deadline. The responses to my Apps were, first, that it was out of time, and then that it had never been received anyway. I may never know the truth of the matter. It would have been nice to have a better coat and more shirts and trousers, but no matter.

PS. Now spoken to H who has just landed from Sofia. Trip went very well. Owner of campervan 'very understanding' about minor prangs and loss of wing mirror. Ah, the insouciance of youth!

13. Friday 29 June, 2018

I am writing this on a Friday, i.e. the start of the weekend. Yes, we have three-day weekends here when there is no work, the weekly 'canteen' orders are delivered, signed for and/or complained about, and fish (or something vaguely fishy) is served for 'tea'. Some people attend chapel for Quaker Meeting or Muslim Prayers, though not together, of course. The Muslims have their own space, though the Quaker chaplain and the Imam seem to be the best of chums! It is also the day for laundry exchange, more in hope than expectation, as previously described. As you observe, neon-green is an odd shade for sheets. I'm not sure if it is intended to be calming, though I find it anything but. Whoever dreamed of pairing pea-green sheets with apricot-orange blankets must have had a bizarre taste in design. Canteen arrived early this morning, 8.30 a.m., so I had to hurriedly don my T shirt and shorts and leap down from the top bunk to greet the officers and sign the sheet acknowledging receipt. This week I took delivery of a tiny tube of 'Stanbul Perfumed Oil' (£2.99) to make myself smell nice for the wing disco (joke). I'm not sure if it's intended as an olfactory reminder of an Istanbul bath house or the Grand Bazaar, but either way it's preferable to BO.

As you surmise, I have been enjoying the recent warm weather during our all-too-brief periods of outdoor exercise. Cell C1-24 faces north-ish, so very little sunlight penetrates the barred and caged windows even now at midsummer. We live either in neon glare or stygian gloom. Cells on the opposite side are much brighter but get so hot on sunny afternoons that their occupants mostly keep the blinds (if installed) down. For myself, I'd happily tolerate the heat to avoid the gloom, though I might express a different view if on the other side. All prisoners are habitual whingers, and I'm no exception. At least on this side we have a fairly open view with a grassy patch (can't exactly call it a lawn) to look out on. This was all Omo white when I first arrived but turned from emerald green to crap brown some weeks ago. Currently it is yellowy and frazzled, dotted with stringy dandelions. The palm trees of my imagination (they are actually Cordyline, I think) look very much at home. It's a shame that the public never get to visit the prison gardens for 'open garden' events. They are extensive, varied and expertly tended by inmates under the eye of professional gardeners (equipped with keys, radios and telescopic truncheons in addition to the more usual trowels, hoes and spades). Their duties include watering the flowerbeds, a task performed by a gang of trusties who cart round a wheeled water tank. This sports a noisy petrol engine to power a pressurised water pump for squirting the plants and, when they think no-one's looking, each other.

On the way to our tarmac exercise yard I can glimpse glasshouses and poly-tunnels, shrubberies and themed herbaceous borders of perennials as well as tubs of showy annuals, just coming into bloom. From a tub in the yard I liberated a musky-scented purple petunia flower but was spotted and berated by an officer. I tried to excuse myself by explaining that picking flowers encourages new growth, but he didn't buy that one. Obviously not a gardener. There are other gardens I have never seen but have been told of, including kitchen gardens, soft fruit beds and a newly-created Mediterranean garden as well as randomly placed exotics such as canna lilies, scarlet hibiscus and bottle-brush shrubs, all of which we grew in Tanzania. It wouldn't surprise me if there's a banana tree lurking somewhere in the micro-environment of our high-walled site.

Which reminds me that yesterday one of the gardeners was working just inside the outer perimeter wall when a substantial parcel came lofting in a neat parabola over the top and landed with a loud thwack at the very feet of a couple of supervising officers.

One can only guess what illegal substances were contained within, but it could hardly have been less appropriately targeted. I may be wet behind the ears but think it unlikely that the intended recipient was an officer or even a C-Wing resident, we all being trusty, upright and law-abiding citizens, as you know.

I have asked Nige, my pad-made, about the work he does in the print shop. It is neither artistic nor very complex, and is mainly printing materials for here and other HMPs such as App sheets, prisoner movement forms (nothing to do with the cell WC) and officers' training manuals. The latter could be quite revealing given time to study them. The whole process is done in-house from design (by computer-literate inmates) to printing on big offset litho machines, guillotining (paper, not inmates), collation, stapling or gluing, binding etc. The workshops are bustling, noisy and sociable places, all of which aspects I would find difficult to cope with. One of the many similarities between prison and boarding school is the lack of quiet privacy.

Most prisoners have very loud voices. Is it just their assertive nature or is it nurtured by the environment? The same goes for most of the officers, especially the more termagant females of the species! Anyone who fancies loud women must have the hots in here. Perhaps they get voice projection training as part of their induction (memo: ask Nige to check that manual), but there's no escape from their stentorian shouts of "Meds!" or "Come on, lads. Get your dinner!" Other common announcements – just to give you a sound-bite of life here – are "Free flow!" and "Lock up and roll count!" Free flow means gather to leave the wing, e.g. for work or exercise. Roll counts are conducted many times every day when officers, armed with click counters, peer through door flaps to check numbers. You'd be amazed how frequently the numbers fail to tally, necessitating re-count after re-count until it is verified that all are present and correct.

In the hope of doing a little good during my time here I have now enrolled as a mentor for the Shannon Trust despite initially having been told, erroneously, that there were no vacancies. The ST is a charitable organisation that trains prisoners to provide support with basic literacy for their non-literate peers. I will have a training session soon (or soon-<u>ish</u>, this being prison) and be rewarded with a free pencil (luckily I already have a sharpener) and two free royal blue T-shirts bearing the slogan 'No Bars to Reading'. Otherwise my intentions are entirely altruistic – honest! The perks may seem rather 'fringe', but it can do me no harm to be seen as a willing stooge and may even earn 'positives' towards achieving 'enhanced' status. Yes, it really is a bit carrot and stick, like primary school gold stars and naughty stools. It pays to keep on the right side of 'Miss'. So far, you may be surprised to learn, I have not been awarded any 'negatives', but nor have I managed to earn a single positive in five months! It's not a game I particularly wish to play, believing that honesty and decency should be their own reward. At least that's my excuse, however pompous it sounds.

The Shannon Trust scheme only provides for absolute beginners, so there are not that many potential students/mentees. No shortage of semi-literate people, though, judging by the number of times I have already been asked for help with writing Apps. I've been familiarising myself with the course materials. These start with a pictorial alphabet to assist with sounding out letters to form words (known to generations of infant teachers as phonics). Words/pictures are mostly chosen for their relevance to prisoners, though the selection does not strike me as very sensitive. Thus A is for App (as above), B is for Bang-Up. No, I just made that up. It's actually for Bed (illustration of iron-framed cell bed same as mine). C is for Court, that fearsome purveyor of 'justice' presided over by J is for Judge, depicted like a whacky auctioneer with gavel and wig – do learners really wish to be reminded of this? D is for Doctor (illustrated brandishing a huge taser gun, or is it perhaps a stethoscope?) E is for Exercise … and so on as far as Y for Yard and Z for Zzzz (illustration of sleeping prisoner). No prizes for guessing that K is for Key and P for Police. R for Rizla is now out of date as all smoking (including W for Weed – just joking!) was banned in January this year. A future issue may need to substitute V for Vape. L is for Libary (sic), but no S for Spelling, or even Speling. I will let you know how the training goes and if they find me a student.

I was touched last Friday to be given three strawberries by a young inmate called Jack who works in the gardens, someone who comes over as a bit of a fuckwit and is regularly 'on the borrow' as a coffee-cadger. Despite warnings about non-repayment of 'loans', this time I got lucky and consider three strawberries (sweet but slightly mushy) a fair exchange rate for a couple of spoons of coffee. They were the only strawberries I shall taste this summer as the entire crop goes to be sold outside the prison. Very unfair, I think.

14. Monday 9 July, 2018

Thanks for both of yours, one of which crossed with mine and the other I have now mislaid, though I have all your previous letters. I've started using an old school exercise book to list correspondence, in and out, but such orderliness doesn't come naturally to me, especially with no computer to assist with record-keeping. It may seem counterintuitive (or just obtuse), but I find it incredibly hard to keep tabs on possessions when confined in such a tiny space. Everything has to be stashed on four open shelves plus bin bags shoved under the bed for clothes. A tidy mind would help, but mine is now surely too old and disordered to be trained. Only in Dar es Salaam did S and I ever achieve a neat and dust-free home, but that was thanks to Margret, our house girl, who used to follow us around the house putting things away. We can't get the staff here!

Which brings me to the latest change in my circumstances since my last letter. This is that my previous companion, Nigel, was 'shipped out' (prison speak) last week to a C-Cat establishment. 'Shipped out' may suggest an exotic posting east of Suez as an officer of the East India Company, but the reality is more mundane – just a road trip locked inside a white container known as a Serco van, AKA sweat-box (more appropriate in this warm weather than during the Arctic blasts of my arrival in February). Nige was rewarded for exemplary conduct by being given a full half hour to throw all his belongings into three bin bags, known as a prisoner's 'volumetric allowance'. Where do they find these phrases? I immediately seized the chance to lift my own bedding down from the top bunk and stake a claim to the lower one. *Carpe Diem*, as they don't often say round here. It seemed like indecent haste, with scarcely a moment to mourn Nigel's passing, but there was no knowing when the next victim of our justice system would be thrust through the door. After four months on top I felt I 'deserved it' (to borrow that annoying advertisers' cliché). I shall miss Nige's reliable shiftiness, but not much.

Sadly, my willing self-demotion to steerage class was short lived. Arthur, who arrived from Crown Court that same evening, valiantly tried to scale the bed-frame's heights but was hampered by his short stature and a poorly foot (collision-damage from some misplaced garden furniture, he claims). Going aloft was clearly a hazardous manoeuvre for him, though I demonstrated a range of stratagems for getting a leg over, so to speak. If Bear Gryllis were doing it for the BBC he would surely be equipped with crampons, hard hat and a stunt man as back-up. Once over the top, Arthur opted to stay put for the first night and did so again the following evening, but after two perilous nights above he gave up the unequal struggle and I more-or-less graciously returned to 'my' top bunk.

Arthur, I should say, is a welcome contrast to his predecessors. He is a first-timer, so I'll get to play the knowing senior partner until he's broken in. Arthur has been something in the City (we are by definition all 'has-beens' here or, more likely, 'might-have-beens'). He has an unremittingly positive and 'can do' outlook on life (will it last?) despite a long professional acquaintance with disaster, doom and death as an insurance underwriter in the City. I can just picture his Pooteresque figure waltzing down Threadneedle Street with bowler and furled brolly. He is also a Morris and clog dancer, accordion player and thespian – mainly amateur but with an Equity card for back-up and Shakespearian roles in his repertoire. I can just see him treading the boards as Falstaff, Dogberry or Bottom, or clad in jester's motley at some great lord's feast. Perhaps fortunately, the cell floor area is too narrow for him to demonstrate his fancy footwork, though he threatens to shred my Sunday newspapers to make a mummer's costume for Christmas.

In the sound effects department, Arthur breaks wind like a bum note on a euphonium; also he has rather smelly feet, but I'll refrain from further comment while I work out a strategy. I won't risk upsetting him so early in our relationship. (Come to think of it, my feet may be spring dew fresh, but my Primark moccasins definitively are not. Surprisingly they have retained their shape but after five months' almost continuous daytime wear they reek like a dead skunk and are long overdue for a scrub with Febreze.) Like me, Arthur is ambivalent about tidiness so the hugger-mugger domesticity of C1-24 suits him just fine.

To return to the Big Issue (the bed), we tried submitting an App, drawing attention to our status as 'gentlemen of a certain age' and requesting a ladder. I'd noticed a bolt-on integral ladder in a neighbouring cell and thought it might be just the job. Our App gained the speediest response ever (next day), saying that bed ladders are now 'verboten' (Arthur feigns pidgin-German) as they can be detached and – you've guessed – used as weapons. Of course I could have put my foot down (literally) at this point and insisted on having a lower bunk on grounds of health and safety. However, this would probably have entailed moving both of us into other cells with agile young tykes who stay up all night, listen to boom boxes and don't know the purpose of soap. No shortage of those, so we judged it a risk too far. We 'oldies' need to stick together 'for fear of finding something worse.'

S reports that her father is now in very poor shape, though at 98 I suppose that is to be expected. He is now back home after a short stay in hospital following a collision with his bed that opened up a nasty wound, but he is profoundly miserable and talks of dying. He puts on a brave act to speak to me on the telephone, but our calls are necessarily brief and hampered by 'noises off' at this end. To my great sadness, I am unlikely to see him again. S has been asking if I will be allowed to attend the funeral when the end comes. I have discussed this with the chaplain, but it seems very unlikely as such arrangements are normally only permitted for parents, children, siblings or spouses, not in-laws. Even if allowed, I would have to be chained to an accompanying officer. Neither I nor the rest of the family would want that, though it would make a memorable topic of conversation for the mourners during the post-funereal canapés.

I sometimes talk here with an older bloke (there are several) who has had a series of hospital appointments where he's always the focus of attention and attracts (mainly sympathetic) stares in the waiting area. Which reminds me that Harry and I shared our last (probably last ever for me) Indian sleeper train journey with a convict on transfer from Panaji to Bangalore Gaol. He was secured to the top bunk (!) by heavy chains and multiple padlocks while his three brown-uniformed captors were enjoying a loud and bibulous party on the seats below, no doubt chuffed to be in stylish AC3 rather than cattle class. The prisoner was a nice guy, spoke excellent English and with a droll sense of humour. If I'd had bolt cutters I'd willingly have set him free.

Must bring this ramble to a close. As I write, Elgar is playing on my little radio and Arthur has fallen asleep and is grunting contentedly on his lower bunk behind me. The headphones effectively blank out most of the wow and flutter of landing life.

15. Wednesday 18 July, 2018

Thanks for your letter and card of faux-heraldic murals in Eyam Church. Walking in the Peak District with the Holiday Fellowship sounds a bundle of fun, especially for the entertainingly eccentric company afforded by that excellent organisation. I suppose I could make comparisons with Her Majesty's Prison Service, which also offers 'fellowship' of a sort, though it hardly matches the normal definition of 'holiday', despite what certain sectors of the press may claim! What sort of masochist would book a holiday – and such a long one too – locked for 22 hours a day in a tiny room with an iron bed, bars at the window and a (possibly incompatible) stranger for a companion? Ah, the Peak District. That brings back memories of a youth hostelling tour on foot with a school friend when I was fourteen – tramping across Mam Tor from Edale to Castleton having first done the obligatory chores of washing up and scouring the stone floors. You don't mention if this forms part of the HF routine. Bravo, John, for striding out with the 'moderate difficulty' group. I would have thought it more suited to hip-hop than hip-op, so I assume that you've the pain under control at last.

Walking tours here are, of course, confined to the exercise yard and limited in practice to about 45 minutes though officially we are allowed 'up to' (prison regulations are full of such weaselly phrases) one hour with a minimum 30 minutes. As with HF, walkers tend to form into three groups. Some pound resolutely round the perimeter for the entire session and then proudly announce to anyone who might feign interest how many miles/circuits they have covered. Others adopt a more nonchalant style, coalesce into pairs or little clusters of three or four, and amble round at a sedate pace apparently deep in serious conversation or putting the world to rights. The third group comprise those (and I am often one of them) who position themselves near the front of the line when the gate into the yard is unlocked at the start of the session, then sprint up the nearside to secure a space on one of the four park bench seats.

The 'screws' also like to sit together here (there are always at least two of them, in regular radio contact with the control room in case of trouble). Occasionally the more compliant prisoners defer to them and offer up their hard-won seats, but only occasionally. For some unknown reason, almost everyone circumambulates left-handwise – widdershins, as our medieval forebears would have said, believing it brought ill luck. This is also counter to Buddhist temple practice, where clockwise rotations are held to purify negative karma for the faithful. We may be missing out on some positive vibes here.

The yard also contains a couple of exercise machines designed, according to their printed instructions, to improve strength and agility. I have only recently plucked up enough courage to sit on one and lever myself up and down on the pull-up apparatus. My arms are now so thin and feeble that I find it quite physically taxing, so I take it at a languorous pace, hoping to convey that I'm really just passing the time without a care in the world and could of course go very much faster if only the fancy took me. S would laugh to see me, and I wouldn't mind, but I don't want to make an exhibition of myself here. It is a rather public spectacle as the machines are directly in front of the benches. I started off in slow bursts of ten, counting just audibly to myself in French, Italian, Turkish, Arabic, Swahili and Hindi (only to eight in the latter). To an (almost) total non-linguist like me, that's a serious intellectual challenge, but it provides an opportunity to exercise the mind as well as the body and perhaps keep dementia at bay a little longer. A pious Pole, noted for his volatile temperament and earnest interest in theology, has been trying to teach me Polish numbers, but I have proved a very poor student. The good news is that my stamina, or at least my staying power, is improving and I now regularly reach 60 pull-ups – well, 58 – ten in each language.

My new pad-mate – though 'pad', as in 'bachelor pad', usually suggests something more discreet and commodious – is settling in well. Arthur is by nature or necessity quite 'driven' and in the habit until recently of rising with the lark in time to catch the 7.20 from Bishops Stortford to Liverpool Street. Thus he spent his first two weeks here catching up on years of missed sleep, since when he has reverted to type and habitually wakes at about 5.30 to boil the kettle for his first coffee of the day. Now that his poorly leg has mended he has nobly taken up residence on the top bunk, so I am awakened by a series of creaks, clanks and thumps as he negotiates the widely-spaced bars to descend from the foot of the bed. He breakfasts on Coco-Pops, then writes (I don't know what) for an hour or so. This at least is a silent occupation allowing me to feign sleep until about 8 a.m. when, by consent, we switch on the Today programme on Radio Four.

Before 9 our cell is unlocked and Arthur, who is now on the list for work (he has no option as he's still a few years off retirement age), goes off to the print shop until mid-afternoon. I regain my cellular solitude while Arthur gets to entertain his co-workers with his banter – and earn his weekly crust. Prison earnings may be a bounty for some – guaranteed, risk-free, untaxed and underwritten by HM Government – but for the likes of Arthur it will take him all week to gross what he could earn in a few minutes in his former City job. At least he is spared the commute. (According to a letter in *Inside Time,* the prison newspaper, French prisoners clear around €500 per week and can amass a useful nest-egg for their release. That might aid rehabilitation, but it would not satisfy the punitive instincts of the Great British Public – or our populist politicians!)

Once installed on the lower bunk, I ordered a prayer mat (so styled on canteen sheet) to use as a bedside rug. This is not a success. It is a floppy, nylon thing of barely blanket thickness, sandy-coloured, but so charged with static that it soon becomes coated with a hoar frost of dust. It seems to have a life of its own, rucks up within moments and becomes a trip hazard. It's now double-folded and shoved under the bed from where I drag it out in the early mornings while padding bare footed round the cell. I've seen the devout prostrate themselves on similar 'mats' in the aisles of aircraft heading towards Doha or Dubai. Here it is going nowhere.

Unlikely request from young inmate:
"Can you lend us a Bible, Guv?"
"Sure, I'll give you a New Testament."
"No sweat, Guv. Any old one will do!"

Which brings me to one rather sweet event last week when Arthur and I were invited to attend the R.C. baptism of a young prisoner (Jack, my strawberry donor). "The Pope's coming," he excitedly told me. I must have looked a smidgen dubious about this, so he qualified it by saying "Maybe it's not the BIG Pope, just the Bishop Pope of Norwich." This sent me to the Episcopal Engagements column of the *Catholic Herald* (freebie from table at back of chapel) and the penny dropped. The local R.C. Bishop is called Bishop Hopes, which he may have heard as "(Bisho) p (H) ope(')s coming". An easily-excusable misunderstanding, I'm sure you'll agree. In the event, neither bishop nor pope put in an appearance and the baptism (portable stainless steel font on castors, possible designed as a washbasin for the bed-bound) was immediately followed by confirmation, Mass, coffee and biscuit (singular), all delivered by a local priest specially imported for the occasion. Our new R.C. was then given a handsome rosary in presentation box, the anticipated acquisition of which was, I suspect from the manner of its acceptance, the main driving force behind his supposed conversion. If only Dr Livingstone had believed in the efficacy of rosaries he might have won more converts.

Good news also on the Lithuanian Goliath * front. Our stone-throwing name-caller and well-deserved object of *odium publicum populi* has finally been removed to a holding facility in Kent prior to deportation to his homeland. His departure prompted a general sigh of relief, especially from our more vulnerable brethren and all residents under six feet tall or aged over about forty (which covers just about everybody). I omitted to mention before that my previous cell-mate had raised concerns with an officer about intimidation and this was very promptly followed up by an evening visit from a lady from 'safeguarding'. In the absence of a formal complaint about any specific incident there was little she could do apart from express sympathy and concern, but it was reassuring to know that the issue was being monitored. There are, inevitably, one or two other loud-mouthed opinionated 'youfs'. Even the most esteemed public schools such as Eton and Harrow have their share of those, before they graduate via the Oxford Bullingdon Club to lucrative careers in the City, journalism, politics, or whatever.

* His nickname is, in fact, Monster (not solely on account of his size!) – apt if not very original. Arthur describes him as a 'great long slick of piss'. Like fisher folk of old, nicknames are rife. The laundry orderly is Pops (on account of his age), Squeaky has a high-pitched voice, and I am known as Colonel. This has nothing to do with rank, seniority or military bearing but merely from my supposed resemblance to a certain purveyor of takeaway chicken!

One horny-handed 'youf', named Kevin (not an Etonian, I suspect), is wont to throw his weight around, though he keeps his legs to himself rather than using them to trip up us geriatrics, a favourite sport of our Lithuanian giant. He has been quite well-disposed towards me since I gave him some ketchup – a little squirt for a little squirt, you might say. Linguistically, Kevin is one of our 'Innits', so called for their fondness for this word that they interject, however ungrammatically, into almost every sentence, as in "I ain't got no effin' coffee in my canteen innit." Kevin delights in queue-barging the dinner line, swearing in his raspy voice at the screws and being generally sparky, noisy, coarse and objectionable. Though not exactly threatening (he's well under six feet tall) he behaves like the archetypal little shit.

Well now all that has changed. Kevin has become all sweetness and light and the occasional coy smile has even been observed on his otherwise mean and gnarly face. The reason for this transformation? Kevin has fallen in with Benny, a mischievous tyke and class clown with a mop of curly blond hair and an infectious laugh. Sartorially they advertise their bond (or bondage?) by tying their joggers below their bums so as to display just enough 'crack' to attract attention but not enough to breach decency rules (which may need updating now this has become a recognised underworld fashion statement). K and B are about the same age (twenty-ish) and have arranged a cell swap and moved in together. Rumour has it that they are 'an item', or 'romantically attached' as the press might say, which sounds a lot better than bent as a pair of sugar tongs. Long may it last, I say, if it keeps them quiet, though I have overheard predictable mutterings from Mr Fundament.

Since starting this, I have received my weekly clean laundry for which I'll generously award three stars. This week's exchange gamble has paid off and I now have a towel that's a bit threadbare and thin but not completely anorexic and full of holes like its predecessor. The 'top' (generally known as a jumper), though labelled XL, is only a little short in the body and arms but neatly accommodating round the chest and expanding paunch. How do those of more extreme proportions manage? (Some here have more rolls of fat than a Michelin man.) Also, I have received three socks despite still having only two feet. For once the sheets are intact, i.e. edges not ripped off, so I may be able to tuck them in. What bliss. I keep most of my own clothing for best (visits, chapel, etc.) in the hope that they'll last out until 2020.

16. Monday 30 July, 2018

Thanks not only for your letters but also post cards of Strelley tomb alabasters, now adorning the wall behind my (lower) bunk. A little different from the more usual cell décor of busty girls (partly clothed), aggressive motorbikes or holiday snaps of Mum on beach (or occasionally all three combined as busty mum rides big bike on beach). Noted your comments on (former) prisoners of your acquaintance – an impressive list, if I may say so, going back to our college friend and inept would-be bank robber Ian. Their stories are a unique take on this country's obsession with retributive justice. This week we've been joined by an 84 year old with a long, long sentence. He is most anxious about his disabled wife whose full-time carer he was. He tells me that the judge explicitly refused to take any account of his age, infirmity or long record of impeccable public service despite his offences dating back more than half a lifetime.

I had to laugh at your description of J's 'uncontrollable gurgling sounds'. Arthur also does a passable impression in his sleep of a hippo smoking a hookah. Unlike his malapropisms it is not deliberate or calculated to amuse, and nor does it. I have now acquired via 'canteen' a pair of bright orange earplugs (not a fashion statement). I find they work best when wet, though they then leave damp patches on the pillow. A benefit of shared cells is that there is (or is meant to be) a curtain or waist high barrier to hide the loo from view. Single cells have no such shield, so the WC is potentially in view from the landing outside. Anyone (officer, male or female, or inmate) who opens the door flap to peer in may find what they don't wish to see in direct line of sight. You could say it's a case of 'point Percy at the peephole'.

Which is how one young man got 'nicked' for masturbating when the officer (young female in bondage-tight uniform skirt) peered through the flap during her early afternoon roll check. To 'get a nicking' involves a formal disciplinary procedure and may result in loss of privileges or, for more serious offences, extra time. He said he didn't know she was about to come; she might have made a similar observation. Public discussion of this topic amongst the younger lads is *de rigueur,* brazen and totally shameless.

One such creamster called Callum is reputed to be almost constantly 'at it'. He's a sad and pathetic character with a flinching, averted way about him who lives in a slum of a cell reeking of armpit, stale breath and spaff. I put my head round his door once but almost gagged and had to retreat. Callum looks permanently haggard and drawn, with the complexion of Lurpak butter. He could pose as a poster boy for Baden-Powell's infamous warning, long since debunked as every schoolboy onanist now knows. Sadly, Callum has not so much been failed by the system as totally abandoned and left to rot (at enormous expense to the taxpayer). He has no friends and no contact with his family or the outside world. His offences are quite minor but as soon as he is released he commits another (exposing himself, I suspect) and awaits the arrival of the police to pick him up and return him here. He can see no future beyond life in prison. The welfare state does not embrace the likes of Callum – 'out of sight, out of mind' is its motto.

Prisons seem to be much in the public eye these days. Even last week's *Catholic Times* (one of several such organs I see) carried a feature labelled 'Prisoners' families are living in fear'. Staffing levels were cut by about a third under the lamentable Chris Grayling/Theresa May partnership. The consequences of this are plain to see in lengthening lock-up periods and reductions in work and training opportunities, not to mention over-stretched, harassed and disillusioned staff seeking early retirement. There is a rather desperate recruitment drive underway at present and we often see groups of wide-eyed potential recruits being shown round, brought here to C-Wing because it is calmer than the volatile wings of young scumbags elsewhere.

We also encounter baby-faced new appointees, straight from school or college, who are trained 'on the job' after their seven-week induction period ends. They often make the mistake of trying to act 'cool' by cosying up to the younger lads. It rarely works for teachers in a school setting, and absolutely never in prison. The job no longer seems to attract ex-military men, once the mainstay of the service. Those few that remain are scathing about the wet-behind-the-ears types who rarely stay the course once reality hits home. One long-serving female officer, who had taken some time out, recently returned to the job to a round of cheers from all the prisoners who know her. She calls us 'my boys' or 'my gentlemen' and has all the qualities found in the best school Senior Mistresses – firm and decisive, detached but not distant, but also humane, warm-hearted and supportive. If only there were more like her.

One of the big issues in prisons everywhere is mental health, as highlighted in last week's TV programme about Durham. Also drugs, from which even C-Wing is not immune. I'm becoming quite familiar with the sweet odour of 'spice' emanating from a couple of cells, and also the dopey demeanour of its users (when not going berserk, that is) as they flop around as spiced up as a vindaloo. Spice is apparently undetectable by prison 'piss-tests' and offers short-term relief from the mental torpor of prison life, which make it the drug of choice whatever its risks. Even prescription drugs (e.g. psychoactive anti-depressants known in prison parlance as 'brake fluid') have a currency and we are told to keep all medications hidden from view – not easy with so little room for hiding places. There are some who will swallow anything they can get their hands on in the hope of inducing a 'high'. One of the young men featured in the Durham programme killed himself with an overdose during the course of filming. It made raw TV viewing, especially as we had only just had a near miss here. Last week one of our likeable but lively lads (that describes several of them) apparently saved up ten days' worth of prescribed pills and then gulped them all down in one massive (over)dose. The next morning, when doors were unlocked for work, the officers could not rouse him. The first inkling Arthur and I had that anything was amiss was the arrival of two dog-collared chaplains (no half measures here!) and a Governor (recognisable as such by his civvy suit and tie), a further bevy of regular officers and SOs (Supervising Officers) and – eventually – a doctor (identifiable by stethoscope). The landing suddenly became crowded. Everyone else was ordered back into their cells and a rare and deep hush descended on the whole wing.

I am greatly relieved to report that the young man in question returned the next day no doubt chastened but not obviously much the worse for his self-inflicted ordeal. (I'm reminded of a boy who ran away from prep school one night and was brought back the next day in a police car, still in his dressing gown. He became an instant hero!) It was that same evening that the Durham documentary was broadcast. How close we were to tragedy. I'm quite easily upset by such happenings though Arthur just lets them wash over him with a shrug. Perhaps because he's so familiar with tragedy of the Shakespearean variety from his acting career, or maybe it's because he's only 'in' for six months. As he wryly commented, it was a 'dumb rue' (Arthurisms might have found their way into the lexicon if Rev. Spooner had not got there first.)

So... like many people here, I just keep taking the pills (as per instructions on box!) hoping thereby to maintain a reasonable equilibrium and level of sanity. As you comment, I do my best to stay positive on the basis that 'if you have a "why" to live, you can bear almost any "how"' – not me, but Nietzsche, more renowned for his insights than his positivity. I suppose it's what sustained Great War soldiers through the horrors of the trenches. But we do have a few eccentrics, though sometimes it's hard to discern the genuinely bonkers from the mere showmen. I offered one guy (our age, educated, wits sharp but tangential) a Polo mint. He took it gladly but said that, if I didn't mind too much, he'd keep it for his 'imaginary friend' later. In his cell he has three lengths of card, inked in to resemble piano keys. Placed end to end on his bed he calls them his 'silent piano' on which he (allegedly) plays Chopin mazurkas noiselessly to himself. On the wing he enjoys snooker, but to an elusive set of rules of his own invention that he likens to Nelson's tactics at the Battle of the Nile. In the yard he clambers over or under the exercise machines in any way except as intended. Eventually an officer will intervene and tell him to get off before he injures himself, to which he responds that he's doing vertical yoga. 'Mad Mick', as he's known, seems to take it as a badge of pride when some of our less 'couth' youths bluntly tell him, "You're a weirdo, mate." Crazy as a one-winged fly? Or is he? It's hard to tell. Either way, his infectious loopiness provides a welcome diversion.

On the whole, most inmates are pretty tolerant of idiosyncrasy in the many forms it can take here, which is just as well. Another guy, an Eastern European called Piotr, practises some variant of an oriental exercise routine (but not Mad Mick's 'vertical yoga'!) and is also an obsessive cleaner. He regularly takes it upon himself to mop the wing floor, an action he performs by working crab-wise across the floor, mop in one hand while thrusting alternate legs into the air. Most blokes ignore him and let him get on with it unmolested, but some lads help him along by purposefully dropping splashes of coffee or pats of sunflower spread (erroneously known in prison as 'butter') to ensure that he never runs out of fresh spillages to clean up. Piotr's most troubling obsession (for the 'screws') is recycling. As soon as the landing bin bags are full he takes them off to his cell to sort the contents – plastic pots here, apple cores and food scraps there; paper here, tea bags there (but in separate piles for used and unused). In the developing world needy people make a living this way (I've seen them at the roadside in Africa and India) but here it merely attracts scorn. Like a Verdi opera plot, it would almost be funny if it were not so tragic.

By the way, our suspicions about Kevin and Benny are confirmed. They have pinned a hand-coloured rainbow flag on their cell card (outside their door) plus a neatly-penned advertisement which reads "C-Wing LGBTQ+ Association". Our resident evangelist Mr Fundament is not amused. He pontificates from his vantage point, both as Bible-bashing Christian and occupant of a cell on the upper landing right opposite K & B's, claiming to have witnessed ABOMINATION (Leviticus 18,22). You can't be holy <u>and</u> horny, he declaims like a tied up yapping dog to which no one listens. He has now, I understand, been officially warned to keep his opprobrium to himself or risk a 'negative' on his record. The Prison Service is hot on the Equality Act's seven Protected Characteristics (only loosely related to the canonical Seven Deadly Sins whatever Mr F might think).

I still haven't had my Shannon Trust training session and now there is another potential mentor also waiting. You ask if there is a library. Yes, we have a 'Libary' (sic) though it occupies a space similar to your smaller spare bedroom and is open only for about 45 minutes once a week. To be fair (a phrase often heard in prison, where things very rarely are), there is another even smaller collection of borrowable books, but that is only accessible to those, such as Arthur, who work in the print or textiles workshops. Arthur is an avid reader who puts me to shame. The books in the wing library are limited in scope as well as number apart from a disproportionately large 'true crime' section, which seems like coals to Newcastle. However, the very helpful and knowledgeable librarian (or 'libarian'?) will order in almost any title through the County inter-library scheme given a week or two's notice. In any case, S and the 'suffering' bishop's wife keep me well supplied.

How I long for a laptop! I'm amazed (+ humbled and grateful) by how effortlessly M hand-writes, filling the pages with entertaining accounts of normal life 'on the out'. I have been jotting this letter down in dribs and drabs all morning between bursts of vigorous hand-washing my personal (as opposed to prison issue) clothes. The washbasin is too small for a full load and I draw the line at using the loo. I'm spared the dreaded and complex chore of re-making the bed this week as there are NO clean sheets available. Ditto socks (not sure about the formless pale blue prison boxers which luckily I don't need, having an ample supply of my own pants). The sock famine has apparently been caused by sock-hoarders not returning their dirties. Just finished writing this in time for lunch – corned beef and pickle sandwich, a weekly delicacy and something I've not eaten willingly since schooldays. They will shortly call 'Lock-up and roll check' (Arthurism: 'cock-up and ball-check') so I will finish this and pop it in an unsealed envelope through the wing office door.

17. Thursday 9 August, 2018

Happy Birthday, Maggie! I hope the arrival of the enclosed card, as you enter your seventh decade, will make amends for all the previous ones I have wilfully neglected. 'Tis the season to be merry…" – first S and John, then Harry and Maggie, almost sharing a day if not a year. Three more are due next month. As I have to register my visitors' details with the visits dept., I am privy to all their ages and have no excuse for forgetting cards, though presents would be difficult to arrange. I may be able to provide a slice of cake when you visit at the end of the month, but you will have to pay! Please remember to bring your photo ID and loose change (banknotes are not permitted). Teresa came down by train from Melton last week. All went like clockwork (if that is an apt simile for a grown-up train) and Sara met her at the station so they could check in together. It must be a nightmare for anyone living far away or without their own transport. When my original cell-mate Sam was incarcerated on the Isle of Wight he did not see his son and family for nearly two years.

Thanks for your favourable report on the new Pope Francis film. I read in the *Catholic Herald/Times/Universe* (free from chapel) that *il Papa* has declared that the death penalty is, in all circumstances, contrary to Church teaching. A pity they didn't know at the time of the Inquisition when *de heretico comburandum* was the order of the day. The Catholic Church never changes – until it does. (The Prison Service demonstrably runs on similar lines). It would be good if the Pope extended this ban to military conflict or at least updated the definition of what constitutes a 'just' war. Something pacifist-minded Quakers don't agonise over. Did I mention that I have been attending Quaker Meeting on Fridays? I now have my very own copy of *Quaker Faith and Practice*, endorsed by *The Tablet* as 'a treasure-house of psychological and spiritual wisdom'.

Ecumenical inclusiveness has its limits, though, even in HMP, and I have now been banned from attending the RC mass on Saturdays. Apparently rules dictate that we cannot be both C of E and RC. Henry VIII has a lot to answer for, not that it troubled the consciences of all those Tudors like my Yorkshire ancestors who attended their Anglican parish church in the morning and then a 'real' mass celebrated by a recusant Roman priest later in the day. I have hesitatingly opted for Anglican worship but note that, since the enforcement of this rule by the Anglican chaplain, his own congregation has tumbled to a mere five last Sunday. Talk about cutting off his parson's nose to spite his face! It seems I was not the only secret syncretist (or 'devil-dodger') who attended both.

I must try and hunt down a copy of the prison rules. I'm told that these consist of PSOs (Prison Service Orders) and PSIs (Instructions, not tyre pressures). What a mine of information and potential source of anecdotes they must be! Anecdotally (since I can't in practice easily obtain a copy – I have tried) PSI 3.4 states that prison libraries <u>must</u> contain a copy of the PSOs and PSIs – so, more in breach than observation then! It would be instructive to see the rules on items that are (or, more likely, are not) allowed to be 'held in possession' (as they say). To choose a few at random, scissors and bladed implements of any type are prohibited, also Blu-Tack and chewing gum, jam jars, umbrellas, explosives, hoodies, black clothing or anything bearing obscene or political slogans. Also 'self-images' – have they not heard the word 'selfie'? Our ID cards with mug-shots don't count, but no narcissist would display anything snapped by that special prison camera that makes everyone smirk like a murderer or a rapist, even those who aren't.

It is said that certain musical instruments are permitted, no doubt under sufferance – guitar, recorder or flute (but not both) and harmonica. One of our number here, a folk singer, asked to have his guitar sent in. Yes, he was told, so he arranged for a family member to bring it in on a visit. Then someone must have checked the rules. Guitar OK, but not strings as they could be a safety risk.

As I always advise when passing on such nuggets of jailhouse wit and wisdom, treat the story with caution. Prisoners often talk 'squit' – but not always. Arthur is threatening to write to *Inside Time*, the prisoner newspaper, about it.

I enjoyed your account of the visit to the Welland Steam Fair. I've been to local steam events in the past and, like Maggie, always indulge in a carousel ride. One of my current colleagues here is the proud owner of a Fowler traction engine of c.1900 which he transports to shows on his own 'artic' lorry, though not as far as Shropshire. I'll see how he responds to being called a 'male operative' (your phrase), which sounds positively seedy, even for a man with a low-loader. Which leads me to observe that just now we have a particularly friendly and supportive group of older residents, mostly well-educated and with interesting life histories. Not that there is much time for socialising, though more for those, like Arthur, who go to work where they can jabber away to each other all day long. It would soon wear me out, but Arthur's Tiggerish bounce seems inexhaustible.

Yesterday afternoon I finally had my training session (more of a brief and cosy introductory chat) for the Shannon Trust reading scheme. I had never before knowingly crossed paths with Colin, the extra-mural (literally) trainer, though it turns out that he was a good friend of my former head of department who tragically died of cancer last year aged only 67. Her last act, the day before she died, was to write a fulsome (but unsuccessful!) testimonial for my court appearance. I was joined for our ST training by a new arrival here, aged 83, who seems admirably public-spirited and not at all crushed by his wholly unexpected fate ('snap' to that). It was good to hear from him how helpful and courteous he finds most of the younger 'lads' who assist him up and down the stairs (which are deep, crisp and uneven) to collect his food. Though there are 'all sorts and conditions of men' here, there is a certain *esprit de corps* born of a common fate. I have never felt threatened or even unsafe, despite the efforts of the late Lithuanian monster.

Back to the Shannon Trust. I may be just a little over-qualified as the sole academic requirement for the role is to have reached Level One in English. I'm not familiar with this particular qualification –

it sounds like a lift destination in Mothercare - but believe it equates to a moderate failure at 'O' Level. As an accredited Mentor I can now lead 20-minute tutorials up to five days a week with a Learner (they are Fond of Capitals in the Course Materials). Not sure who (or whom) to expect, but I am now wearing the blue elasticated wrist-band (music festival style) provided to advertise my services as a Mentor to potential clients. The two free T-shirts will follow if they can find some in my size (most are sized for the grossly obese, not a look I covet) and there will also be a laminated MENTOR card to go outside my door. From now on I will be on call for anyone needing help with specific reading or writing tasks such as letter-writing or interpretation of abstruse or ambiguous official notices. (The prison authorities could also benefit from a lesson on apostrophes – or should that be 'apostrophe's'? – but I'm not pushing that one. It's a lost cause.) Unofficially I used to help my first cellmate Sam with the legal letters he received, usually from public bodies demanding money. My assistance was rarely appreciated, certainly not by his lawyers whose letters invariably ended up in the bin, unanswered, despite my best endeavours.

Word may already have got around. While waiting for Sunday chapel, a fellow attendee asked if I could explain a couple of words he'd read in a book. On his left forearm he'd carefully written in biro the words 'nostalgia' and 'nauseous'. In chapel I was asked to read a long OT lesson (Prophet Nathan castigates King David for his marital infidelities) and afterwards one of the accompanying officers (normally two of them doze at the back) said, "Cracking reading, mate." I must have given him a perplexed look because he then said, "No piss-take, that really was a cracking reading." It was genuinely kind of him (compliments are rare), though I have had a lot of practice.

Last Friday I had another little surprise which truly was a 'piss-take'. I was unlocked for afternoon exercise and, as usual, had a pee, a necessary precaution before going out to the yard for up to an hour (we get the full whack on sunny days as the officers also like being outside). As we were leaving I was called aside by name and told that I must provide a 'sample' for a random drugs test (RDT for short, but generally known as a 'piss test'). "But I've only just gone, I protested. "They all say that," he responded, none too reassuringly. So I was led over to the druggy unit (or whatever it's called) where I was obliged to read and witness various forms before being handed a calibrated jar to be part-filled within four hours. Evidently an 'electronic random number generator' in London (regrettably not ERNIE of premium bond fame) had selected me for this month's jackpot. I was allowed to drink a single plastic cup of water to speed delivery (any more might dilute the results), but it's not something I can produce to order. I tried sitting, pacing up and down, gazing out of the window, or just standing, staring and regretting that I was not outside with the other chaps, but to no avail. The 'screws', two of them, were not in the least put out. One briefly nodded off to sleep, the other twiddled nonchalantly with his computer. They were in no hurry. I guess anything was preferable to a duty on A-Wing, the possible alternative. After 1½ hours, I was finally able to comply. Phew! I was told that every month they test 5% of the entire national prison population (about 4,000 tests for 80,000 prisoners in England and Wales), of whom 20% test positive for drugs. (I think that's what he said, but don't quote me). It sounds plausible, though here on C-Wing there is no <u>obvious</u> drug problem, or perhaps I just don't recognise the symptoms.

I'm interested to read your comments about the HMP Durham fly-on-the-wall documentary. What cheerful holiday viewing! Inevitably it portrayed the prison as a sin-bin for the unhinged and focused on certain 'characters', sparky incidents and issues that make for dramatic telly-viewing but failed to convey the sheer tedium of the typical day. The most familiar features for me (and you, by now long-suffering readers of my letters) were the plastic eating utensils (I must have a 'thing' about these), identical cell size, layout and fittings, green sheets (yuk), 'uniform' fleece tops and pocketless grey jogging bottoms that endow the misfortuned wearer with an air of wantonness. Some of the leading characters, with their tattoos and confrontational swagger could have walked straight off the set of any prison in the land. So could some of the issues, such as self-harm. I'm sorry to say that we lost someone off this wing last week in similar circumstances. I'll save that for a future letter. It's still a bit raw.

PS: I'm also a tad sad to report that the Kevin and Benny 'affair' (interpret that how you will) is now history. Last week, Benny was shipped out to a C-Category prison somewhere on the far side of the country. Kevin has a new pad-mate who is impervious to intimacies, and the little rainbow flag has disappeared from their door. Kev has regressed to his old sour self and vents his frustrations by cursing and kicking his door at the slightest provocation. His 'characteristics' were not 'protected' after all. From the landing above, Mr Fundament observed the removal process as keenly as he had allegedly watched their lewd shenanigans. He wore a self-satisfied smirk as wide as the very jaws of hell.

18. Wednesday 22 August, 2018

Your last letter must again have crossed with mine which I hope arrived in time for Maggie's birthday. Nothing here is ever certain until it happens, especially when the vagaries of the GPO are combined with those of the PPO, if you get my meaning. When my stock of stamps was very low I resorted to the 'free' WL (weekly letter) system only to have a letter to Christine returned unposted after a week with a note saying that I had exceeded my allowance of one per week. I had, in fact, been most careful not to send out more than one that week, but such official responses brook no argument. I mentioned it to an officer on the wing who shrugged her shoulders and said that the post-room clerks (aptly, she pronounced it to rhyme with 'berks') are not very bright. Sara has now sent in another batch of stamps, and so have you, for which, many thanks. I've had a surfeit of correspondence recently, not all of it welcome. Call me naïve, but I had mistakenly imagined that 'legal aid' was as good as its name and that their initial assessment (and my payment of several thousand pounds) constituted the full and final reckoning. Not so. They (in the form of Rossendales, an outsourced collection agency) have now sent a further much larger bill that more than wipes out my entire retirement savings at one go. To add injury to insult, they now threaten everything from bailiffs to bankruptcy if they are not paid in full within thirty days. I'm afraid poor (especially now) longsuffering S will have to sort this one out as best she can. In here I am powerless.

You asked me about self-harm, a topic aired in the HMP Durham documentaries. This seems to be a widespread problem throughout the Prison Service. What sheltered lives we have led to have encountered it so rarely, if ever, though I recall a school friend of Harry's used to cut her arm from time to time. I don't know the statistics, but here on C-Wing there are several men, mainly in their twenties and thirties, with visibly lacerated limbs. Those with old wounds have parallel or cross-hatched patterns of raised wheals, mainly on their lower arms but sometimes also on their legs or inner thighs (occasionally visible now that shorts are *de rigueur* on warm days). Current practitioners sport arms bandaged with wadding held in place with sticking plaster, oozing gobs of congealing blood. They are usually put on an ACCT – not sure what it stands for *, but it means they are subject to regular supervision (i.e. officers peeping through their door flaps to check up on them). Strange to say, cutting serves as a stress-release mechanism and a coping strategy, especially for those with existing mental health issues exacerbated by the close confinement and punitive environment of prison. According to *Inside Time*, numbers of self-harm incidents are rising quite steeply just now, exacerbated no doubt by government cutbacks, overcrowding and staff shortages.

* ACCT = Assessment, Care in Custody and Teamwork.

I mentioned last time that we had 'lost' one of our number in distressing circumstances. The young man in question had a single cell on one of the upper landings and I can't say I'd even recognise him. Ronald, who I've mentioned before, apparently knew him quite well and they had met up for a coffee and a chat that same lunchtime. He tells me that the man was a bit jittery and anxious about some personal issues, but not unduly so, nor did he show any hint of suicidal thoughts or intentions. He was a known self-harmer but not, I think, subject to an ACCT. However, later in the afternoon, when his door was next unlocked he was found slumped on the floor in a pool of blood from a self-inflicted wound in his groin. The rumour going round is that he had been pressing his bell and shouting but that no one had responded, which would suggest a tragic accident – a cut that went too deep and the help that could have saved him never arrived. Pending an investigation and (presumably) inquest his cell has been sealed up but left untouched, not even mopped out and I'm told a trickle of congealed blood is visible under his door. I'm glad I don't have to walk past it on the landing.

Yes, mental illness is very much an issue, and not just at Durham. Prisons have become a bit of a dumping ground not just for the seriously criminally insane but for many who really ought to be receiving specialist psychological help beyond the capacity of the overstretched prison psychological services. Our night times are usually almost eerily silent here on C-Wing, but not so last Monday. A very angry new arrival was located on 'the twos' almost directly above this cell. As soon as his door clanged shut he began complaining, and by 2 am was shouting, swearing and banging at regular intervals. It is said that he flooded his cell and was handed a mop. Big mistake. Mop handle rammed rapidly against iron cell doors sounds like gunfire and, just below, we felt we were under siege in the trenches. We could hear officers shouting at him through the locked door, but all attempts at pacification failed. Mercifully he was led away elsewhere early the following morning, possibly to the vicinity of the snappy Alsatians' kennels as something then seemed to set them off. There are other stories I could tell – about the 'Staff Wellbeing Day' that signally failed to live up to its name. And how the Acting Governor 'accidentally' got locked in a cell, only to discover that the response to the so-called emergency bell was far from swift (see above). But I'll keep those until we meet!

If life 'inside' sounds a little scary at times, that's nothing to life 'on the out' for those who have spent long years in prison. This was brought home to me at last Friday's Quaker meeting (something I always look forward to). We usually start with coffee and biscuits – the reverse of the Anglican routine – then sit in the comfy chairs at the back of the chapel for half an hour or so of general chat before sharing a short reading to set the mood for a period of silent meditation. Last week was the final meeting attended by Dave, an articulate and perceptive member of the group (and, according to Matthew, the chaplain, a brilliant writer) who has now been released. Dave is 40-ish and has been in prison ever since his mid-teens when he stabbed and killed his father to stop many years of abuse. The world is so much changed since his youth that he is anxious – no, frightened – about how he will cope. He has never learned to drive, used a computer or owned a mobile 'phone. On the positive side, his mother has agreed to take him back having refused all contact for many years. But Dave is a mass of tangled emotions and fears about freedom, family and personal relationships, the brain-numbing temptations of drugs and alcohol, and how to face up to so many demons from the past. We talked about his home town, which I know from years ago, and a favourite walk along the river bank that we both remember. We all wish him well, hope that he makes it and that we will not see him back here any time soon.

I enjoyed your story of the B&B with decrepit landlady, threadbare towels and mouldy jam. I'm sure you told me just to make me feel more positive about my current domestic arrangements. Nice of you. But I'm intrigued that said landlady had 'done some hovering' prior to your arrival. Levitating – at eighty? You amaze me.

You also ask about our 'kitchen provision'. Nice phrase. No, it doesn't take much heed of the seasons, let alone climatic fluctuations, and is broadly designed to satisfy the basic needs of gastronomic retards. Spuds feature prominently and are eaten in prodigious amounts. Fodder for the poor, I suppose. You may recall that Malthus (clergyman/economist, a most unseemly combination!) disapproved of potatoes, observing that the poor were more compliant when hungry. He would not have agreed with the old proverb that 'a hungry man is an angry man'. Here we have many angry men – but not for want of spuds! Back to our 'kitchen provision'. Where else would anyone choose to eat sprouts during an August heat wave (if ever)? The dietary (to use the old workhouse term) works on a four-week cycle throughout the year which, like half-board in cheap tourist hotels of our acquaintance, allows us to repeat our successes or avoid our failures. That said, we are currently being treated to some 'home grown' produce (a concept that stretches the normal understanding of 'home') from the prison market gardens. This includes nice waxy new potatoes, courgettes and marrow, runner beans and the occasional 'salad sandwich' lunch of crisp lettuce, aromatic tomatoes and flavoursome but knobbly cucumbers that might otherwise end up in the supermarket reject tray. Strawberries are grown in poly-tunnels, but we don't get to sample those unless by the bounty of some light- and sticky-fingered gardener. It's a cruel deprivation for a strawberry-lover like myself.

Just had a strangely busy lunchtime. We were unlocked to collect our lunch, then locked up again (as usual) after 15 minutes or so, then unlocked, re-locked and re-counted again twice over. Instead of the usual one officer on duty there were several in attendance, mostly unfamiliar faces on this wing. The explanation, we now know, is that they are new recruits observing 'bang-up and roll-check' procedures as part of their training. Like most policemen these days, they all look very young to us oldies. I wonder how many of this latest cohort will stay the course?

In my new Shannon Trust role I have been asked by Andy, an amiable thirty-something, to help with some writing. Andy has forms to complete for a compensation claim following an altercation with a prisoner from B-Wing. As previously explained, residents of A and B wings are supposed never to meet those of us on C. Given the contiguous layout, and our sharing of the assembly area known as the bubble, this at times requires complex manoeuvres that might tax a military display team. Even escorting a lone prisoner, say to Healthcare or for a legal visit, demands vigilance and advance radio co-ordination to ensure that the route is clear lest some aggressive B-winger should mount an ambush. Which is what happened last week to Andy. The accompanying officer, perhaps distracted, failed to notice some other prisoners, one of whom sprang out and kicked Andy viciously (his word) on the shins and punched him full on the face. He is now nursing hurt pride and a purple plum of a swelling beneath his half-closed left eye; he tries to portray himself as a war-wounded hero, but it doesn't quite wash. But look on the bright side. He has already acquired the necessary papers to apply for compensation. The written word is not Andy's natural *metier*, so he has sought my help to throw together some choice phrases to describe his ordeal just within the bounds of credulity. He hopes to earn £500 (as the table prescribes) towards savings for his release next year on grounds of dereliction of duty of care by the prison. He has a point.

Why this aggression? Even prisoners on A and B wings –

murderers, drug dealers, fraudsters, burglars and perpetrators of the whole gamut of lesser crimes – need to feel superior to someone. That someone probably resides on C-Wing, which is believed (erroneously) to be populated solely by 'scum' such as rapists and child-molesters AKA 'nonces'. Andy is not a 'nonce', but how was his assailant to know that? Besides, the assault probably earned the attacker dollops of 'street cred' with his fellow 'gangstas', well worth the short-term inconvenience of whatever punishment the prison authorities dished out to him.

Attacks like this may be rare on C-Wing, but are not the only annoyances. On these balmy summer evenings I am glad not to live on the south side of the wing as this faces 'enemy' territory. B-Wingers delight in singing through their open windows a chorus of 'Paedo….; Paeee….do; Paeeee….doooo!' sung fortissimo to a falling minor third and sounding like a whole forest of sick cuckoos. That is not their only trick. I was long ago warned off the self-service gravy and custard that comes with Sunday lunch. The kitchens, you see, are manned by prisoners from other wings who are said to delight in adulterating food destined for C-Wing by peeing in the gravy and ejaculating into the custard. Or is it the other way round? I'm not sure I believe this, but either way both gravy and custard are surprisingly tasty! And 'needs must' – I have always had difficulty swallowing dry food.

Looking forward to seeing you soon – don't forget the photo ID!

19. Tuesday 11 September, 2018

Many thanks for your letter and, of course, yet again for your visit. Well beyond any call of duty! You must have had a long and tiring day with changes of train, taxis and so forth, and as you admit, all for so little time here. This is a bit of a bone of contention, and not just for me. The official line is that prison guidelines allow for a *minimum* one-hour visiting time, so anything beyond that (and we usually get at least half an hour more) is a bonus, not an entitlement. That's what 'Miss' (a friendly and supportive landing officer) says, so all she could offer was sympathy. It's a lottery. Mid-week afternoons are always full, rushed and noisy with a carnival of small children careering around and showing off to

Daddy. For the reasons I explained last time, C-Wing residents have to be escorted over, searched, processed and admitted entirely separately and on the opposite side of the hall from A and B Wings. Often it's a case of first in, first out, which in practice means that we tend to get less time with visitors who are not admitted until all prisoners are seated at their allocated tables. Which makes me all the more grateful that you put yourself to so much trouble for so little benefit. I cannot imagine how someone whose family live at the other end of the country must feel when there are delays in escorting us over to the visits hall. The tension is palpable.

I'm so lucky to have family relatively close by. On Thursday S came in with her sister Jo and, it being a morning session, we had over 1 ½ hours together. However, Rog was also booked in and duly came along, only to be turned away at the first hurdle. He forgot to bring his wallet and was thus unable to present a driving licence as photo ID and only had a single bank card to proffer. In the absence of a photo, two other forms of ID are required. All very frustrating – he was, after all, properly booked in, named on my 'approved list' and accompanied by his wife with the same address and (unusual) surname, so he could hardly have been an impostor! Also, as a mild-mannered seventy-year old, no-one could look less like a gangster or drug dealer, but I guess it's hard to tell these days. Some prisoners are masters of disguise.

I am still much as you found me, counting my days here in a sort of purgatorial pending tray awaiting 'shipment' elsewhere. I've put in an App to request a meeting with my OS (not Ordnance Survey or Outsize, but Offender Supervisor) to discuss any plans she may have for me, or not as the case may be. I have never met the OS and did not, until last week, know that such a person existed. When I enquired after her I was told, depending on which officer I asked, that she 1) was very busy; 2) was on long-term sick leave; 3) may have moved to another department; or 4) "Dunno mate. Never 'eard of her." This is not reassuring.

What prompted my enquiries was the arrival of Re-Categorisation paperwork which is, apparently, issued every six months. This states that I cannot be re-categorised (yet) as it is 'too early in my sentence to be considered for open conditions' * and that I 'have no sentence plan [true, but hardly my fault unless they were expecting me to write it for myself!] Hence my request. Meanwhile time ticks on. By the end of this month I shall already have served a quarter of my sentence (hurray!), and there's Christmas to look forward to. We may expect a cooked breakfast and passable roast turkey for lunch, but maybe not much opportunity for carol singing. Maybe just as well.

* [Postscript: This was not true. PSI 40/2011 states that prisoners are eligible for transfer to D-Category open prisons within 24 months of release date. As of Sep 2018 I had 22 months to serve]

Yes, all cells are equipped with electric kettles of the small white plastic 'travel kettle' variety. If Arthur and I have a spare tenner (we don't), we could upgrade by purchasing, via the weekly canteen list, a shiny new stainless steel model. I think you already know that we have a small TV made out of clear plastic so we can see all its inner organs and differently-coloured cabling, like an anatomical model or pathologist's guide to autopsy. I initially interpreted this as a design statement, but gather the clear case is to prevent us hiding contraband such as drugs or mini-cellphones (both of which may be hidden 'anatomically', so to speak, though that must be a pain in the butt.) We each pay 50p per week for the TV which works on a cable system with a limited range of channels, not including BBC4 – a shame as it has some of the best cultural offerings, but clearly not the 'right' sort of culture for prisoners! There are also a couple of amateurish (squelchy soundtrack and jerky picture) in-house prison channels offering basic information on prison procedures, dos and don'ts (mostly the latter) and some sort of basic English tuition. I wonder what it says about apostrophe's? Which reminds me – many thanks for the cards. I love the *Apostrophe Man* cartoon. He would be very busy here, with so many notice's, menu's and (especially) rule's and regulation's for the screw's to enforce.

Life here is, as you surmise, pretty equable and I try to follow the wartime injunction to 'keep calm and carry on.' However, I had a heart-stopping moment when I returned from your visit to find a letter shoved under my cell door. Official HMP header at top, and strap line 'We see the person not the prisoner', like a gratuitous fart at the bottom – so far, so unconcerning. But as I casually scanned its contents, what sprang out at me like a punch in the gut was the emboldened heading **NEGATIVE**. You may imagine my immediate anxiety as 'negatives' are punishments for misconduct and may result in 'nickings'. What had I done wrong? What pettifogging rule had I unwittingly transgressed? Would I ever be allowed to progress to 'enhanced' status? Then I looked more closely to find that it was in fact a Certificate of Achievement for a *NEGATIVE* Result (they also like capitals) in my recent RDT (Random Drugs Test). It's one of those tests you must fail in order to pass, so to speak. I will keep it for posterity – and possible future display in the downstairs loo at home – amongst my growing collection of prison memorabilia.

Chapel attendance has fallen (again) since the Sunday before last when the B-Wing lot tried to steal the toaster from the chapel kitchen. You just can't trust anyone nowadays! The incident, and the (failed) investigation that followed caused such long delays that us C-Wing attendees, who are on second shift, were rationed to two hymns but still arrived back late for Sunday lunch (roast chicken leg – halal version recommended as it's coated with a spicy glaze – and aforementioned gravy). Next week the Rev referred to the incident in his expostulatory sermon, a rare instance of an electrical appliance used in a parable to illustrate the Word of God.

We (that is, this 'nick') also feature in this month's *Inside Time* under the heading 'Prison Staff Not Happy.' As a headline it's about as unremarkable as the celebrated, but possibly apocryphal, one from *The Catholic Universe* 'Reverend Mother Stung by Bee'. *Inside Time* relates that we are currently forty staff short, mostly on sick leave, and 'everyone is at the end of their tether'. As stories go it's a bit of a damp squid and the headline lacks grit (just to mix a few more metaphors!) Others from the latest *IT* include: 'Chickens get better treated' (HMP Bromsgrove – nothing halal about that); 'Religious Discrimination' (HMP Peterborough – the letter begins, 'I am an active Pagan witch…'); 'Falling to Bits' (HMP Dartmoor); and 'Side Affects' (sic – HMP Holme House). The front page headline screams 'THE WORST EVER PRISON' and concerns HMP Birmingham, which you have surely read about elsewhere. I am pleased to report that here we are not at present infested with rats, mice, ants, cockroaches, bed-bugs or even fleas. C-Wing is kept shiny-clean, thanks to the daily endeavours of a team of orderlies, notably Piotr (as previously described) who has an OCD in litter-picking from the University of Life.

To answer your question about the prison population, on this wing there are relatively few non-native Brits, viz. a few East Europeans (including Piotr and the 7ft tall Lithuanian who finally left last month to the relief of everyone shorter, i.e. everyone) plus a few black and Asian residents, so broadly-speaking representative of the local population beyond the walls. The prison authorities are properly very hot on equality issues and most prisoners seem to me to be commendably colour-blind. I could go further and say that, by and large, prisoners here are supportive of each other irrespective of age, background, race or any other markers. However temporarily, what unites us trumps what might otherwise divide us outside. The Lithuanian was not disliked for his nationality, but because he was a bully.

I'm intrigued by your description of the 'classy magazines' in our visitors' waiting area, but not entirely surprised that they are so little used. Apart from our own orders, we only have access to a few free-to-take magazines in the briefly-open weekly library, mainly of the *War-Gaming Monthly* variety. The chapel also has free reading matter, though its appeal is very limited and I'm clearly the only reader of *The Catholic Herald* and *The Tablet* (I'm still permitted to read these despite the ban on my Catholic chapel attendance). A new inmate – unsuccessfully – requested a large-print Bible, explaining that he has 'catalysts' in both eyes. (Another one complained to me that his pad-mate is a 'maniac-depressive'). On your recommendation, I will ask our helpful librarian (he works for the County Library Service, not the prison) to source a copy of *The Underground Man* and hope it will get me grinning. Meanwhile I have submitted six mini-reviews for my bronze level Library Challenge Award and await laminated certificate (another one to frame for the loo?) and motivational mini-dictionary. Arthur has already earned his Silver Certificate, but he's an unreconstructed swot straight out of the pages of *How to be Topp*. True, I write more letters (all logged in my notebook) than Arthur, but he has now taken up art as well.

Is there no end to Arthur's aspirations? What a legend he is! He has produced some still-lives (lifes?) that are recognisably based on the apples and oranges in our communal fruit bowl, albeit in rather psychedelic colours, possibly the consequence of Arthur's over-indulgence in prison tea. These, along with some other even weirder offerings, are now laminated and displayed on a wing notice board under the heading PRISONER ART. It's nice to see talents celebrated and they have not yet been defaced, though some of our number seem to live in such a state of terminal torpor that they may not even have noticed them.

Did I mention that I have applied to become a Listener? You may have seen something of this scheme in action during recent TV prison documentaries. It is not just worthy; it can be a genuine life-saver for prisoners at the end of their tether and contemplating suicide. And for others too who just need someone sympathetic and non-judgemental to unburden their anxieties to. Almost all prisons now have a Listener scheme run on a voluntary basis by the Samaritans and it's well tried and tested here. Orderly Darren told me of it during my induction (how long ago that now seems!) and I know of several people, including one of my previous cell-mates, who have benefited from it. There is a selection process to go through, of course, and a series of training sessions that are based on Samaritans training but adapted to the peculiar circumstances of prison life. Watch this space.

Nothing further on our recent death. I do hope there will be an inquest to establish the facts. The official line suggests suicide, but the bush telegraph leans towards an entirely avoidable accident.

20. Thursday 8 October, 2018

Your latest letter's anecdotes about the train trip 'down south', those London galleries, and your friends' lavish nuptials have kept us in C1-24 heartily amused. (I hope you don't mind my sharing them with Arthur – there's little space for secrets when sharing an eleven-by-seven.) I'm glad the wedding was a 'decent' affair, though as you were only B-list guests, whatever excesses must have indulged the A-listers?

Writing 'decent' reminds me that today we have had a 'decency inspection' conducted by a member of the Management Team. I don't know if the grey-suited gentleman who came to check our cell (supported by female assistant brandishing clip board) was the new Governor * (arrived Monday) as he didn't introduce himself and I couldn't read his name badge without invading his personal space and appearing nosy, short-sighted or intimidating. We had been handed a warning notice in advance (like a tip-off prior to an unannounced OFSTED inspection) so Arthur and I had a little flick of the duster and general tidy up and I gamely volunteered to wash the floor while A was out at work.

* *He wasn't, as I now know.*

Despite this, the 'Guv' – not a man to mince his words – asked what 'all that crap under the bed' was. It's our clothing, in bin bags! Where else are we supposed to store it? I was relieved that he didn't inspect the <u>under</u>side of the top bunk. Here, some long-departed former occupant has deeply scratched on the metal webbing directly above my eyes, 'I had a great wank here. Ha ha!' The mental picture of some tattooed reprobate tossing off where I now lie does nothing for my own much diminished libido. The Gov asked his PA (or whatever) to note down on her clipboard that we need a paint job and expressed his view that our plethora of pictures looks messy, but stopped short of ordering us to actually take them down. Just as well as most are covering up holes in the plasterwork. There is no way we can aspire to the gleaming and perfectly ordered spotlessness he seems to expect. The Gov also said we should ask for de-scaler to clean the loo. A kind thought - how sweetly domesticated of him. But in truth we have repeatedly asked for this very substance, only to be told that it is not currently available from stores. Maybe some desperado has been drinking it. I also notice a charming attempt at re-branding our living quarters in the advance-warning letter which refers to cells as 'rooms' and prisoners as 'residents'. The jolly cartoon-like illustration [Caption: 'A sparkling clean room, a happier ☺ you'] appears to have been cut and pasted from an advert for Premier Inn or similar and shows a twin-bed motel-style suite rather than anything remotely resembling an actual prison cell. Good try, Gov, but you can't fool us!

Another official communication arrived last Friday with, perhaps, the latest twist in the 'staff not happy' saga as reported in *Inside Time*. The letter, pushed under our doors at 8.30 am, said that 'normal regime activity' will be delayed 'due to' (sic – the pedant in me would like to correct this to 'owing to') action by the Prison Officers' Association (POA). Friday mornings are normally pretty quiet, but even less happens with the 'screws' on strike. It's supposed to be the day when canteen orders (drinks, stationery, snacks, vapes, etc.) are delivered, but they can surely wait while we have yet another 'change of normal regime' or, in prisoner-speak, 'extended f - - - ing bang-up'. There's little doubt that most prisons are coming loose at the seams and the whole system shudders and creaks like the Titanic in its death-throes. I'm not sure how striking 'screws' will help the situation, but I think most inmates are broadly sympathetic to their cause. We're all in this together – same shit but different, as they say.

I am sorry to hear, John, of your worsening issues with your leg/spine/hip which must be a worry, especially for one used to being so physically active. At least you have an unassailable excuse for <u>not</u> de-scaling the loo or dusting under the beds. Good luck with your new range of exercises, whatever they may entail. I've previously described how I sit coyly and lever myself up and down on the shoulder-press machine in the exercise yard here. Arthur does the same, but in his case with an expression of such innocent insouciance that it looks like effortless enjoyment. I've now worked up to doing 100 leverages in three or four sets, a sort of snacking menu of 30 or 40 physical jerks at a time. I'm very conscious of the need for more activity, and Teresa keeps sending me helpful hints about exercise routines (though it's really the kitchens that would benefit from her expertise). Meanwhile my blood pressure remains stubbornly high along with other possibly heart-related issues such as chest pains (a.m.) and swollen ankles (p.m.) The doctor here (who I much like) is monitoring my condition while doling out more and more pills. My Dad died suddenly of a coronary when he was exactly the age I am now, something to concentrate the mind.

'Wellness' is a current buzz-word here and the current round of wing and cell inspections seems to be part of a drive for order and cleanliness. On this wing, at least, general cleanliness would do justice to many a hospital ward. The chief cleaner is a tattooed Desperate Dan lookalike who calls me 'bruv' and has tried but failed to recruit me into their team. If he knew me as well as you do, he would realise that my talents do not extend to cleaning or tidying. Our wing's general cleanliness has, in no small way, been the product of Piotr-the-Litter-Picker's efforts, so there was some concern that standards might drop following his release on Friday last week. We need not have worried. He was already back again by Monday morning wearing a very hang-dog expression. I asked him what on earth had happened since I knew how anxious he was to re-connect with his young son currently in foster care. Sorrowfully he told me how he had shared a bottle of vodka with a friend over the week-end; their jollification turned into an argument, then a fight, and he ended up laying the friend out cold on the pavement. (Piotr is a strong guy who can do limitless shoulder-press pull-ups using <u>one hand</u> only!) So now, after a sobering-up night in a police cell, he's come back to resume his old job of floor-cleaner in chief. I feel very sad for him.

You ask after my reading. *The Underground Man* is still on order through the library but meanwhile I have enjoyed Bernard Cornwell's *Fools and Mortals* (also from the library), passed on by Arthur. It's a jolly romp through Shakespeare's London with a decidedly ripe turn of phrase – one reason why it appealed to Arthur, who is a master raconteur of ribaldry. I've not heard of *McMafia* and think I'd prefer to distance myself from the criminal underworld (not so easy in prison!). Crime – both 'true life' and fictional – seems to be popular with 'our residents' (to borrow the Gov's euphemism), and that's just their reading matter. Did I mention that I have read the typescript of an (as-yet) unpublished novel written by an older (or 'even older') inmate? A lyrical romantic story set mainly in Botswana (where we stayed with Tim on our first African trip). The author is 87 and has now been moved to another wing where the facilities are better adapted for care of prisoners with limited mobility or other disabilities. It is called L-Wing, though I'm not sure if that's because it's L-shaped (which it is) or that it mainly houses elderly 'Lifers', or perhaps 'cos it's the last stage on the way to 'ell for its residents. I'm sorry our elderly author has gone as we used to enjoy reminiscing about southern Africa where he has been on many safaris with his wife.

Bad news on the 'phone front. As you know, I telephone S every day, usually during the one hour's 'association' time between afternoon exercise and our evening meal. I also call Harry on Saturdays and altogether use up to £9 per week worth of 'phone credits. You might think they'd bring the price down if they really wanted prisoners to maintain contact with their families outside, as they claim. We have three 'phones on this landing but only at weekends does much of a queue begin to form. Well now a time restriction has been imposed (without any prior warning). After about ten minutes into a call there is now a loud beep and the 'phone cuts out just one minute later. We then have to wait for perhaps half an hour before being able to re-connect. It was thus in three stages that I relayed to S instructions on how to switch the home central heating to come on. Very confusing. This has made me realise, only too late, how important it is to share and explain such domestic details in case one is unexpectedly left home alone.

Good news, however, on the Listener front. Five candidates from this wing have been vetted, interviewed and selected to join the team. I don't know how many put in applications though rumour has it that at least one expectant applicant was 'weeded out', wisely in my view. The interviews were conducted by Samaritans of the 'sixty year old, smiling public man' (Yeats) type (though in this case, mostly women) who are well represented amongst the various volunteers from outside who freely give up their time and energies to support prisoners in one way or another. The IMB (Independent Monitoring Board) is another such group, and, of course, Prisoner Visitors who act as friends and mentors to individual prisoners, plus others from the 'free world' who occasionally pop in to assist, for example, with education or chapel. Anyway, an initial training session is scheduled for tomorrow, so I will report back in my next letter. Wish me luck.

21. Tuesday 8 October, 2018

Your account of your German visitors' stay made me almost glad of our more limited social circle. How your hearts must have sunk when you saw all that luggage heaped in your hall and realised that they would need entertaining for a full eleven days! You are so generous and sociable, you quite put S and me to shame – though our lack of sociability may have helped draw us together in the first place. One of the most draining aspects of prison life, I find, is to be thrown together in an at times rowdy bustle, with some who would not normally be companions of choice (to word it generously). That said, Arthur's allocation to 'my' cell was a serendipitous move. Of course, he talks far too much, though not half as much as Sam! But at least Arthur talks sense – or intelligent nonsense – most of the time, unlike Joe who spewed out a constant stream of crap. I wonder who has to put up with him now?

There's a sequel to my decency inspection story. Certain persons whose cells were found to be spotless and chillingly Spartan (not muddled and homely like ours) were instantly upgraded to Enhanced status. We (Arthur and I) were never contenders, but do feel slightly discriminated against, both of us in our different ways being congenitally untidy. This is not how the system is supposed to work. Even Miss G, one of our best-loved wing officers, agrees.

The Listener induction has now started in earnest with a schedule of nine afternoon sessions to be held over the next three weeks in the 'Training Suite' (located under Healthcare – a cold, bare room ornamented with nothing beyond a flip chart and tea-making facilities). There are five trainees from A and B wings and a further five of 'our lads'. It is most unusual, even irregular, for the wings to mingle, but I guess being chosen as a Listener indicates a degree of trustworthiness, so I have no fears of being biffed on the bonce by a B-Winger. Our five are all likeable guys in their different ways and include my former cell-mate Nige (alias Hopalong or 'Prof. Jingles' after a celebrated Lowestoft Punch and Judy man) plus a notable recent addition to our ranks called Bob. At least, that's what we all thought, until one of the trainers addressed him as Crispin. Like several others who were long-ago Christened with posh-sounding names, in prison he has opted for the demotic and we have all sworn to keep his secret, as befits good Listeners (it's part of the training). 'Bob' is in his thirties, conventionally tall, dark and handsome (potential nickname = Alfonso), and with an upright bearing, plus the rounded vowels and crisp consonants of a peachy public school voice. Despite his crumpled prison garments he conveys a certain aura of authority. He has compassionate, enquiring eyes and, if he can exorcise his own demons, may be well placed to help others dispel theirs. Unfortunately Bob talks too much – much too much. This could become an issue. We are meant to be listeners, not talkers!

The other trainee Listeners all present as thoughtful, insightful and compassionate people (this does not necessarily apply to the prison population as a whole!) and I am impressed by their commitment. The expectation is that, once trained, we will be on a call-out rota to meet with anyone who is distressed or at risk. This can be at any time of the day or night. Each wing has a 'Listener suite'. I have now seen ours (at one end of the 'twos' landing) and it would stretch even the most charitable blind man's imagination to call it a 'suite'. It's just a regular tatty old cell with unshielded lavatory, two hard chairs, a soft one (stuffing erupting from seat cushions), and a low coffee table with bog roll (for mopping tears, not crap, though we may hear quite a lot of that). It has echo-chamber acoustics for lack of beds, curtains or personal impedimenta. A therapist who met clients in such surroundings would surely be struck off. No matter. It may help focus attention on the issues.

Our training course is professionally delivered and, in the way of such things, heavy on small group work and role play (ouch!). So far we have concentrated on the confidentiality issue and it's been firmly rammed home to us that, like a priest's 'seal of the confessional', we must never, ever divulge what we may be told in confidence. So don't expect future letters to be laced with racy anecdotes from the Listener Suite! Our role is to listen (hence the name) and help our 'callers' (Samaritan speak) to explore their own feelings and consider available courses of action. We are not allowed to proffer advice or express opinions, so phrases such as 'If I were you I'd….' or 'I think that…' or 'Why don't you…' are banned. That is a difficult ask for those of us with instinctively controlling personalities. Some unlearning to do there! We have been role-playing likely scenarios (a bit scary) and also practising asking 'open' questions to enable us to tease out our callers' thoughts and feelings rather than risk shutting them down with 'closed' yes-no answers. One such game was a version of *What's My Line?* where we must discover the other person's occupation (from list provided) but without asking any questions that can be answered by yes or no. It's a tricky one (for this exercise I role-played a market trader, an accountant and a dentist – ouch).

Re. your question about wall hooks in the cell, the answer is no, there are no 'official' hooks. I'm not sure why, but it may have something to do with hanging. However, such is the resourcefulness of prisoners that hooks of a sort can be made out of headless matchsticks glued together into a U-shape then stuck onto the wall. There are some here in C1-24, made by previous occupants, and very useful they are too, e.g. for hanging up our outdoor coats or keys (joke – keys are something we live without). I never realised PVA was so strong. Matchstick modelling is an 'approved' craft and materials (headless matches, glue, paints) are available for purchase. Matchsticks may be shaped or cut with blades liberated from prison-issue razors, which are not very sharp by design. I have seen some most detailed models (cars, planes, houses) which, with permission, may be passed on to children to take home from visits. They are the modern equivalent of those intricate bone or straw models made by French POWs during the Napoleonic Wars – examples often found in maritime and other museums. Peterborough Museum has a fascinating collection made at the nearby Norman Cross prison where my great-great-grandfather was steward (bet you never knew of my long family association with prisons, right back to the one who was held in the Tower and famously executed in 1535).

Since starting this on Tuesday, Maggie's letter (postmarked 1st October) has been delivered. Don't ask who or what held it up, we'll just blame Royal Mail. Likewise, there's no knowing what Stasi-like scrutiny incoming letters are subjected to pending release to addressees. Rumour has it that senders sometimes impregnate notepaper with 'spice' (not the sort sold at Sainsbury's). At the least suspicion of this, photocopies are made for delivery to recipients – all yours have so far passed, but go easy on the cinnamon and nutmeg if you're writing in the kitchen. The only 'high' I get from your letters is their literary style and, of course, my joy at hearing your news. It would be instructive to know how long this letter takes to reach you and I will affix a first class stamp to expedite delivery.

What little triumphs help make life bearable! Today I have at last managed to secure a blue plastic tray to help with collecting meals from the servery. These zealously-guarded trophies are supposed to be available for ailing or elderly prisoners (in this case, anyone over fifty) but have a way of falling into the hands of sundry 'heavies' and young tykes instead. As I was let out of the cell just now I spotted a low pile of brand new trays sitting on the table tennis table and grabbed one while I still could. This means that I can finally jettison the much gravy-stained and slightly soggy cardboard box that has had to serve until now.

PS. My App to my OS re sentence plan etc. failed to elicit the courtesy of a reply. Having waited a month, I bit my tongue and submitted a second, grovelly, App ('I realise you must be very busy, but…') though I have not as yet received any response. Grrr…!

22. Wednesday 24 October, 2018

Your letters, like Reith's BBC, never fail to inform, educate and entertain. Where would I be without them? They make my little perspectives on prison life seem quite inconsequential and droll by comparison. So here's another one. The Gov's request for us to de-scale the loo still awaits the required chemicals. However we have had a further defect to report – a leaky tap that has been drip-dripping with increasing determination since the start of the month. I reported this to the landing officer who filled out a requisition form and in due course the Men from Maintenance came to take a peek. "That's dripping," they observed. "It needs attending to or it will only get worse." Not wishing to hurt their feelings, Arthur and I feigned polite surprise and chorused our appreciation of their diagnosis. They left. A week or so later, after a further prod from the 'screws', two more men came and went, and a further two such visits ensued, usually in pairs (one to do the job, the other for protection in case we – being criminals – turn nasty). By now we were using our waste bin as a bucket to catch the drips from the U-bend, and the regular *splat, splat* was becoming an irritation, especially during the night. Finally, yesterday afternoon while I was out calming myself at Buddhist meditation, someone with the right thingamajig came along and I'm pleased to report that we are now drip-free.

A fellow 'resident' called Rod – a cynic if ever there was one – informs me that in the 'old days' (Rod has done a lot of 'bird', as they say) the problem would have been sorted out promptly and in-house, but now plumbing and maintenance are out-sourced, so every call-out notches up another generous fee for private enterprise. Naturally I treat all such observations with the scepticism they deserve, but this one does seem plausible. Rod blames Mrs Thatcher, though not personally of course. I'm not sure she would have known how to handle a plumber's plunger.

I realise that I'm feeling deprived of the sights and sounds of autumn. How strange not to be able to see any trees apart from the diminutive palms/cordyline or indeed anything much to mark the passage of the seasons apart from the earlier onset of darkness outside and the sometimes warm heating pipes within. Most prisoners are hardy types and eschew warm clothing in favour of shorts and T-shirts (or, horror of horrors, string vests – where do they get them? – that make a revealing complement for displays of extensive tattoos). I feel a bit of a misfit in my warm fleecy top and outsize grey/orange donkey jacket.

As part of our Listener training course we had a couple of sessions on self-harm, an ever present issue, as I have mentioned before. Our role as Listeners is not to prevent, criticise or deter self-harmers, but to acknowledge their feelings, empathise and reassure them and respect their wishes. Self-harm can take many forms from mild scratching, hair-pulling or scalding to head-banging, cutting (as with our recent tragedy), asphyxiation or ingesting sharp objects e.g. razor blades. Why? Apparently it can give an immediate sense of stress release and taking control, so – however counterintuitive it may seem – it can be a positive experience. It's rarely a one-off, though. They do it again and again, as their scars and stripes bear witness.

Anyway, training has now finished and we all passed – sessions ended as they began with a one-to-one interview. There was a passing-out parade in the Training Suite (heating on for once!) at which we were all photographed wearing our new green T-shirts and holding our certificates. We now have a rota on the wing to ensure that everyone is called in rotation, though initially we are doubling up to learn the ropes with experienced Listeners. I am paired with Shane, a gritty fellow in his forties (also 'done bird' before) who has a good heart and a no-nonsense approach that earns him widespread respect on the wing. The first call out we had – I hope I'm breaking no confidences here – Shane warned me that the bloke was notorious for trying to scrounge extra vapes (on a 'payyoubackhonestbruv' basis) on the pretext of feeling low, etc. We went through the motions, but Shane was right and was not budging an inch re. 'loan' of vapes, though the bloke later sweet-talked an officer into parting with one. Was this an abuse of our Listener service? Maybe, but it is definitely not typical.

Now for a change of tune. We have a new arrival on the wing, Clifford, who is (or was) an organist, formerly of a local non-conformist chapel though he was brought up in an Anglican household and is now a Mormon. (How's that for 'devil-dodging'?) I have talked him into forming a little choir to sing at the Christmas carol service in chapel, a proposal that momentarily gave our generally stolid chaplain a fit of the giggles. We have a quartet of willing singers and, if the chaplain can find the organ key, Cliff may even be allowed to accompany us on the Wurlitzer itself rather than the pre-recorded boom box. The Rev has agreed to a service of <u>five</u> lessons and carols, rather than the conventional nine, on the basis that any more would be beyond the congregation's attention span. A pity he doesn't apply the same criterion to his sermons! We're a bit stuck for music, but I've asked S to bring in my old copy of *Carols for Choirs* (first edition – showing its age, and mine) and Clifford is hoping to source a further two copies via a visitor. I'm not sure when or where we'll be able to practise as the logistics of getting a group of C-Wingers over to the chapel out of hours, so to speak, may prove insurmountable. We basses are down here on the 'ones' but our tenor (appropriately) is up top on the 'threes' and a baritone is on the mid-level (in both senses) so meeting up on the wing may also be difficult. I suppose there's always the exercise yard, where we do meet up and, indeed, most of our planning has taken place. But that's no place for a sing-along, especially in the bleak midwinter.

But let's remain optimistic. With no instrument for rehearsals, not even a guitar (strings banned, remember *) and no tuning fork, we shall be relying on Cliff to give us our notes. Ingeniously, if he removes the ferrule from his tubular walking stick and blows not too vigorously across the open end it produces a clear and audible A. Just what every choirmaster needs! I'm now conducting a recruiting drive. Arthur, despite a distaste for religious ritual, has agreed to sing the tunes in his booming but rather folksy tones. I shall sing bass, of course. Our tenor is (or was... same old story!) a lawyer as well as an opera buff and composer of jingles for Romanian TV adverts. Versatile chap, bit of a polymath (alumnus of your old school, John). During exercise periods he is often to be seen deep in conversation with our Romanian brethren for whom he acts as interpreter and dispenser of free legal advice. I would treat his opinions with some caution given his apparent lack of success on his own behalf. Finally there is Crispin, alias Bob, who, like me, survived school and college choirs with his vocal cords intact.

It will be good to sing in parts again, harmonious parts that is – much of the singing I hear in chapel is at best approximate. Even so, I enjoy a bit of a sing (to CDs played on the boom box) at Sunday chapel, though the Rev. tends to favour modern jingles over 'old favourites' on the basis that most people here don't know the traditional tunes. In truth, they don't know the new ones either!

* To his great delight, Arthur's letter on this topic is published in this month's *Inside Time* and has won their 'Star Letter of the Month' prize of £25 (to be credited to A's 'spends account'). The letter begins, 'Sometimes you have to wonder where the system's brain is at when they implement the most outrageous and nonsensical rules. We now call these rules the Guitar String Paradox, or GSP, and here's why...' Yes, Arthur has a way with words! I suppose we must give credit to HMPS for allowing such a letter to be sent, published and then circulated through every prison in the land.

Guy Fawkes' Night is only two weeks away and already we hear the occasional whizz and pop of fireworks being prematurely let off by unseen persons beyond the prison walls. I have been chatting during fine exercise periods to a little arsonist, podgy as a pudding, who is already excited in anticipation of the 'big night'. It is very rare for anyone here to talk about their convictions, but our arsonist is an exception. His gnome-like face lights up as he gleefully describes how he set his house alight thus imperilling his own and his neighbours' lives. Perhaps I am glad of that well-greased plughole half way up every cell door (through which my pills were poked on night one) that is designed to take a hose to douse any fires within.

You may remember my account of being called out one afternoon for a drugs test. This was a Statutory Drugs Test or SDT as opposed to an STD, for which they also test, but only on request. Last time I tested Negative, so should have been awarded a Positive on my records. Confusing innit? (Sorry – I must be picking up the habit.) Well, would you believe it, at the start of this week I was called out again, this time roused from bed at 8.15 am, so they did not have so long to wait for me to produce the goods. The 'electronic random number indicator equipment' (ERNIE) either has it in for me, or they have genuine suspicions. The ever-friendly officers in the drugs emporium showed me how the collection jar has an integral temperature gauge so they can check that the sample is warm. Apparently prisoners who consider themselves at risk of testing positive sometimes carry around a small jar of what the officer termed 'counterfeit piss' from a 'clean' donor, with which they can surreptitiously fill the collecting jar. Another source explained to me the ways and whereabouts of concealing this at body temperature, but we needn't go there. Is there no end to prisoners' ingenuity?

Thank you for the reminder that this month is the fiftieth anniversary of our first meeting. You have both stayed the course through so many downs as well as ups, and I am humbly grateful. I hope I have not caused you too much heartache or embarrassment over the years and I am fortunate to have such true and loyal friends.

23. Wednesday 7 November, 2018

Thanks for the letter and postcard from Llandudno with 'X marks the spot' to locate your hotel room-with-a-view. If I could, I'd return the compliment with an aerial view of my current 'holiday' accommodation with X for C-Wing, but that would probably be a security breach. You could try Google Earth unless this counts as a sensitive site permanently obscured by mist. Should you consider sending in a drone (as per recent national news footage) with e.g. some squishy French cheese or a bottle of vintage port for Christmas, forget it. All our windows have external metal cages with strong but rusting slats to prevent ingress or egress. They made good cool boxes for keeping milk fresh in the summer. You certainly enjoyed a much better view in Llandudno than I do here, the only similarity being the presence of mobster seagulls that (when not raiding the bin bags) like to hop around on the grass outside my window loudly squawking to each other. Sociable birds, gulls. I listen to them early in the morning and imagine myself afloat in some foreign yacht harbour. The bunks are similar too (narrow and firm), but there the comparison ends. Happy days!

For the first time ever I have availed myself of the offer of a 'flu jab. Not that I have been laid low by 'flu for many a long year, but I fear that in this hothouse if one goes down with it, everyone risks catching it. So, better safe than supine, I think. My blood pressure has been persistently high for several months but is now slowly dropping thanks to yet another daily pill. I currently take five every morning and a further three before bed. No wonder the NHS is on its knees, even if I am not.

Your account of the 'munching men' lunch, John, had me salivating at its sheer deliciousness and excess. But I have to ask, why did you not <u>accept</u> the garlic bread with the lasagne, then 'trade' it for, say, a couple of extra sachets of ketchup not wanted by another diner? That's what we'd do here. Like the ancient Egyptians, we have no access to coinage for trades. They commonly used sandals as a convenient unit of currency (everyone wore them and their price was not subject to fluctuations). Here almost anything will do from chocolate bars to milk cartons, 'vapes' to Vosene.

I too am hoping to lose a little weight having put on 7lbs since my arrival here. This is starting to show around and (especially) above waist level so getting into some of my cherished own clothes is becoming a squeeze (not prison issue, which have infinitely expandable waists). The prison male nurse brings electronic scales onto the wing at least once a week, mainly for the benefit/consternation of us less active 'older gentlemen', and these read 74 somethings (about 11 ½ st, I believe). I now opt for fruit instead of stodgy puddings – which also resolves any lingering doubts over dodgily adulterated custard. I have recently discovered that the quiche and salad that form the vegetarian option on alternate Tuesdays is really rather good, also the baked beans and baked potato (Saturdays), though it can make for a rather 'windy' cell if we both have it. Otherwise I usually stick to meat (fish on Fridays) as the vegetarian choices tend to be variations on a theme of soft grey/brown mush. I was told they sometimes taste better than they look, and put it to the test by trying the baked mushrooms. These are presented in foil containers and resemble bowls of steaming turds, but (with eyes closed and nose pinched) they taste disarmingly palatable.

Even without comfort eating, the carbs are hard to avoid and I'm trying to persuade the servery helpers (fellow inmates) not to give me so much food. It's a losing battle. They seem to be pre-programmed to heap food to the very limits and compete to see who can create the tallest pyramid of mashed potato on a 9-inch plastic plate, far more than it (or my stomach) can safely hold. Our food servers are not a happy bunch, it seems. Maybe it's because the very sight of brawny, tattooed prisoners in white coats, elasticated pork-pie hats and blue rubber gloves (for handing out boiled potatoes!) would move most people to mirth. Not that I would dare laugh out loud. Their feelings may be softer than they'd care to show. My meek, "Not so much, please!" used to be met by No. 1 Rude Boy (of the fairground Traveller community, and a Catholic to boot) with a curt "You'll get what you're given, mate" as yet another weighty splat of mash landed on the plate. Much of it ended up down the loo unless either 1) I was feeling charitable towards the marauding seagulls and put it in the bin bag to go outside instead, or 2) Arthur scooped the surplus off my plate. He is slightly shorter than me but even more amply proportioned round the middle, despite which he maintains that he has actually lost weight since arriving here. No mean feat if true. Anyway, this particular RC Rude Boy has this week been 'decanted' (another curious prison usage) to Highpoint. Much joy may they have of him. We never did.

The religious reference above reminds me that Faith is another of the Protected Characteristics the HMPS is committed to uphold. Also that the cell-mate of the aforementioned RB was confirmed yesterday at a special chapel service taken by the C of E suffragan bishop. The candidate was suitably awed by the bish, especially by his cope and mitre, all cream satin emblazoned with flames of red and gold thread. He had never seen a bishop (or a mitre) before ("only on the telly"), and even I admit that it looked a trifle incongruous in these downbeat surroundings. "Where did you get that hat?" he (almost) asked.

I'm surprised and sorry to hear that on your Samaritan friend's patch they only have one Listener per prison. This morning we had our monthly meeting with the Samaritan co-ordinators (first time since I qualified) with fourteen of us present from across the different wings. We've certainly been busy on C-Wing where we normally operate in pairs (reassuring, since all except Shane are new recruits) to cover evening and night-time call-outs. During 'workshop hours' I'm usually the only Listener left on the wing, but that is an unlikely time for a call. So far I have been on seven calls, though some have had more. Every one is different – so many issues – but interesting, like being on the set of a TV soap or drama, and giving an insight into the often-chaotic lifestyles of others. Feedback from callers is reassuringly positive. We need to be self-disciplined – we don't judge, won't give advice, must avoid talking about ourselves and always maintain confidentiality, though we may share information with other Listeners when appropriate. Same rules as for Samaritans, I guess. If an officer asks, "What's the problem with so-and-so?" the answer is "Why don't you ask him yourself?" By and large the staff seem to be supportive of Listeners, though a few odd-ball characters have the attitude that we are pandering to weakness and prisoners need to 'man up'…

As a Listener, I sometimes suspect that I'm only being thrown selective fragments of a much longer, darker tale. Take fears about life after prison, for example. The longer the 'bird' served, the greater the anxiety. I talked recently to a young man, soon to be released, who had always seemed to have everything going for him – a swaggering braggadocio, handsome and popular; well-heeled supportive family and loving partner; own home, good job and prospects …Except that, as he tearfully admitted, none of it was true. In reality he has no money, no home, no job, and his family have all disowned him. Back in the spring I wrote of someone who attended our Quaker meetings – an articulate, insightful guy who had spent over twenty years (all his adult life) in prison for murdering his abusive father. He was understandably anxious about coping with life after release, especially as he was returning to live with his mother who had never fully forgiven him for murdering her partner. Very sadly, we learned this week that he quickly succumbed to old demons and died of a heroin overdose. I find tears welling up as I write this. Goodness – I hardly knew the bloke, but what a tragically wasted life. RIP.

You may have seen recent reports of filthy conditions in some prisons – rats, bugs, fleas and the like that seem able to evade the generally stringent entry requirements for visitors. As I've previously reported, the cleaning orderlies here do a decent job despite the worst habits of a few bad boys. So I was a little bemused the other day on leaving my cell to find a group of residents gathered round a creeping insect as it made a bid for freedom and scuttled across the floor. "It's a cockroach. Kill it! Squash it!" came the call. I looked carefully. It was the most strange-looking 'cockroach' I have ever seen (and I saw a lot in East Africa) with black and yellow bands across its abdomen. Now I know I never studied, let alone passed, O level Biology at school, but even I know a wasp when I see one. To the best of my knowledge it was allowed to escape with its life prospects untrodden on, unlike most of our human residents here.

Your last letter is unusually full of improbabilities, e.g. Norwich City top of the First Division, Rochdale re-branded as Venice of the North, and consumption of two bananas per day extends life by 7%. The last mentioned is the most germane to my present situation as for the past few weeks I have been buying bananas via the weekly 'canteen' sheet. Only enough for one per day, so I now expect to live 3½% longer. But longer than what? Would I have had to start daily banana consumption in infancy, or will I get the same benefit by waiting until my seventieth year before splurging on bananas? I've always loved bananas. We had a lot of them in Africa, some from our own trees.

The truly good news is that, as of the start of this month, I have finally 'achieved' Enhanced status. To qualify for this one must not only not be naughty (i.e. no Negatives or 'nickings'), but must also earn some Positives. This is problematic for someone like myself who does not go to work, where Positives are more readily attainable, though I may have gained them for passing drugs tests and reading challenges at bronze and now silver level. Positives are like piles – in the end every arsehole gets one. Being a (still dormant) literacy mentor and accredited Listener may count for something, and Miss G said she would 'put in a good word' with the CM (Custody Manager). The principal benefit from being Enhanced is that I gain an extra visit, thus four per month (3 + 1 for good behaviour). Also, depending on staff willingness/availability, we get an extra hour or so of unlocked time on Mon-Thurs evenings plus access to a sort of common room with leatherette sofas, microwave and toaster (for the still-hungry to make toasted cheese sandwiches). It's like being a school prefect but without the responsibilities or having to toady to the masters (deliberate archaism).

Good news also on the musical front. We may be allowed to use the Enhanced Room for practices and have chosen our carols – *Torches*, the Coventry Carol and *Infant Holy,* all of which work well in three (male) part harmony. Unfortunately we still have just the one copy of the carol book (mine) as the two that were brought in for Cliff (choirmaster) were disallowed by the duty officer in Visits that day. Rejecting a book of Christmas carols seems a disingenuous use of an officer's discretion, but I guess some 'screws' may find the Jesus-story subversive, on account of its message of peace and love, hope and forgiveness.

24. Wednesday 21 November, 2018

Your letters are so full of entertaining anecdotes of visits, family, social and cultural events that I wonder what you must make of my modest reflections on life in the slow lane or, more aptly just now, on the hard shoulder. Still, I always enjoy your exploits vicariously… so long as you don't go into too many mouth-watering details about food and drink! I usually pass on the *Observer's Food Monthly* supplement unread to a young man here who knew Harry at school. He has now been released and hopes to train as a chef.

Bonfire Night came and went peacefully enough with just a few fire-rockets, fountains and parachutes sparkling above the walls from outside. My arsonist friend hopped around all day like a jumping jack in anticipation of a major conflagration that in the event was little more than a damp squib. Not a patch on Diwali!

If Guy Fawkes was a disappointment, Remembrance Sunday events this year were more than usually poignant being the centenary of the Great War Armistice. I was able to watch a range of televised events. Indeed, they were hard to avoid. I was particularly fascinated by the newly-colourised film footage from the trenches but was called out on a 'Listen' half way through. There's no catch-up TV in here, so I must watch out for the inevitable repeats. I watched all 25 or so episodes of *The Great War* on greyscale telly at school, remembered mainly because it was such a rare treat to see any TV at all. The following year we were summoned to watch Churchill's state funeral (still black and white, of course) which I thought tedious, but preferable to double Latin.

Our regular C-Wing Sunday chapel service more or less coincided with Remembrance events at the Cenotaph. The chaplain had (unusually) gone out of his way to put together a special service for the occasion, the altar decorated with a profusion of poppies and lit by a row of unscented tea lights. We arrived a little ahead of time, but he asked us all to stand to begin the service with the customary two minutes' silence. We then sat down while the Rev launched into the opening prayers whereupon an officer (appropriately an Afghanistan veteran with prosthetic leg) flounced in at the back, interrupted the chaplain, and announced that 11am was about to strike so we should all stand for (another) two minutes' silence. So we endured rather a lot of silence – unusual in prison – though everyone was on best behaviour given the solemnity of the occasion. No one protested, at least not audibly.

Later in the service the Rev handed me a poem to read, *The Men I Marched Beside'* (Anon). It was, arguably, from the wrong war, something I suspect the chaplain, being young and Nigerian, may not have realised. I did my best to dramatise it and bring out the marching rhythm of the metre and at the end won a spontaneous round of applause. We then sang *Onward Christian Soldiers*, excruciating but inevitable I suppose. At least most attendees knew the tune.

With chapel in mind, I am looking forward to the carol service, with the bishop possibly in attendance once more (same suffragan – he has diocesan oversight of prisons). As I feared, any thought that we singers might be escorted over to the chapel to practise has been ruled totally out of the question. However, the more helpful of our regular officers (that's about half of them) have agreed to let us use the Enhanced Room during evening association as long as we don't shut the door or fiddle with the toaster. On the positive side, the ever-helpful librarian has managed to source two more copies of the carol book and has offered to photocopy more as standbys. Word has got around the wing and we now have a couple more volunteer singers, though as neither of them can sing/croak in tune or read music (or perhaps even read) their contribution will be somewhat muted, I earnestly hope. Choral singing may not be a 'protected characteristic' but we certainly wouldn't turn anyone away.

I enjoyed your cheesy story, though Melton Mowbray seems a long old way to go just for a slab of Stilton. The cheese we get here comes ready-grated and I suspect from its blandness of taste and elasticity of texture that it may be missing one of its vital ingredients, like milk, for example. That said, the kitchens produce a more than passable macaroni cheese topped with tasty crusty bits (alternate Wednesdays) and tonight I have put down for 'Mediteranean (sic) Fish Bake'. This also incorporates cheese plus vaguely piscine pink bits and is a favourite with me. Nonetheless, I could murder for a nip of spicy Dolcelatté or creamy Brie. So much for avoiding the food topic!

Since my last letter the wing walls have been bedecked with a series of colourful posters and also a 'prisoner poetry corner'. Some of the posters depict calming views of mountains, lakes, rolling hills and dales, none of them bearing the least resemblance to the local landscape that lies without these walls. Others are seascapes, mainly flat calm or with pink-hued wavelets rather than thundering billows, the sort of thing you'd find on the walls of a funeral parlour, or perhaps a dental surgery. Another series are, I suspect, home produced in the graphics section of the prison print shop. These feature motivational slogans such as "If you can dream it you can do it" (which for some inmates may account for their being here in the first place), or "You only fail when you stop trying" (questionable) or "To finish you first must start" (bleedin' obvious). I don't think anyone else (apart from Arthur and me – we have had a philosophical discussion) has even noticed let alone commented on this rash of cod wisdom, but at least their graphics add a little colour to the magnolia and pale turquoise blandness of the walls. Prison staff are not exempt from the sound bite sagacity of the walls. Above the staff staircase (in the 'bubble' assembly point beyond our doors) is the exhortation, "When you think of quitting, remember why you joined".

'Poets' Corner' has, though, attracted some attention. I don't know who the poets are as their works are wisely unsigned, but their offerings (versified, rhyming) are almost all about self-harm, suicide, loneliness and despair, the most anguished imaginable cries for help which I can't bear to quote lest I spoil your weekend. It's a wonder that the authorities ever allowed them to be pinned up. My guess is that they never even bothered to read them.

The sudden arrival of cold weather outside leaves the cell too cool for my liking with the heating pipes barely warm at times and the Perspex windows working loose and draughty. I think we must be at the end of the pipe's circulation route as the cells opposite are toasty warm. I feel for the unfortunate Lithuanian guy (a different one, average height and dopey, not a bully) in the next cell where both windows are permanently jammed slightly ajar. Of course he's repeatedly reported it but… Undoubtedly I feel the cold more than most who regard shivering in a T-shirt as a badge of manliness. Even Arthur has only just started using a single blanket on his bed whereas I have four, possibly exceeding some official allowance. As I write, the sun has just come out, so I may don two jerseys and coat and risk venturing outside for this afternoon's exercise period.

25. Tuesday 4 December, 2018

As usual, your droll descriptions of social engagements bring a smile to my face, especially the Chinese concert, waterways talk and charity sale of last year's unwanted Christmas gifts (a great idea as long as the previous recipients don't turn up). I'm wondering what to get Arthur. He deserves something for being an all-round good egg, though on second thoughts he can probably manage without as he is due for release between Christmas and New Year (lucky bastard!) so will no doubt get many on his return to Essex. A more charitably disposed organisation than HMPS would surely release him a few days early in time for Christmas at home, and save a bit of taxpayers' 'hard-earned' cash (as politicians say).

I'm enclosing this with your Christmas card. HMP suppliers do not 'do' holy cards (though I know you're not much into religion either) and the choice available from canteen is restricted to reindeer with a ruddy-faced Fr Christmas ("More sherry, Father?") or Fr C with Snowman, both with sumptuous sprinklings of glitter. Fr Christmas with Big Bunch of Keys might be a bringer of greater cheer to the incarcerated. This one is ever so slightly better than the above as I was able to swap a packet of prison custard cream biscuits for a couple of better quality cards sent in from outside to someone else who felt disinclined to use them (or couldn't afford the stamps). We can order 'quality' individual cards from canteen, named for Wife, Son, Dad and so on but can never be sure what will turn up. I have successfully secured a Wife card for S, but one bloke ordered a 'For my Wonderful Wife' card only to receive a 'Husband' one in error. How very modern! Definitely not appropriate in his case, and he vented his feelings in very macho male style lest anyone be in any doubt. In most respects this is a pretty macho environment. There are about 120 of us on the wing, that's 119 blokes plus Penelope, who is trans, but seems to fit in well without obvious discrimination and is allowed a single cell. She has long blond hair and wears a bra but jeans rather than a skirt, which might be a temptation too far for a few of the guys. Just at the moment there's a good sense of community amongst the residents, especially down here where a certain 'camaraderie amongst convicts', if not honour among thieves, rules the day.

Forgive me if my handwriting is (even) less fluent than usual. For the past several days I have been nursing a painful right thumb whose joint is swollen and snaps audibly to and fro instead of hinging smoothly as thumbs were designed to do. I suspect the culprit is some form of writer's cramp. Arthur says I've brought it upon myself by writing too many long letters, gripping my BIC biro too tightly and/or constantly wiggling my thumb to control it. It is, of course, as nothing to your severed finger-tip, Maggie (commiserations), and I'm glad that the latter is almost repaired. At least you could with a clear conscience excuse yourself from washing up after the charity tea, even if you were alarmed at the volunteers' prodigality with hot water. Here we have a seemingly limitless supply of hot and cold, unless someone breaks their sink, wedges the tap on and deliberately floods their cell until the water runs out under the door, across the landing and splashes down onto the landing below. There is a separate stop tap to every cell, but that depends on an officer with the right thingummy getting there fast enough to prevent a flood.

Thus far, no major probs with the thumb. I wish I could have a fountain pen, though, but of course they are on the contraband list along with almost anything sharp, even wits.

I'm gaining more experience, and confidence, as a Listener and have been called out twelve times over the past three weeks, including once at midnight! One of the promised 'benefits' of becoming a Listener was supposed to be that we would not be moved to other prisons within the first three months. In practice that turns out not to be the case and two of our new recruits have already been shipped off elsewhere. Despite our diminished numbers we still operate in pairs here and I am learning a lot from another guy, a smooth talker, who is a Buddhist with a long experience of 'inside' and a degree in psychology. Or so he claims. I'm not so sure. I'm still at the probationary stage and like to have a quick glance at my notes (do's and don'ts, useful phrases, things to avoid saying, etc.) before going up to the suite to engage with callers. Mr Smooth-Talker has a well-rehearsed patter and is really good at putting others at ease and encouraging them to open up about their issues. With Christmas coming up, separation from family and loved ones is a major issue, as is uncertainty about legal processes, though we must avoid appearing to dispense advice even when requested.

The Lithuanian guy next door, despite my repeated failure to get his draughty window sealed, has latched onto me as a source of help, though not in my Listener capacity. Unlike his now departed compatriot, he is neither monster nor bully but a bit of a softie. Currently he is grappling with wording a letter to the authorities setting out why he should <u>not</u> be deported. With no address, no job, no money, no family in the UK and a list of petty offences as long as his leg, his chances of remaining here must be pretty slender. But who am I to tread on his dreams? His most recent conviction was for pinching a girl's bottom on a bus in Haverhill. He doesn't deny it, but totally fails to see why it is an offence as it is acceptable, even laudable, behaviour back home in Lithuania, or so he claims. It took some explaining.

His language levels are a good deal lower than his libido, in which respect either he's severely myopic or his appetites are peculiarly undiscriminating. If I correctly interpreted his wordless gesture and Malvolian leer, while alone with him in his cell he invited me to 'perform a sex act on him' as the papers coyly say. He's not such a softie after all. Either that or there was a snake loose in his joggers. Somewhat taken aback at this unexpected turn of events, I politely declined his offer, and withdrew to the security of C1-24 to ponder what had just happened. (This, you may recall, is my second such incident. Why me? I'm totally flummoxed.)

Apart from the above, we've had a rapid turnover of occupants of the adjacent cells in recent weeks and are currently neighbours (on the other side) to a couple of quietly-spoken older gents. One tells me that he was last 'inside' thirty years ago and is amazed at how much more relaxed and informal things are nowadays. Don't tell the *D. Mail*, though I suspect his observation is only true of C-Wing. Over on B-Wing there are regular emergency alarms, plus not infrequent visits from officers in full riot gear backed up by the snappy security-dog team. It all helps create a circus atmosphere in the run-up to Christmas as our lads gather round the glazed doors, hoping for a glimpse of the performance next door. Our new neighbour also tells me that 'back in the day', many/most of the 'screws' were ex-army types who stood no nonsense. They are a dying breed, but we still have just a few, recognisable by their upright bearing and mirror polish on their black toe-capped shoes (or brown if they were officers, though our officers were rarely Officers). I especially respect these all-in-a-day's-work types and those who make the most of what can be a pretty grotty job. Shirkers, moaners and jobsworths don't command much respect.

Our greatest menace is to have YOs (Young Offenders) banged up nearby, especially those youfs (like Kev) who shout to, or at, each other through open windows until late at night. Currently, most of 'the kids', as we call them, are up on the threes (top landing) but that doesn't stop them disturbing the peace down here when they have a mind to. But, as I've said before, generally things are pretty calm on this wing and most prisoners are considerate and supportive, which goes for the staff too. Truly there is some 'honour among thieves'… and muggers, fraudsters, rapists, drug lords, even murderers. Yes, we have our share of those, though they come over as pretty decent 'chaps' most of the time.

As well as 'listening' I now have a student on the Shannon Trust literacy scheme. He is someone who (or so he tells me) fathered a child at 13, dropped out of school and worked as a farm labourer. He's now in his thirties with family and would like to be able to help his young children when he gets out of prison. He can read and write, just, but only at basic kindergarten level. To appease his self-esteem, we initially started the course on Book Two but it was soon apparent to both of us how, for example, he still confuses vowel sounds so we have gone right back to the beginning. We share an interest in classic cars so, as a break from practising phonics like 'hat, hit, hot, hut', I have made flashcards with 'Ford Cortina', 'Triumph Stag' and 'MG' (an easy one, that!).

Sorry for the shorter than usual offering. It's the season of Christmas letters, and I have several more to do. Thumb still holding up, just.

26. Thursday 20 Dec, 2018

Many thanks for your latest plus card of jolly japes in the snow at Wollaton Hall. Here my washing line (the one made out of knotted strips of J-Cloth – it's holding up well) is now festooned with 30+ cards (a record on the wing, I'm told) and I have cleared the clutter from the top shelf to stand up some sturdier ones like yours. The officer on yesterday's cell inspection – the regular check-up when they yank at the window bars and look for holes in the floor – complained that the cards could be a fire risk. As he did not insist on me immediately taking them down, my attempts at festive embellishment survives – for now. Otherwise I'm sorry to say there's not much Christmas spirit around, and definitely none of the alcoholic variety. Arthur, however, is more frisky than usual being demob happy pending his release just before New Year. I guess his wife and family will have deferred Christmas and he talks of holding a grand and boozy party at the pub. Arthur, despite getting himself into whatever mess brought him here, still sees life gold-side upwards. That's a gift I find it easier to admire than emulate.

This may be my last letter from C1-24 as, all being well, I shall be moving on Friday. Not far, of course, just diagonally across the landing to C1-01. This is an unusually commodious cell for which there is strong competition. Intended primarily for wheelchair users or disabled prisoners, it's a sort of semi-detached cell with an open but curtained archway through to the adjacent C1-02. Each cell has just a single occupant, despite both retaining their bunk beds on which basis they are laughably known as a 'dorm'. On (what I hope will be) 'my' side there is no loo or wash basin (for which I'll have to go through to C1-02) which makes the whole cell seem much more spacious/less claustrophobic.

On the other side lives Terry, who I very much like. He's a popular bloke in his fifties, a graduate engineer who has spent most of his working life 'in oil' in far-flung places across the globe. We already trade travellers' tales, me of marauding buffalo on the Zambezi, he of frisky nightlife in downtown Tashkent. I suspect Terry is an inveterate workaholic. Instead of using his enforced idleness to be, well, just plain idle, he is now up to his eyes in textbooks and essays studying for an OU Sociology degree. That's why he wants a quiet and considerate companion, like me. Terry despises television and has disconnected and hidden his set under the bed to avoid its distractions. I have promised only to use mine with headphones connected. However, we will be able to share newspapers as he favours *The Times* on Saturdays and *Observer* on Sundays. So I'm just keeping fingers crossed. We have sweet-talked all the relevant officers into authorising the move, but of course nothing is ever certain here until it happens and even then may be reversed on a whim. Wish me luck.

With Christmas now just round the corner, life on the wing has become a little edgy. It's never easy being separated from family and friends, but especially at this time of year. The 'young bloods' are becoming more than usually fractious and noisy, messaging each other by rapping vigorously on the water pipes with metallic clangs that carry right round the wing and quickly bring shouts of "Shut the f... up" or threats of worse. We have a doe-eyed 13-year old on the wing, a rambunctious kid called Alan who delights in farting and making silly high-pitched cackles or girly titters to amuse the other young-uns. No, of course he's not actually 13 (he must be 18 to be here at all), but he looks and acts like Noddy with testosterone. Maybe he'll be Foreign Secretary (or PM) one day? Alan flashes his flirty eyelashes at almost anything with two legs hoping they'll come running. They don't – despite his pearly complexion and youthful looks he is regarded more as an irritant than an embellishment to the establishment. Nonetheless, the older and wiser prisoners are quite protective of him and some of the female officers give him much-needed mothering. Alan and his current cell-mate, an intelligent and likeable but rather sad deaf boy, are both terrified of being sent to Young Offenders Institutions where bullying is said to be rife. They feel safe here, but I feel for the deaf lad who has been disowned by his family and sees no future for himself outside prison. Like everyone, he needs hugs, but I doubt he'll get any in here.

A couple of nights ago there was a noisy altercation between three of our more excitable and hard-bitten youfs that quickly escalated from shouting match to fisticuffs. Immediately, alarm claxons began to wail (almost the first time I've heard them used on this wing), open doors automatically slammed shut and officers came running from all directions to separate the combatants. I've no idea what it was over, no doubt some trivial issue quickly forgotten as they are already friends again, but all three lads 'got a nicking' and had to appear before a governor for adjudication. Not the best way to celebrate Christmas.

More seriously, it is salutary to be confronted on Listener call-outs with the traumas and tribulations of the lives of others. These may impinge on everyone on the wing, not just the Listeners, especially when normally equable and contented characters suffer psychotic episodes and resort to prolonged banging or, even worse, head-butting their cell doors to attract attention or relieve their stress. This happened last Tuesday when someone hammered on his door continuously for over an hour. As you may imagine, not all fellow prisoners were sympathetic and many would willingly have strung him up by the nadgers. Such behaviour is a real problem for officers especially with numbers being so stretched. Depression is widespread and, though most people learn to cope (with or without the happy pills), some go round wearing permanent hang-dog expressions. The bloke I hand on my newspaper to is one such. Arthur, a virtuoso of choice turns of phrase, describes him as having a face 'like a boiled pig's bum'.

For much of the Christmas period, 'normal regime' will be suspended and a new timetable has been pinned up outside the servery. As work is cancelled until after the New Year, everyone will be banged up in their cells for much, much longer than usual. To compensate, there will be extra 'association' periods during the afternoons and some of the more public-spirited prisoners have organised tournaments. I put my name down for backgammon but was knocked out in the first round. It would have helped to have known the rules but I had my arm twisted to make up numbers.

I've also entered dominoes ('cos it's easy and I have my own set). There is also a quiz, though the questions (as yet unseen but plagiarised from quiz books) are said to be 'killers'. I suspect they will mostly be about football, pop music and TV sitcoms, so I confidently expect to score zero. The authorities have agreed to award prizes of £3, £2 and £1 for the first, second and third in each category, so it's not exactly *Who Wants to be a Millionaire* and the general opinion about the prizes is 'we'll believe it when we see it'.* As I can't play table tennis and am wholly out of practice at pool and billiards, I haven't entered those tournaments but we now have a second pool table so I may try my hand at some point. There is a near-complete Scrabble set that we can borrow from the landing office. Last night four of us (plus a changing cast of self-appointed helpers hovering behind with gratuitous and usually misinformed suggestions) had a thoroughly enjoyable game during the evening social time for us Enhanced inmates.

* The cynics were right. No prize money ever was paid out.

The long-foretold Christmas Carol Service took place yesterday afternoon and was very much enjoyed by all attendees. The Bishop did not appear after all, and there were only twenty or so prisoners in the congregation plus a few guests such as the ancient and scrawny Methodist gent who helps at Sunday chapel and a couple of Catholic ladies devoutly fingering their rosaries. Inexplicably, only regular chapel-goers (CofE and RC but not Buddhist or Pagan) were permitted to attend. Our organist Clifford accompanied the singing on the mighty organ, the first time I have heard it played. Once the gremlins causing crackles and flutter on the bottom were identified and rectified it sounded great, indeed thunderous. Our little quartet of part-singers sang *Torches* and the *Coventry Carol* for which we were roundly applauded. Afterwards tea and mince pies (not home-made but of the stodgy corner shop variety) were served. I read from Luke's nativity narrative, cheekily interposing some of the King James Bible language in place of the bland modern wording the Rev had printed on the service sheet. So my Mary was 'great with child' rather than bluntly 'pregnant', the shepherds were 'sore afraid' and my baby Jesus wrapped in 'swaddling bands' rather than merely 'frightened' and 'cloths' respectively. I'm sure nobody else noticed, but it gave me a slight frisson of control, something we don't often feel in here.

S and Harry are spending Christmas and Boxing Days over at 'Grandpa's', then coming in here to see me on 27th. I can't wait. The following week H flies out to Zanzibar for a music project sponsored by the British Council. Envy! I hope that you have had an entertaining Christmas and wish you all the very best for 2019.

27. Wednesday 2 January, 2019

HAPPY NEW YEAR!

You seem to have had an entertaining and energetic Christmas starting with your At Home for neighbours. We used to do something similar, the highlight of which (or so I fondly imagine, though it may be self-delusion) was my annual quiz based, room by room, on pictures and artefacts around the house. Though ostensibly aimed at the few children present, most of the adults also took part to win bags of sweeties left over from Trick or Treat. Sample questions: 1) 'How were inmates punished in Hamburg Workhouse?' and 2) 'What skeletal snapper has lost some teeth?' (Answers at end). As I have – Hurray! – now moved to more spacious quarters (see below), I could conceivably have held an 'In Cell At Home' for a very select number of my prison friends. I would have offered Dairylea cheese on Ritz crackers (as sold on Canteen) washed down with apple juice (or 'cider' if I'd left it open near the heating pipe until it 'accidentally' morphed into something resembling draught scrumpy). A sociable chap who has now left used to do just that, and was kind enough to have me on his invitation list. We could sing a carol or two, after which, by way of entertainment, the Christmas cards draped along the bed frame could provide scope for a quiz, e.g. what is the infant Jesus wrapped in? (Not 'cloths'!)

So, I was allowed to transfer to C1-01 on Friday morning and had my belongings bagged up and ready to move in just as soon as the previous occupant left. I wasted no time on the basis that possession is nine-tenths of the law. If I procrastinated, someone else would probably invent an excuse to claim it. Despite this, my well-rehearsed move was very nearly thwarted by the arrival, fresh from court the previous evening, of a very angry new inmate who proceeded to comprehensively trash his cell. It was all utterly bizarre. A group of us trusty enhanced types nonchalantly sat there at the portable tables chatting, playing cards or whatever as if completely oblivious of all this crashing, banging and cussing going on above our heads. It reminded me of Breughel's *Fall of Icarus*, where 'everything turns away quite leisurely from the disaster', as Auden observed. Before long, water started to swill out from under his cell door (sink waste pipe smashed) while officers gathered up old sheets and towels to stem the flood until they found the thingummy to shut off the stop tap. Finally, little pieces of torn paper were dropped, confetti like, from above the door. Initially, the upshot of this was that, with the vandal's allocated cell effectively out of commission, he would need to be accommodated here in C1-01. In the event, there were protests all round and I garnered sufficient support from officers for my move to go ahead as planned with the vandal banged up elsewhere. Poor old Arthur, who had hoped to spend his first and last Christmas in custody on his own, thus acquired a scarily uncongenial companion. I would not willingly have brought this upon him, but at least it was only for a few days. He (Arthur) has now been released.

My chest may be better but my thumb still troubles. I try to control the biro with flicks of the wrist rather than the hand. No, that's not quite true, but I minimise thumb movements as it will only articulate by stages with a series of jerks and an audible click sounding like a Geiger counter concealed in my right hand. On Friday I braved the freezing outdoors and dreaded Healthcare waiting room where the vile youfs seemed inordinately concerned with 'odours', as TV adverts say, and insisted on opening the window. I saw the doctor, the nice black one (they are colour coded) known as 'Dr Hardcore' (a lazy rhyme with his actual name) who I prefer to his rather off-hand white colleague. Dr H is thorough and courteous and addresses me as 'Sir', which, needless to say, is not the norm in prison (or outside, come to that). He explains that my condition is called 'trigger thumb', is age-related and exacerbated by occupational wear and tear, e.g. writing, a bit like tennis elbow, housemaid's knee, smoker's cough, wanker's wrist or parson's nose (not really!) He went on to say that if I had a neck problem it might be 'trigger neck'. I gave him a logophilic look at this and he pealed with mirth and said he'd just made that up to make me laugh. He subscribes to the old adage that laughter is the best medicine. Now he has prescribed some anti-inflammatories and if they don't work, steroid injections should do the trick. It's a pain, in every sense. I am so dependent on my right hand and have not a trace of ambidexterity, unlike my artist great-uncle Cyril who could draw and paint with both hands simultaneously.

Christmas was a proper ol' curate's egg – good in parts. Unlike the melodramatic old *Christmas Day in the Workhouse* monologue, where "The cold grey walls are bright / with garlands of green and holly / And the place is a pleasant sight…", we had no tree or decorations of any sort on the wing. Nor can I honestly describe it as 'a pleasant sight' – just same old, same old. There <u>was</u> a tree in the chapel – decorated, perversely, <u>after</u> the service by 'the lads' but with no lights as they had (allegedly) been nicked! Christmas Communion for C-Wing Anglicans was held on the afternoon of Christmas Eve, or what Catholics call an 'anticipatory Mass'. The Catholics ended up with no service at all as their Mass was cancelled without explanation or apology. No one seemed particularly surprised or put out, apart from me, on their behalf.

We Anglicans by comparison hit the ecclesiastical jackpot with another visit from Bishop Jonathan with his now-famous flaming mitre, chasuble and crook. As if there weren't enough crooks in here already! Arthur, true to form, made his ritual observation about him being only a suffragan/suffering/stinking bishop (a rather cheesy joke). We assembled mid-afternoon for more carols, again energetically accompanied on the chapel Wurlitzer by our resident organist. The Bish preached the best sermon we've heard all year, and not just because it was the shortest. He enlivened it with a song, for which he received polite applause (it was not an audience of cognoscenti). He is renowned in the Diocese for this eccentricity and (he admitted to me over more mince pies afterwards) was using us as guinea pigs for his Midnight Mass sermon later on in another parish. We felt truly blessed, not least because the Rt. Rev. showed some awareness of his audience's fuzzy fidelity and limited attention span, unlike our regular preacher whose offerings are as prolix as they are incomprehensible.

Christmas Day began with a full English fry-up – bacon, sausage, tomato, egg, black pudding (v.g.), b-beans and hash brown, a once a year treat, all served canteen-style with a rare if brisk courtesy. They did us proud and the breakfast was my personal highlight of the day. With all that dished up at 9 am, there was hardly room for roast turkey at 12 followed by Xmas pud with mere custard – no brandy butter, obvs! In the evening we were treated to a cold buffet with really tasty ham. Such prodigality was there that I kept some back for a Bunterish midnight feast, trying not to wake Terry, who was enjoying the sleep of the just on the other side of the curtain.

Unfortunately the suspension of 'normal regime' for two whole long weeks (no work, long bang-ups, no newspaper deliveries – aargh!) led to boredom setting in and some inmates becoming more than usually fractious. Even I, usually so even-tempered (or so I like to think), became jittery and argumentative and had a very public stand-up row. Was this over some real or imagined slight? Or some breach of the unwritten prisoner code of conduct, e.g. by entering another's cell without permission or 'snitching' to a 'screw'? Not a bit of it. It was whether or not 'Jain' is an allowable word in Scrabble.

As anticipated, we Listeners had our work cut out in the lead up to Christmas. Then all went uncannily quiet apart from one near miss when two of us were called out to talk to a young man who had tried to hang himself in his cell. He was spotted completely by chance when an officer looked through his flap for a routine check. He was cut down not a moment too soon having already passed out. I spoke to him again today and he does seem a little more positive.

S and Harry came in to see me together the day after Boxing Day and it was good to see them looking so relaxed and enjoying each other's company. Christmas Day at 'Grandpa's house' went well with Grandpa himself – just turned 98 – on good form and enjoying having the family round him. He has asked to visit me here, so I have filled in the application form to add him to my 'approved visitor' list, possibly the oldest person ever to apply! I had not expected to see him again, so am greatly cheered at the prospect.

This comes with best wishes for the whatever befalls us in 2019.

P.S. Quiz answers: 1) Suspended in a basket above the Guardians' table so they could watch them eat (old framed print); 2) The baby crocodile skull on the piano.

P.P.S. It was decided by 3:1 majority to allow 'Jain' adjectivally (as Christian or Buddhist would be). Red-faced Albert disagreed, accusing us of cheating by inventing a 'fictitious' word. He was summarily dispatched to Brixton yesterday. That'll teach him!

28. Wednesday 16 January, 2019

What sumptuous feasts you seem to have enjoyed during your Shropshire family celebrations, reminiscent of Henry VIII at Whitehall or Hampton Court. Ours was mean fayre by comparison (apart from the memorable fry-up), but at the time welcome as a change from the regular diet. I've already mentioned that the general goodwill and bonhomie of Christmas was looking a trifle tatty a week later. We eased our way into New Year almost imperceptibly and there was a general sigh of relief when 'normal regime' of work etc. was renewed on 2nd January. The crashes and bangs around midnight on New Year's Eve were external, from extra-mural fireworks parties out on the heath rather than from cell-destroying activities within. Our resident arsonist, a little Christmas pudding of a fellow, was deeply disappointed at the paucity of fireworks but told me how much he had enjoyed the smell of extra candles at the Christmas services in chapel. (Protestants of a more Puritan persuasion, such as our Rev, are generally not much into burning things – candles, incense, sanctuary lamps – except perhaps the odd recusant priest in Tudor times.)

I was very interested to read, Maggie, of your mother's lifelong battle with claustrophobia and how she had to avoid train compartments and aircraft. A good reason for her to avoid prison cells too. I'm not sure how claustrophobics (is that a word? Too long for Scrabble!) cope in here and hope they are allowed single cells. It's amazing how the size of a cell seems to shrink as soon as a second person enters.

I'm pleased to report that Arthur is now enjoying his liberty to the full, at least as full as his licence conditions allow. His wife has written (he is not allowed to) enclosing a photo of him ensconced at the bar of his 'local', frothing pint in hand, and no doubt regaling other regulars with chucklesome tales of prison life. Touchingly, she thanks 'all his prison mates' for taking such good care of him while he was inside. She also quotes a typically Arthurish observation about his licence, that 'the illiteracy of its expression is only exceeded by the absurdity of its content.' Do I miss Arthur? Yes, in many ways. Especially his generosity of spirit and seemingly bottomless trove of hilarious and often saucy anecdotes. Though not for his effervescent farting and stertorous snoring, like pebbles rattling in an empty bean can. But that's another epic. Terry, with whom I now share these semi-detached cells, is much less flatulent at either end. His snores are a Debussy lullaby after Arthur's Wagnerian chorus. If they were Norfolk villages, they'd be Great Snoring and Little Snoring respectively.

Arthur could be a bit of a smarty-pants, but that was a refreshing change from the dour demeanour of so many people here. Only now do I fathom just how claustrophobic I felt in C1-24, shut in that little double cell, forever waltzing round my pad-mate to get to the desk, boil the kettle, open the window, climb precariously onto the top bunk, use the en-suite loo and so forth. Whatever my initial misgivings when sharing with Sam, I have so far been uniquely blessed to have such considerate and easy-going companions. Locking up two potentially incompatible strangers in the grinding proximity of a tiny cell can be a recipe for conflict. However, since moving here to the more spacious surroundings of C1-01, the early morning tightness in my chest has significantly loosened. Cell (or Room) 1-01 has a familiar ring to it. I hope my present abode has more in common with the BBC TV comedy show than the Ministry of Love torture chamber in Orwell's 1984. Time will tell.

My new bunk (lower level: upper berth unoccupied) has an even more pronounced banana-shaped sag in its centre so I feel very secure. A previous occupant (Pops the Laundry Orderly) has scratched his name indelibly on the metal webbing just above my head. Big mistake. It is hallowed prison lore that to inscribe your name on your bed brings bad luck – you are sure to find yourself back 'in the clink' again before long. Since the departure of tyrannical Pops, the laundry room has become almost democratic. Mind you, I'm still wary of removing other people's clothing from the dryer until it is bone dry, starting to bake and crackling with static. Even then I make a point of leaving it folded and neatly piled on the shelf. Prisoners, having so little they can call their own, can be aggressively possessive of their few belongings.

As you may have seen, Durham gaol has been back on the small screen for another instalment of 'prison porn'. Of course it had to feature intimidation, black eyes and broken bones, scaldings and slashings with blood and gore on the floor, none of which have been part of my everyday experience here. Over the eleven months since I arrived there have been only four or five incidents of this type, all quite minor and mostly involving hot-headed YOs (Young Offenders). Of course this wing is not typical of the prison as a whole, but the programme illustrates how the media may distort public perceptions in the interest of drama. Maybe *Porridge*, however quaint it seems nowadays, was closer to the mark after all. As Terry observed the other day, we may not regard all our fellow prisoners as friends, but there are very few whom we have much cause to actively dislike. (Which doesn't mean we would ever wish to share cells with some/most of them!)

I have been here for almost eleven months so far and have now served rather over one third of my sentence but with no hint, as yet, of if or when I will be moved elsewhere. You may have wondered why I didn't report back on the requested meeting with my OS (Offender Supervisor). That is because it never took place. I tried three Apps on successive months but all were ignored. So I still don't have any 'sentence plan', which was their reason for not re-classifying me after the first six months here. I sometimes wonder what is the purpose of so expensively keeping me here. How can it possibly be rehabilitation (as claimed) if no-one ever engages with me to discuss my alleged crimes and re-direct me onto the paths of righteousness?

Thank you for your enclosed post cards. Christine also sends one (of the Yorkshire Dales) with every letter and so does local friend Ros who has a great store of art and architectural cards from long-ago travels with her architect late husband. In my new cell I have a pin board and have ordered a box of drawing pins from 'canteen'. We didn't have boards in No 24, though they are listed as standard basic equipment. This omission was dutifully noted down without fail at every inspection (including the one by the suited Gov and his PA) but never rectified. Anyway, I now have a circulating gallery of cards, so many that I'm thinking of setting up a monthly loan scheme paid for in mini-milk cartons (a convenient form of currency for low-level transactions). On my board and walls here I currently have our old college court in seasonal snow, your tram on Great Orme's Head (so like the wonderful but fast disappearing Calcutta trams) and lovely Lübeck, all from your recent travels. Keep them coming! Did I mention that I was asked to take down one of my pictures, a laminated A4 image of the Buddha, which I had stuck on the wall next to the window. Why? Not because it was indecent, offensive or affronted the officer's religious sensibilities, but because it 'compromised the integrity of the wall'. Integrity is not a quality often associated with prisons, so it is good to know that at least the walls possess it.

I love your collective noun of a 'gloomery' for comatose old ladies in care homes. It's a scary prospect that before long some of us may be joining their ranks. So may I recommend a short spell in prison by way of preparation for contracting horizons and institutional orderliness? My father-in-law is so lucky still to be in his own home at 98, but we do wonder how much longer it can continue. He has just about exhausted a whole series of carers, even with S or one of her sisters also in residence most of the time. He is now officially booked in to visit me here on 26th January and S has arranged to reserve the visitor wheelchair for his use. Fingers crossed!

Your Turkish film sounds entertaining in an off-beat sort of way. How very avant-garde Nottingham has become to screen such shows! I note your comments about the apparent universality of smart phones and gleaming white teeth (in Turkey and beyond), neither of which are much in evidence here. The former are obviously banned, which is not to say there are none, just that their existence is privily concealed. As for the latter, I notice that most young men here already have wonky, stained, chipped or missing teeth. Many older inmates, if they have any teeth left at all, have gums set with blackened stumps like Passchendaele after a bombardment. I recently donated a decent brush and toothpaste to one needy young man in the hope that it would incentivise him to take care of his few remaining teeth. The prison <u>does</u> supply free brushes and paste (called Segem), but it seems to be a badge of honour not to use them for their intended purpose (though the paste is good for sticking pictures to the wall). I sympathise. The white 'Government' brushes have moulting bristles so loosely secured that they get stuck between the teeth and pull out.

My own teeth, it must be admitted, are not a good advertisement for British dentistry, though I still have most of them. Fifty years ago the University dentist subjected them to a brutal and un-anaesthetised assault with pneumatic drills and adamantine fillings, painful at the time but still in place. Here there is a fully-equipped dental surgery in the Daycare Centre. Any self-respecting dentist must regard prison patients with despair, so I have no wish to join their ranks at present.

So much for gobs. When it comes to bums, HM Prison Service has gone soft and issues single-ply absorbent toilet paper (also effective as draught-excluder). You will remember the days when Civil Service departmental loos had paper of the shiny, medicated (impregnated with carbolic acid) Izal variety with every sheet individually printed GOVERNMENT PROPERTY. It doubled as tracing paper, for which it was arguably better suited than its intended purpose. I guess the cost of printing and the advent of soft paper in the 60s put paid to printed paper in prisons.

Prisoners may not count for much in the eyes of society, but we are much counted. At regular times throughout the day and night, officers come round with 'clicker' tally-counters to check numbers in cells. Sometimes the count involves a cursory glance through the glazed door flap, sometimes a more thorough check. The young officer on duty yesterday (maybe a new graduate recruit – something of a rarity) came in, gave me a conspiratorial wink, and peered under the bed 'in case somebody's hiding there.' He seemed ill at ease, encased in a crisp new uniform which he wore like a Tudor traitor's gibbet. A long-serving officer (military type) tells me that when the original Victorian wing (with windows high up the wall) was still in use, officers had to climb up and strike the bars with a metal rod. If they did not 'ping' clearly, it indicated that someone was attempting to file through them, though what with I cannot imagine.

From time to time more thorough checks are conducted, officially at least twice a week but daily if government inspectors are anticipated. These are known as 'AFCs' which (I've just asked) stands for 'Allocation Fabric Checks', a typical bit of official gobbledegook. AFCs involve checking the emergency bells, lights (including externally switched dimmer switch), lavatory seats and window bars. These are yanked to check they haven't been loosened. Every month or so the Works Dept blokes come round to test the smoke alarms that are fixed over the doors outside every cell. It's not a popular procedure when 96 sets of ear-splitting beeps are set off in quick succession. The alarms are highly sensitive and prone to going off at almost any time, day or night, with or without actual smoke. In the event of a real fire in a cell, there is a 1 ¼ inch hole in the door (usually plugged with a well-greased bolt) through which a fire hose can be poked to quench the flames and drench the occupant. An effective deterrent for anyone thinking of burning their bedding as a protest. Unfortunately our smoke detectors are not able to sniff out 'spice', though I have become quite familiar with its distinctively syrupy, druggy odour outside certain cells. One young man is said to fund his spice habit by selling sexual favours. Nothing would surprise me.

Counts are still held several times a day, announced over the tannoy by 'Lock-up and roll-check' or, if numbers don't reconcile, 'Re-count', sometimes two or three times in quick succession. Similar rules apply whenever people move round the site and we are checked against lists at almost every door or gate we pass through. Just about everything requires a new list to be generated, e.g. for work, exercise, gym (for those who do), healthcare, visits, chapel and so forth. It is hardly surprising that errors creep in, hence all the re-counts. These are not well-received, especially when we have just been let out of our cells only to be ushered back in or told to stand by the doors to be re-counted. Those who have served time in other HMPs maintain that counts are far more frequent here, but I take this with a pinch of the proverbial. Prisoners must always have something to grouse about.

I've had a letter, out of the blue, from someone (friend of friend) who I slightly knew at Uni (as the young ones now say) and who 'did time' a few years ago in Dartmoor. As a prisoner, that is, not some sort of sociological experiment, though I guess it comes to much the same thing in the end. He writes warmly of his time 'inside' and the unexpected friendships he made there. Since his release he has been back to visit some of his prison pals and has helped others find employment and a roof over their heads on release. He is a businessman with significant means as well as first-rate communication skills and, for example, mentions talks he gave (e.g. about JS Bach, with musical examples played on the chapel organ) to the prisoners' Over-50s Club. Now there's an idea... I have made enquiries and discover that there used to be just such a club here, but it became an early casualty of staffing cuts.

29. Wednesday 30 January, 2019

This is the letter in which I hoped to report on the success of father-in-law's visit. In the event it was an unmitigated disaster, a tragedy verging on farce. As I told you, I added his details to my approved visitor list (at 98 possibly the oldest ever visitor) and S booked his visit by email in the usual way. In addition, she telephoned in advance to reserve the wheelchair for his use and also to request that we should be allocated a seat in a quiet corner of the hall. Like most hearing aid users he finds background noise distracting. So far so good. On the morning of the visit S drove over to collect him and found him eager but understandably a little anxious of what might lie ahead. In all his years he had never before visited a prison. Getting him ready was no mean feat, not least finding permissible photo ID as he longer has a passport or a driving licence, and just getting him in and out of our low-slung car can be heavy work. They arrived here, parked up, and S collected the wheelchair, as pre-arranged, and trundled him back to the reception area. At about the same time I was being escorted over to the hall with the other guys where I was duly allocated the corner seat. Again, so far so good. There I sat, keeping my eye on the far end of the hall as visitors began to dribble in, in ones and twos as usual. After twenty minutes or so everyone was in and seated, but with no sign of S and her Dad. I called an officer over and he went to enquire, reporting back that there was 'some problem', he didn't know what.

S meanwhile, with her Dad bewildered and increasingly anxious in his prison wheelchair, was told that he would not be allowed in as his name did not appear on the list for that day. How could this be? S had been more than usually thorough in making the booking. The officers on duty checked and agreed that f-i-l was on my list of approved visitors, but that the name of his daughter M-J (same surname) had been entered in error as my visitor for that day. Without his name on the list, they were not authorised to admit him. Clearly it was a simple confusion by the bookings clerk, one that could have been remedied with the use of a little discretion and common sense by the officers on the door. Such attributes are evidently not highly rated in HMPS.

The officers concerned were plainly embarrassed by the situation, especially when faced by an increasingly agitated 98-year old in a wheelchair, but said they could not allow him in. By this time, S was pretty irate (not something to be taken lightly!) and insisted that they 'phone through to the Duty Governor for his authorisation. Simple enough, surely? The DG, however, was having none of it. He was, he said, _far_ too busy to come down to the Visits Hall in person. If the visitor's name was not on that day's list, he could not be admitted. End of story. Poor S had to wheel her confused and disappointed Dad back to the car. Of course, in a prison above all, rules are there to be followed. But given all the circumstances, especially that the error was so obviously down to the prison staff (either that or my wife is a blatant liar willing to subject her ancient and frail father to an embarrassing ordeal for no reason), one might have hoped for a little flexibility and common humanity. Qualities manifestly not possessed by this particular Duty Governor.

The first I knew of all this was when S thundered into the hall, fuming at the nostrils like a bull at Pamplona, to hastily explain to me what had happened before driving her Dad back home. The officers apologised to me and were genuinely sympathetic, but said it was up to the Duty Governor to determine.

Back on the wing, I felt miserable and disorientated but, above all, sad for S and her father who had gone to such lengths to plan what should have been a happy event for us all. S and her sisters now, quite reasonably, feel that they cannot risk another such fiasco, which means that – almost certainly – I shall never see my much-loved father-in-law again. His health is failing and he will be almost 100 by the time I'm released next year. I spoke later to one of our wing officers, and older man who has worked here for many years. When I mentioned the DG's name he rolled his eyes and said, "I might have guessed. That man is a bully and a liar and I hate him with a vengeance." Nuf said!

S will, of course, be writing to complain to the No 1 Governor and I shall raise the issue with the IMB (Independent Monitoring Board). I'll also acquaint myself with the formal complaints procedure, a three stage affair, each with its own set of forms (Comp 1, 1a and 2) to complete. In ten months I have never felt moved to make written complaints, though I know some prisoners who submit at least one Comp 1 every week, however trivial, 'just to keep them on their toes. I have a well-founded suspicion that the 'top brass' will simply close ranks and shrug off my complaint. Truly they must have more pressing matters to attend to, but I do feel that the governor responsible should be taken to task.

Amidst all this angst I can't find much to be positive about just now. So maybe I should focus on my forthcoming 70 th birthday and emulate your friend by drawing up a list of seventy fun things to do with the rest of my life. Most of them would require energy, imagination and freedom (and cash!), all of which are in short supply just now. Our mutual friend writes enthusiastically of all the worthy causes he supports, the prominent personages he meets and places he visits in his various voluntary capacities. I can only admire his zeal.

I had thought that my days of committees and meetings were over, but I have recently been asked to sit as Landing Rep on the Wing Council. (I was approached by the Supervising Officer, not elected by the inmates. Prisons are not democratic institutions!) I feel genuinely honoured, though the task is not onerous, involving little more than monthly meetings with a couple of senior officers. I suspect that it is a box-ticking exercise intended merely to demonstrate (should anyone such as an Inspector ask) how the prison engages with inmates' concerns. I had several times tried, but failed, to find out when the meeting would take place so that I could talk to 'the lads' in advance about any issues or problems they might like raised. (You may guess what was top of my personal list!) Nobody in authority knew, or cared, or was prepared to divulge when the meeting would be scheduled. So I was a little surprised to be dug out of bed early last Sunday morning and given ten minutes to get ready. Fortunately I had already jotted down a few matters to raise in a small notebook labelled 'Wing Council' (old habits die hard).

It was not a stimulating meeting, not least because Crispin/Bob (Rep for the Threes landing) talked so much, though I concede he made some perceptive observations. On one point, at least, I may have scored. I objected to guys being referred to in the minutes and on notices as 'Offenders', when (say) 'Residents' would be more appropriate, and is occasionally used elsewhere. I'm not just looking for a weaselly word to avoid the bloomin' obvious; the fact is that by no means all inmates are proven offenders. This being a B-Cat local prison, many are here on remand, statistically about a third of whom are likely to be acquitted and released. Others may already have been acquitted and are held here pending deportation. So 'offenders' is inaccurate as well as pejorative. I hope that some of the other issues raised (mainly routinely boring practical matters such as laundry, food, the on-going saga of the broken floor buffer, etc.) will be addressed prior to the February meeting, for which a date has been fixed, at my suggestion /insistence.

Of course I raised the father-in-law's visit issue. The SO was sympathetic but otherwise non-committal and stony-faced. He can be scarily forthright and has a reputation for 'fighting dirty' when (occasionally) he has to restrain errant prisoners, a procedure known as 'bending up', which is self-explanatory. I have witnessed it only once and it was certainly not painless. However, I suspect that when it comes to dealing with his superiors, the SO may be just another 'jobsworth'. Until now I've had only limited dealings with him, but he has always been perfectly civil, at least to my face.

30. Friday 15 February 2019

Thanks for yours, plus more cards for the circulating gallery, especially the intriguing translucent stained glass pictures which I have sellotaped to the window. My apologies for the delayed reply. My little brain has been preoccupied with other issues and I have given in to the allure of lying low (as befits my current mood) and listening to music through the headphones. I hope you won't mind a rather cheeky request but perhaps when you send cards you could leave the obverse blank to give me the option of re-using them for (occasional) brief messages rather than full letters. How lazy I become – though, in my defence, this is my 237th letter since I started counting last May! I hope you approve the changed appearance of this letter. I am now writing on an 'art pad' as lined paper has been unobtainable from 'canteen' since before Christmas. What's available or what turns up (e.g. cards for 'husbands', as previously mentioned) is a bit of a lottery and errors are not readily rectified as orders are made up at another prison. They are none too scrupulous about checking. Either that or they enjoy a laugh at our expense – the other week I was sent custard powder instead of washing powder. What a mess it made of my shirts! Incidentally, shortly after the Wing Council meeting, the tumble dryer broke down and now the washing machine has followed suit, the laundry orderlies have downed tools and it's back to hand-washing smalls and shirts and drying them on the heating pipe.

S came in yesterday for a Valentine's Day visit with the visits hall more than usually busy for a weekday. Disappointingly the card I posted first class on Monday still hadn't arrived, possibly a casualty of Tuesday's lock-down for a staff training day. But the thought was there, and it was good to share some time alone (if you can call it that with 100+ other people in the room). She frequently brings someone with her, not that she needs a chaperone at her age, but because there is a long list of local people who seem to regard prison visiting as a pleasure rather than a duty or a chore (some people have a strange sense of fun). S reports that her dad has got over (or forgotten all about) his prison visit debacle, distressing as it was at the time, but her sisters are adamant that we cannot risk a repeat. That's disappointing, but I entirely see their point. The response to my initial complaint (on 'Comp 1' form) from the governor concerned was less than satisfactory – defensive, evasive and mealy-mouthed (and semi-literate, e.g. he says he 'emphasises' with the situation). He said that 'procedures were followed' (they weren't) and therefore he could not offer any apology (he could have). This entirely misses the point. I am now following it up through other avenues (Comp 2 and IMB), as is S.

I was amused by your description of the contents of *Good Housekeeping* magazine, especially the adverts. I'm sure it was never as saucy as that in the days when my mother subscribed 50+ years ago. Maybe I should start taking it for the recipes when I take over some of the cooking duties at home, as S insists I shall be doing. Her resolve may not last long when she starts to suffer the consequences... *GH* is not on the approved list here (unlike *GQ, OK* and *LO*) and which mags actually percolate through the shredder seems to depend largely on the whim of the censor on the day. Terry sometimes receives his monthly *Sky at Night* and *History* magazines (both published by that subversive leftie organisation known as the BBC), but sometimes not if they are held back by some censorious lowly paid fuckwit of a clerk in the post room. In which case Terry receives a memo marked 'NFI', the prison abbreviation for 'Not For Issue' (alternative: 'No Effing Idea'). They are then sent to 'Prop' for storage pending his release. The same fate sometimes befalls my fortnightly *Private Eye*, though *The Oldie* always arrives without fail. Prisoners are not allowed to write to the press (except *Inside Time* and *Jail Mail*) otherwise I would congratulate *The Oldie* editorial team on this improbable endorsement by HMPS. Magazines, inc. *The Oldie*, are delivered with their outer wrappings removed. A sensible precaution lest their national distributors had generously slipped in some porn or powdered drugs as a free bonus for incarcerated 'oldies'.

Just collected my lunch. "There you are, Boss," said the servery worker (prisoner) as he slapped the wrinkly baked potato down on my plastic plate. "That's not the boss," said another, "That's Tom." I must be getting assimilated at last. As I've written before, I do genuinely like a lot of the people I meet in here, which goes for the staff too. We have been speculating on the likelihood of the Duke of Edinburgh joining our ranks if he is prosecuted for dangerous driving following his recent prang. I guess he'd be made welcome by the older gents, probably enjoy a respite from royal duties, and soon feel at home, if only for a short while. He'd be our oldest resident, though not by much.

Tuesday was our meditation session with Rodney the Buddhist chaplain, one of my weekly highlights. When I first started we spent the best part of an hour in silent meditation, ending with a 'ping' on Rodney's electronic timer, a must-have for budding Buddhists. Then follows a chat and a bit of Buddhist teaching. I rather wish we could go over to the chapel (as the Quakers do) where it would be quieter. Rodney is resistant to this idea so we usually meet either in the classroom on the second landing or the Enhanced Room on the top floor. Though he times his visits to coincide with outdoor exercise, the wing is rarely completely quiet. We must contend with the cleaners' music, clattering of mops and brooms and some pretty ripe and un-Buddhist language from just outside the room. Recently we have started unpacking the fundamentals of human existence by way of course notes on Buddhist principles and philosophy. These are read aloud (usually by me, there being no other willing volunteers) followed by discussion. As the Ancients go, it's pretty inscrutable stuff – Aristotle reads like Enid Blyton by comparison. I'm not sure what the others (usually four of us) make of it all but I'm giving it my best shot and have bought highlighters to colour code the various concepts and strands of thought in the notes. If I realise one thing it is that, despite all the revelations of 2½ millennia of science, we humans haven't advanced much in understanding ourselves. Much of our church-based Christian teaching (in parish as much as in prison) is pretty feeble by comparison. Of course I value ritual, symbolism, singing and so forth, but I sometimes wish we could spend more time talking <u>about</u> beliefs. It might help sort out a few bizarre misconceptions, e.g.

Q. "What's the difference between Christian and Catholic?"

A. "Catholics worship two Gods but Christians only have one."

My few fellow proto-Buddhists are earnest types, if at times baffled by some of the teaching, as am I. But we all greatly like and respect Rodney who dispenses wise counsel of a practical nature as well as Noble Truths and ethical precepts. Only one of our number (who, appropriately, is also a Listener) is fully signed-up as a Buddhist with the Prison Service, so 'Buddha-curious' might be a better tag for the rest of us. We have a new recruit who is anxious to get his name on the official list as this will entitle him to acquire incense sticks via the chaplaincy. Surely Catholics (Anglo- and Roman) should also be accorded this dubious privilege? I won't press the point. I suspect Rodney may be a little suspicious of the young man's motives, and with good reason.

My new abode, C1-01, is near the main entrance to the wing and is thus a good vantage point to observe the comings and goings of visitors. Also, it's the first cell they come across on entry (the one opposite being adjacent to the showers, into which visitors are not advised to peer). This means that my cell is frequently used to show people what a 'typical' cell (and occupant) is like. Except, of course, that this cell, with its air of relative spaciousness, is far from typical. When asked, I am of course delighted to show people round (there's not much to see) but I make a point of explaining the several details in which it is superior to a regular cell, and for good measure hint at the potential horrors of sharing. This week we have had two groups of strangers being given the tour by a suited governor. Mostly female, they were dressed in understated M&S smart casual wear and sensible shoes, and I wondered if they might be from the WI. They were accompanied by a few male hangers-on, possibly partners drafted in as protection squad. I could call them 'lambs to the slaughter' but the age profile is wrong, so perhaps 'sheep gone astray' is more apt. I guessed from their reticence that they had been cautioned not to speak to residents, like not feeding monkeys at the zoo. Not to be ignored, I approached one lady, smiled sweetly and asked the purpose of their visit. "We're considering applying to become prison officers," was her unlikely answer. I had to bite my tongue to stop myself saying "You must be mad!" or some such. Instead I just wished her the very best of luck, to be interpreted however she wished. I doubt if they were taken into B-Wing.

Outside the shower room is an orange warning cone labelled SLIPPERY FLOOR. Some wag, with a permanent marker and a better grasp of humour than spelling, has added ANAL DIALATOR. Hum. An officer wisely removed it in the nick of time before the above delegation came round on their tour.

I've just offered someone a biscuit. "Thanks. Can I have two?" he said. I'd call that 'taking the biscuit'.

31. Tuesday 5 March 2019

Your letters arrived promptly this time and, for once, did not cross with mine. To my delight I also received my first issue of National Geographic magazine, a gift subscription from my niece who is an occasional contributor. Only 'surprised' because the package was inexplicably addressed to 'Mr TT'. Fortunately in these parts I am also known by my number, though it is not yet tattooed on my forearm. I am greatly relieved to hear of your all-clear on the health front and am impressed that you managed to stay so cheerful and positive for several anxious weeks. It's amazing what we can tolerate when we have to, as the past year has taught me.

A very minor inconvenience here since Christmas has been the progressive attrition of laundry facilities. First the industrial washing machine went *hors de combat*, then the tumble dryer. This, I can report, has now been fixed and thanks to the ministrations of the laundry orderly once again delivers up piles of warm, crumpled and slightly moist clothing ready for ironing. Except that the iron and ironing board have both gone AWOL. The sight of burly blokes meticulously pressing their pants on the landing (use of iron in cell is banned) was as heart-warming as it was incongruous. It's no fashion parade, but one must keep up appearances and we are obliged to maintain a modicum of 'decency', as you know. Mops and brooms are available on request from the landing office, though they have a tendency to disappear for days on end. Some residents are obsessive about cleanliness, though (as you may guess) I am not one of them, having only a nodding acquaintance with conventional notions of tidiness. If I could pay someone (in kind) to wash the cell floor I would – there would be several willing mopsters – but it would set a poor precedent. We must maintain a semblance of equality *. On a positive note, we have received a delivery of vanloads of new bed sheets, stitched in some other nick. Same livid green colour, but less pilled and with their edges hemmed and as yet intact. For now, at least, we shall be able to tuck sheets in on all sides and avoid a ridge of rucked-up fabric forming down the spine.

* This reminds me that last year, when I struggled to support my trousers without a belt, a prisoner opposite – a member of the Traveller community with a scheming, oleaginous manner reminiscent of Trollope's Mr Slope – called me over to show me his belt. It was beautifully soft and rosy as a maiden's blush with intricately tooled patterns of Islamic swirls and curlicues. It smelled fresh from a Fes Medina tannery, and looked very expensive. "I could get you one of these," he offered, conspiratorially, "But you wouldn't be able to afford it." How observant of him!

I am writing this at my little desk (which I no longer have to share!) but feeling slightly chilly as the heating pipe is barely warm. It must be me as most people go round in T-shirts and even open their windows, whereas mine is still permanently sealed with strips of J-cloth in lieu of draught excluder. Last week I went outside in shorts, but today I endured a whole hour's icy blast in the yard. Big mistake. Exercise is voluntary, but once outside we're committed to the full hour at the end of which my fingers were icicles and my nose dribbled frozen snot. I was glad to return to the cell for a brew of hot Yorkshire tea while coddled in my homely dressing gown and fleecy moccasin slippers.

When 'the sun does shine' (remember that title?) it shines in my cell from about 2.30 pm onwards and I watch the shadows of the window bars creep slowly across the wall and floor. Perhaps I should mark out a sundial? Which reminds me that I used the word 'gnomon' in a Scrabble game last week, and with Albert safely in Brixton, there was no one around to object. Piotr (litter-picker) 'liberated' a handful of wind-blown daffodils from a flowerbed on the way back from chapel last Sunday and kindly presented them to me. They now stand tall in a cut down Robinson's squash bottle on the desk and I am enjoying their musky smell of early spring. I have now been here over a year!

Thank you so much for the unwritten-on postcards. I have already used one to acknowledge the date of my (former) vicar's next visit. The west window of Southwell Minster seemed appropriately ecclesiastical, but I shall keep the card of the famous chapter house carved stone leaves for my local friend Ros with her love of the vernacular. Please don't pre-stamp cards as I have a bit of a surfeit. Not only has S sent me all her unused and now unseasonal Christmas stamps, but I must always enclose cards in an envelope so that I can indicate my name, number and location in the approved manner.

Not much follow-up, as yet, to any of the issues raised in the Wing Council meeting. However I have been grilled by the strutting supremo of the servery. This smarmy tosser and self-appointed Great High Inquisitor of the Wing called me aside recently and sort of warned me off becoming the landing rep. He said that:
a) it's a pointless waste of time because it never achieves anything, and
b) I may be accused of being a 'grass' or screw's lackey and will henceforth be blamed for <u>everything</u> that goes wrong. I would take his observations more seriously had he not added that
c) he is, in reality, <u>extremely miffed</u> at not being invited to take on the role himself.

The GHI (above) may be right about the meetings achieving little, but I can already report one minor victory. This is that, as of now, we older chaps (retirees, infirm and disabled) are to be allowed to associate out of cells during the mornings when the young and fit are over at the workshops. This, apparently, has always been the HMPS-wide rule, but not observed here within recent memory. It came to light in rather surprising circumstances. As previously mentioned, our printing workshops produce materials for other prisons nationally, e.g. such things as Apps, menus, post-room records books and movement forms. Also, officers' training materials and bound booklets of labyrinthine regulations, targets and so forth issued by the Ministry. Now these can make interesting reading, not, of course, that anyone in the print shop would have the time or inclination to study them. Maybe it was a mistake of the workshop supervisor to tell his team so emphatically not to read them – like telling a teenager not to look at porn – and on no account to remove copies from the workshop. But what if there is a shortfall of a couple of covers, and the unbound, incomplete copies get tossed in the re-cycling bin? What possible objection could there be to someone surreptitiously slipping one of these into his bag, for re-use as scrap paper, perhaps? All purely hypothetical, of course.

Which is the rather indirect explanation of how I come to have a copy of just such a document that describes in exacting detail the 'Expectations' (that's its title) of prison inspectors. It is very clear that, under a general heading of prisoner welfare, we are not supposed to be banged up all morning (and most afternoons and evenings too). I raised this issue at the Wing Council and also with the IMB people who visited me in my cell and then promised to take up the matter with senior management. It helped to be able to quote chapter and verse, though without revealing my sources of course. I promised to keep shtum about that. The IMB are said to 'have the ear' of the Number One – I must look out for a grey-suited gent with a bandaged head, like Van Gogh – and he gave them a favourable hearing. So from now on we Oldies are to be let out of our cells once the younger lads have left the wing for work. (That's what's meant to happen, but the regular officers are remarkably resistant to change and take some persuading.) I have no great wish to wander round all morning gossiping with the other old farts, but what a difference it makes psychologically just to have the door open!

This morning Terry voluntarily joined the tea-packing team, a modern equivalent of picking oakum, perhaps. Between half a dozen of them, they bagged up (in mini freezer bags) 11,000 tea bags, along with cereal, café-style fingers of sugar and sachets of coffee whitener, enough to supply the daily desires of every prisoner here for the coming week. Terry says it is a mindless task, but sociable with badinage and banter, and earns him an extra pittance on top of his weekly wage. It's a mean reward for a man who once earned £100k in the badlands of Uzbekistan.

Along with most of the other Listeners, I recently attended a SASH training course. That's **S**uicide **A**nd **S**elf-**H**arm awareness. This is now an essential part of prison officers' basic training, and they went through the same materials to give us background information and a better understanding of official policies and procedures. It was certainly an instructive experience, not least because every one of us (officers included) had at some time lost a relative or close friend to suicide. Over the years there has been a steady rise in prisoner suicides and, as you know, self-harm by cutting (or worse) is all too common, so it is good to know that the Prison Service gives a high priority to addressing the issue. It's not something I could ever contemplate as I'm freaked out by the sight of blood, though there are other less bloody means. We were told of a prisoner who poked radio aerials down his throat and another who swallowed batteries. It doesn't bear thinking about, but that probably also applies to the levels of distress they must be suffering. There does seem to be a relationship between staffing ratios and self-harm as, in women's prisons where staffing levels have improved, the incidence of suicide and self-harm has gone down.

It was also gratifying, for once, to be treated like adults whose views were worth listening to. Bob alias Crispin, true to form, talked a lot. He's really into self-harm – not his own, of course (despite his public school upbringing he's not into flagellation) but analysing the secretive practices of others. He let slip that he'd like to re-train as a therapist following his release, something it might have been wiser to keep to himself. It was an enlightening day, though disappointing that a few of the Listeners absented themselves on the grounds that they did not want to be 'manipulated' by officers.

You ask again about the issue of S's father's visit. The time has come to draw a line under this. Following receipt of my Comp 2 form and, possibly a nudge from the IMB stooges, the Deputy

Governor (not the one who caused the upset) has written placatory letters to S and me saying that it 'could and should have been handled better and with some compassion.... and I wish to apologise on behalf of HMPS'. The understatement of the year, but it must have been difficult to write from an organisation that rarely admits error, so I appreciate it. They have allocated me additional visits and offered the use of a private room if we wish to re-arrange father-in-law's visit. Meanwhile S has had a further letter of apology from the Visits Department acknowledging that the error was entirely theirs. In a more humane establishment surely someone from management might have thought to visit me to apologise in person? It would have been a small but thoughtful gesture. So much for 'We see the person, not the prisoner!'

32. Monday 18 March 2019

Thank you so much for the surprise cards of York, looking delightfully daffodilly in the spring sunshine. I'm glad you enjoyed the Railway Museum, somewhere I once organised a two-day training event (though not on Suicide and Self Harm!), and where I'll return one day when I have my freedom back. I'm reminded of Hardy's poem about the convict on the station platform:
"And the man in the handcuffs
Suddenly sang with grimful glee:
'This life so free is the thing for me!'
I quite often feel 'grimful glee' at present, and the sight of hosts of dancing daffs round the grim site stimulates some glee. They have taken a battering in the recent powerful winds, a good excuse to pick some of the fallen ones to add a splash of good cheer to the cell. Nobody seems to mind, though I'm wary of 'taking the not-offered' (one of the Buddhist precepts we've been studying with Rodney) having been told off last year for plucking a petunia in the exercise yard. (If that sounds like a euphemism for some dubious or deviant practice, it is not, so far as I am aware.)

I'm interested to read your critique of the Djanogli Gallery's Bauhaus exhibition having recently read a review of the new biography of Walter Gropius. Females of his generation seem to have readily fallen under his spell, and not just for his buildings.

The exhibition sounds like an excellent way for Nottingham Trent to promote the work of graphics students. There's a talented student artist here just now who has covered his entire cell walls with his own work, some of it pretty impressive (several notches up from Arthur's *Still Life with Oranges on a Blue Plastic Plate* which is still displayed on the walls almost three months after his liberation). Our student hopes to return to his studies in September following his involuntary 'sabbatical' as a guest of Her Majesty. He comes over as the archetypal art student – amiable, self-effacing, casual tending towards scruffy, bit of a drop-out (like most of Harry's mates) – so I was really surprised / horrified to hear him come out with some startlingly illiberal pro-Brexit prejudices. I must try and re-educate him while there is still time. For the record, the great debates of the day (e.g. Brexit and its aftermath) rarely raise so much as an eyebrow in here. It's another world 'outside'. No wonder successive UK governments have got away with ignoring EU demands to give prisoners the vote.

Workmen were on the wing all last week renovating the showers. This is something else we have been pressing for in the Wing Council, though I suspect it was long-planned so I won't award myself a pat on the back just yet. There may be a connection with rumours of an impending 'surprise' inspection: evidence the fact that one day last week we had a scrum of <u>eight</u> suited governors on the wing. Whatever is going on? Normally we rarely see any of the big bosses from one week's end to the next. Sadly, the workmen tell me that they are contracted to work only on the ground floor showers, not the upper landings. This will not be well-received by the lads up top. When I say 'renovate' I actually mean 'remodel' as they have installed chest-high barriers to create cubicles as a very long-overdue concession to modesty and decorum. It took the workmen an inordinately long time to complete the job, perhaps because in here every plumber, tiler, plasterer and painter has to be protected at all times by a specially designated prison officer. I wonder what the risk assessment says? Our showers are now noticeably more popular (good news for all cell-sharers) and the old prison advice about 'don't drop the soap' is no longer apposite, if it ever was.

You ask how my Shannon Trust student is getting on with his reading. Sadly he has dropped out, despite my best endeavours. Having reached the whole book stage (albeit only at *Bob the Builder* level but with more adult illustrations though similar subject matter) he decided he'd gone far enough or, to borrow his phrase, it was 'doing his head in'. He has now been decanted * to another prison. He was not a popular guy here, mainly because he was a bit of a fantasist, forever bragging that he was 'about to be' enhanced, or re-categorised to D-Cat, or moved to an open prison, or allowed extra family visits or whatever. Everything was 'about to be' but none of it was true. Also, I negotiated a concession so I could mentor him during the evening enhanced periods on the strict understanding that he remained in his cell, a restriction that he refused to abide by, wandering off mid-session to my embarrassment and the annoyance of just about everyone else.

* Quaintly figurative prison usage: "Kindly pass the port, Guv'nor. I wish to decant another prisoner." I suppose every profession (to use the word somewhat loosely) has its own distinctive vocabulary.

Though I have lost my regular Shannon Trust student, I still get asked to help others with occasional letter writing or form filling or act as a more-or-less willing living dictionary (quicker than looking up a word, especially if you don't know how to spell it). My own letter writing has been noticed and widely commented on, mainly "Can't imagine what you write about as nothing ever happens in here." But as an unpaid scribe, I also get to correspond with lawyers, government departments, prison officials, debt collectors and, of course, the families and friends of my less literate colleagues. One lad – a genial dolt, scruffy, overweight, blotchy trousers held up with string – begins his letter, 'hi mum i hat you just jokeing how is the old tart' (he means his Dad!) and so on. I hope Mum appreciates it. It takes all types, and there are some rum ones here.

We have now had our March meeting of the Wing Council, though the SO has not (as yet) compiled the minutes for February. He was not enthusiastic about writing up the latest meeting either and readily accepted my offer to do so. It must be a long time since public bodies kept books of handwritten minutes (I remember poring over ledgers of immaculate Victorian workhouse guardians' minutes, whose standard agenda was disturbingly similar to ours). I've no wish to be the SO's stooge, but it strikes me that writing up the minutes may give me some slight control over what gets recorded and therefore actioned. We shall see.

Unlike the Mother of Parliaments, the Wing Council is not an example of democracy at its best. Its function is at most purely advisory like, say, a cross-party parliamentary catering committee or a village amenity pressure group. Nevertheless, all the regular gripes got another airing this month, e.g. the continued malfunction of the washing machine, lack of advance information about regime changes, allegations of bullying, issues with visits, etc. I make it my business to consult the residents in advance over issues they'd like mentioned. Thus I raised grumbles about the Sunday custard being doled out from a seat adjacent to the rubbish bin; also that a rat (a rodent, not a wayward resident) had been spotted scuttling across the servery floor, conjuring up visions of Manuel's pet rat/hamster in *Fawlty Towers* (named Basil 'because chef puts a lot of basil in the ratatouille'!) One of my fellow 'Reps' must have spilt the beans in the servery, metaphorically at least, and the following day the Great High Inquisitor himself (a pillock of the community who talks a lot of froth) summoned me to his Star Chamber in the servery for a further roasting. He was not unduly perturbed by the rat (they freely saunter in and out via the drain cover, apparently) but was very miffed about the custard complaint. I put up a stout defence and am pleased to say that I placated him on this and other matters and he is now my 'new best friend'. He described me as 'the most polite person on the wing'. Little did he know that I'd referred to him in the meeting as 'an odious twat'! Someone else said, 'I wouldn't piss on him if he caught fire.' I didn't tell him that either.

One of my pet schemes (ref. my former friend from Dartmoor) is to revive the Over-50s Club that used to operate here and is still advertised on various A4 posters around the place. The idea would be to invite occasional speakers from outside on a range of interesting/useful topics, anything from art history to zoology. We could guarantee them an even more exclusive audience than your Dante Society or National Women's Register. In years gone by some of my former colleagues used to come in with entertaining talks about historic crime and punishment, bringing along appropriate museum artefacts such as thumbscrews and knuckle-dusters, handcuffs, Georgian truncheons, broadsheet posters advertising public hangings and other amusing ephemera from the good old days. Do let me know if you have any suggestions for speakers or topics. Meanwhile I am trying to get names and email addresses of local branches of organisations such as U3A and WEA that may be able to help. I'm not optimistic, but worth a try.

33. All Fools Day, Monday 1 April, 2019

Thanks for your letters and cards of Edinburgh. How enterprising to sit in on a debate in the Scottish Parliament. I like your description of its 'many protestations of good intent but no concrete proposals' which just about sums up our Wing Council (though of course that is not a democratic body). Sorry to read of your latest run-in with the NHS, loss of medical records and (now) John's broken tooth. In the light of which, I make a mental note, pending my release, never to confuse a steamed dumpling with a hotel hand towel. Last week I was summoned to see the ever-jocular Dr Hardcore again, this time to be told that recent blood tests reveal a potassium deficiency for which I must take a course of supplements (prescribed) and eat more bananas. I asked if he could also prescribe the bananas (I'm a convict of limited means) to which he replied that it would be easier to arrange a private audience with President Trump than persuade the prison authorities to provide free bananas. It seemed an odd analogy. Dr H doesn't present as someone with Republican sentiments, but he certainly knows a thing or two about prisons and bananas.

As I have now been here over one year, a re-categorisation review has been held *in absentia* and I am delighted to report that I am now officially a D-Cat prisoner, i.e. the lowest risk level. I now know, thanks to certain documents I was not meant to see, that a) I could have been 'D-Catted' (as they say) last August, and b) I should have been told of this review in advance and given the opportunity to make representations. It's no surprise, then, that I have still not been given a sentence plan (a need highlighted eight months ago!) or indeed had any contact whatsoever with my so-called Offender

Supervisor, if indeed this person actually exists. Maybe he/she is, like my Personal Officer, just a vague aspiration or figment of the Ministry of Justice's fevered imagination. No matter.

You may recall that, not long after my arrival, I was advised that I would shortly be sent to a C-Cat prison. Well that idea went right out of the window. I'm now told that C-Cats are in practice for people they want to do courses (e.g. anger management or sex offender programmes), neither of which includes me. (You may have read that new research shows that certain sex offender courses may in fact reinforce offending behaviour by encouraging prisoners to discuss and swap notes on their offences!) To be positive, as a D-Cat prisoner I am now notionally eligible for transfer to an open prison. There are two such on this side of the country, both affording fresh sea breezes and healthy agricultural smells from their rare breeds pigs and sheep. One is Hollesley Bay, where I once visited in another capacity. It would be handy for that well-known riverside hostelry the Ramsholt Arms, but I doubt if the openness of an open prison extends as far as a pint at the pub. The other is North Sea Camp, near Boston. A distant relative of mine was MP for Boston in the 1850s and a more recent MP, Lord Jeffrey Archer, is an alumnus of the 'Camp'. So it has 'pedigree', and that's not just its rare breed pigs.

My pad-mate Terry is also now D-Cat, as is a fellow wing-councillor, and we are all three considering applying for a transfer if that is feasible. We are not optimistic. The SO tells us that places in open prisons are in short supply and usually reserved for prisoners who are coming towards the end of long sentences as a way of easing them back into the community. Not applicable in my case. Also, I would not be keen to move so far from home that it would be difficult to S to visit regularly, as she has until now. So I guess it's a case of 'here I stand', to borrow Luther's declamation.

My attention was drawn recently to a notice, pinned outside the dispensary (why only there when we have a board within the wing?), inviting prisoners to apply to attend so-called Equalities Strands meetings. Equalities refers to the relevant 'protected characteristics' under the DDA, being Age, Disability/Mental Health, Race, Religion/Belief and Sexual Orientation. By the time I saw the notice (on my weekly visit to collect meds) the deadline was only days away, so I submitted an App requesting attendance at Age and/or Religion meetings and also asked landing officers to telephone the governor responsible. Answer came there none, so I submitted a second App and persuaded another officer to contact the governor named on the notice. I must say he showed extreme reluctance to do so, and, not for the first time, I formed the impression that communication between regular 'screws' and the gents in suits is at best uneasy, if not actually discouraged. The same applies to prisoners, and my impression is that we are not expected to speak to governors unless first spoken to (as I was advised when presented to the Queen Mum).

Notwithstanding, soon after I spotted a governor on the wing (about as rare a sighting as a bittern in the reed-beds) and had the temerity to speak to him on the issue. He seemed to be completely unaware of the Equalities Strands meetings but said he would 'look into it'. Eventually, however, I received a rather garbled verbal message to say that the meetings had already taken place but that, in any case, I could not have attended as they 'were held in another part of the prison to which C-Wing prisoners do not have access.' Brilliant! So why advertise meetings to people who cannot attend? Just to make us feel like second-class citizens? So much for 'equalities'! Not ready yet to succumb to such absurd opacity, I spoke to the IMB people (by now they must think me a trouble-maker!) who agreed to take up the matter. They have since come back with the response that I may – just may – get an invitation to attend 'next time' (if there is one). I'm not holding my breath, but I'll certainly have plenty to say about internal communications, along with a list of issues re. Age and/or Religion.

The above is not the only example of retirees being in the wrong place at the wrong time. This is why I cannot attend the Rev's weekly Bible Study sessions, which are held over at the workshops. That may be God's doing, as I would probably be a disruptive influence. Likewise I am unable to join the monthly Book Group, which truly is a shame. Terry attends and enjoys it a lot. This week they had to present a poem of their own choice. On my recommendation Terry read *The Execution* by Alden Nowlan. Check it out and you will understand why it provoked a lot of discussion!

On which point, yesterday some Evangelical minister from a local free church visited the workshops to chat to (i.e. 'convert') prisoners and handed out leaflets to Terry and everyone else. Reading it later, I thought its tone was positively medieval, an observation I made to Terry, who was so shocked (he is not of a religious mien), that he promptly ripped the leaflet to shreds and cast it into the bin like Daniel into the lion's den. I have now retrieved and painstakingly reassembled the pieces. It is all about sin, death and eternal damnation. I quote: "As the Last Judgement follows death, so an everlasting Hell follows Last Judgement. Hell is a place of everlasting torment, where there will be weeping and gnashing of teeth." Surely prisoners have enough to grapple with without shitting their pants at such nightmare-inducing proselytising? (Small consolation – their teeth are often too rotten to gnash.) The solution, according to the leaflet, is to "join a church that believes in the Bible, such as [name of church]… We are living in an age when many churches have forgotten what Christianity is…" Is this sort of stuff acceptable in Her Majesty's Prisons? Would they allow a firebrand Imam to use similar threats to recruit for Isis? I must have a quiet word with the Chaplain whose tiresome Sunday exhortations are as balm by comparison.

I'm intrigued by your cousin Sue's opinions on the iniquities of radiotherapy and the races! S and I have only been once, to the Queen Elizabeth Gold Cup in Calcutta, and a very splendid day it was too. Terry organised a sweepstake here for the Cheltenham Gold Cup (race-goers must be fond of gold) with wagers taken in cartons of prison-issue UHT milk. I wagered my very last milk carton on a horse called Presenting Percy at 4:1. Unfortunately Percy came in fifth so I had to breakfast the next morning on Weetabix with orange squash, a combination I can't recommend.

Last week's brief burst of springtime has brought the prison gardens (what little I can see on the way to exercise or chapel) to life. The daffs are already decayed, even though Easter is still three weeks off, but there are plenty of neatly-planted rows of dwarf wallflowers and velvety midnight blue pansies just opening out. I pointed out the latter to a rather fey young man who said he'd often heard the word pansy but never knew it was a flower. I've been helping a remand prisoner with correspondence as he struggles to piece together a credible explanation of how he came to be arrested. It's a bizarre story involving a stranger, a camera and a pretty wild flower – by process of elimination, possibly *ranunculus* – that was growing in a wood where some young girls just happened to be playing. The poor man knows absolutely nothing of botany. Perhaps he should borrow a book on wildflowers from the library and swot up on *ranunculi* before relying on their identification for his defence. Everyone is entitled to an occasional fib, but some here seem to have made a lifetime's career out of it.

Another bloke I help is nicknamed Neanderthal. You'd understand if you saw him, with his big hairy 33-year old body loosely attached to a head encasing a brain like an Emmental cheese. Neanderthal has taken up writing a story for me to read and correct. He's now on the fifteenth page of big, loopy, un-joined, un-punctuated and un-paragraphed narrative. Actually, not entirely un-punctuated, as he likes to throw in quotation marks about as randomly as prison drugs tests. Example: "and then jamse sed git in the car 'so jon git in' and then they…" and so on, and on! An averagely well-taught six year old could do better, albeit with less specifically 'adult' content and fewer swear words (or maybe not nowadays?) Oddly I find it quite a privilege to help him. Well that's one way of looking at it. He offered me a cup of tea, but I politely declined on health grounds. I'm not sure if he understands the purpose of soap and his once-white pottery mug is stained as black as an inkwell.

A few days ago we had an 'incident' on the wing when a volatile rough-diamond of a new arrival, a man with a tuba voice but a piccolo brain, lost his cool with the 'screws'. Jimmy (not his real name) is one brick short of a load, as they say, and made such a scene over some trivial issue that he had to be roughly 'bundled' back into his cell by the SO, who proceeded to remove his television. This is often used as a first line of punishment. Jimmy was having none of it and threatened to 'flatpack' his cell unless the TV was returned. It was not. To save face, Jimmy then proceeded to carry out his threat. 'Flatpack', an unlikely verb not yet in the OED, neatly describes the process of trashing or smashing up every last piece of furniture, then breaking the glass in the door observation slit and feeding the detritus through it bit by bit onto the landing outside. Having rendered his cell effectively uninhabitable, Jimmy was later removed to another wing. The following day, as I was sitting in the Visits Hall waiting for my visitors to arrive, a large lorry with a cherry picker could be seen reversing alongside one of the other wings. In jest I said to the bloke at the next table, "Perhaps Jimmy's on the roof?" Someone else must have partly overheard me and shouted out for all to hear, "Hey lads, Jimmy's on the roof!" A crowd promptly gathered round the windows, but with no sight of Jimmy who, I now know, is safely locked away in 'Seg', as the segregation unit is known. He must be regretting his smashing spree. Call it Chinese whispers, but now I understand how easy it is to start a rumour.

34. Wednesday 17 April, 2019

Thanks for the updates on your health issues and concerned enquiries about mine. I'm approaching the big seven-oh with some trepidation, though Dr Hardcore has not managed to find much wrong despite his best endeavours. I stuff myself with daily doses of –lols, –pines, -statins and –zides, some of which merely cancel out the unwanted side-effects of others. Life was so much simpler in the days when (powdered) rhubarb was cure-all physic and a glass or two of good port before bed purportedly kept gout at bay. I have already completed my course of rather nice fizzy potassium pills, a cross between WC de-scalers and G & T (minus the G), and am taking my daily banana as recommended but not prescribed. One of my correspondents claims that her late father, an Irish clergyman, had Guinness on prescription, and my Victorian grandmother used to swear by the same medicine, or perhaps it was Mackeson. Regrettably neither of these health-giving potions is obtainable here.

This has been an uneventful week, even by prison standards. No visits, no medical appointments (thinks: must book dental check-up), no 'incidents', no meetings and not even any Listener call-outs. That, at least, must be a positive sign that all is well on the wing. It is, however, Holy Week, and I greatly enjoyed listening through my headphones to the entire *St John Passion* from Amsterdam on Palm Sunday. I missed *The Magic Flute* you mention but did catch and enjoyed *Tosca* (from the Met). *Tosca* was the first opera I ever saw live (Rome Opera House 1963), that is if you discount the N. Lincs Amateur Operatic Soc's *Merry Widow* in Cleethorpes c. 1960.

I had hoped that we might re-convene our little chapel choir that proved such a hit with Christmas carols to sing some Passiontide music (albeit not Allegri's *Miserere!*) However, the organist and two of our choristers were released mid-Lent, which is a shame, though not for them. Singing is one of the things I really miss. Singing along with pre-recorded jingles on the chapel boom box does not quite hit the spot. Occasionally we have a stand-in vicar from a local parish who brings in his guitar for accompaniment. It makes a welcome change, despite his rasping voice and choice of hymn-lite jingles. * Thankfully we had a few of the traditional hymns on Good Friday. Their words and melodies may have been mournful, but at least not quite as banal as some of the 'worship songs' the Rev imagines people prefer. On Palm Sunday I started a lusty rendering of *Ride on, ride on in majesty* hoping to encourage the others to open their lungs, only to realise that the pre-recorded accompaniment was quite different, a weak and feeble substitute for the traditional tune.

* While I may not much care for his voice, this gentleman's down-to-earth manner and obvious sincerity make him a winner with 'the lads'. He invites them to go to his church after release where he promises a warm welcome and practical support in finding accommodation and employment. If only more were like that.

This year's palm cross, distributed last Sunday, now joins its predecessor from last year tucked into a book on the windowsill (which serves as my overspill bookshelf). By the time I have a third cross I shall be counting down the days to release. This year's Passion reading had to be cancelled for lack of time after a late start following an alarm elsewhere. However I was allowed to attend the RC Mass on Saturday and took the star role of Narrator while their flame-haired lady lay-chaplain took the part of Christ. We must be inclusive nowadays when some Christians question Jesus's gender-identity. I can't imagine what St Paul would have made of it given his strictures about women not speaking in church. Sunday's Epistle was read by the little evangelical known for his views as Mr

Fundament, or more usually Comb-over, from his bald patch and self-trimmed old-school hairstyle. He announced his reading as 'St Paul's Letter to the Philippines' – I never knew the Apostle was so well travelled! Comb-over and I enjoy winding each other up, mainly over his (or my, as he would contend) selective interpretations of Scripture.

Here's another prison eccentricity. Standard C of E practice on receiving Communion is to respond 'Amen'. Here, almost everyone on having the wafer placed in the hand responds, 'Thank you'. How very polite, and English! Our mutual friend P, who knows our local bishop well, says how much he likes preaching here because we are such an attentive audience. He may just be misreading that glazed-eye prisoner look. P, as you will know, can be hard on us retirees and writes "One should take one's social responsibilities seriously. Few people do. They say that, despite being retired, they are too busy. In fact they're mostly busy going on holiday." So there! I try to do my bit, though it's not always welcome in here. There can be a thin line between genuinely helpful and merely meddlesome.

I was intrigued by your account of visiting the Spiritualist church in Edinburgh, not least because I never knew such institutions still existed (Conan-Doyle was an enthusiastic exponent, I recall). I must ask Hopalong, my former pad-mate, about it as he's a Pagan who has dabbled in Spiritualism. He's unusually (for him) evasive about his experiences in those realms, but lays claim to some singular out-of-body encounters. He also clearly recalls events from some of his previous lives. He tells me that he was formerly a slave in a Greek galley that sank in the Gulf of Corinth with the loss of all hands. In his current embodiment he is training to be a copy-editor and proof-reader (or 'pruff-reader' as he says – he's from King's Lynn) for which he has acquired ring binders and an enormously heavy dictionary. Hopalong (aka Prof. Jingles) is a keen Scrabble player with an encyclopaedic vocabulary, perhaps acquired from his spirit friends or during previous incarnations. He can be a bit chippy about his lack of formal qualifications, referring to graduates Terry, Crispin/Bob and me as 'the three degrees'. He takes great delight in beating us at Scrabble, which he frequently does.

Current pad-mate Terry, on the other hand, has quite limited vocabulary and even worse spelling (I check his OU Sociology essays to pick out the more obvious howlers) but an amazing ability at Sudoku, at which I am terrible. He manages to knock off the 'killer Sudoku' in the Sunday *Observer* in next to no time while I struggle for hours even with the easy one. Terry is determined to leave prison better educated than he came in, though he already has a B.Eng. which once earned him pots of money. His cleaning, it must be said, is no better than his spelling, a fact which he excuses on the grounds that he worked mainly abroad and always had a maid for menial tasks. We discussed advertising amongst fellow prisoners for a cell-cleaner (payment in milk cartons or vapes) but decided it would not be a good look, so we must learn to live with a bit of fluff, as I suspect Terry also did when he worked 'in oil'.

The prison nurses appeared in force on the wing last week armed with an old-fashioned pump-action blood pressure monitor and impressive digital scales. A rather large lad called Larry took to the scales ahead of me, but at his first two attempts the screen read ERROR. When they finally produced a reading it showed 158 kg, more than twice my own miserly 74 kg. Even this modest score is a little up on when I entered the prison fourteen months ago. I'm now trying to reduce my sugar intake and walk a few extra circuits every time I brave the exercise yard. I envy you your energy as well as your opportunities for purposeful walks amongst the hills and vales or along the banks of those canals you so love.

I hope that this will reach you in time for the Easter week-end and forecast bout of warm sunny weather. Terry has ordered a couple of chocolate eggs from canteen to hide in the cell for me to find when I return from chapel on Easter Sunday morning. The annual egg hunt has long been part of our family ritual at home and will continue this year, though S says they must all be at eye level as her Dad now finds it too painful to stoop. Terry will need some ingenuity to conceal the eggs in this tiny shared space, but thank goodness we are not at HMP Peterborough where (according to an IMB visitor from there) the cells are smaller – I mean 'even smaller' – than ours. I guess they don't hold Easter egg hunts there either.

I chanced two milk cartons on last week's Grand National sweepstake. This time I fared even worse as my horse *Monbeg Notorious* retired after the first fence! There must be a moral in that.

Happy Easter!

35. Monday 4 to Wednesday 6 May, 2019

Full marks to Terry for his ingenuity in hiding my cream (or 'crème') egg on Easter Sunday, though I was lamentably unable to find it despite searching high and low on my return from chapel. I asked for a hint, at which he flapped his elbows and made clucking noises as if he'd freshly laid it just for me. In the end I had to admit defeat whereupon he pointed to my box of chicken-flavoured cup-a-soup sachets, where I found it nestling within. No wonder he's so good at Sudoku.

'Neanderthal', the lumpen lad (aged 33) I tried to help with his writing, finally reached page 23 of his interminable low-life story. It did not improve as it went on (and on and on…) , and I gently tried to persuade him that quantity is not the same as quality, though perhaps in his world it is. He doesn't do subtlety but must have suspected that my patience was wearing almost as threadbare as his stained joggers. Last week he presented me with the gift of a five-inch wooden cross made out of glued matchsticks stained dark brown (like his once-white mug) with tea. So prison tea has some uses after all. The very next day he was gone, shipped out to serve the remainder of his sentence at some other jail where I hope he will get better support than here. He has a good heart, but is totally devoid of any ambition or hope of betterment and accepts his lot in life without demur. He would have made a good scullion or lay-brother in a medieval monastery, or perhaps (like Nige in a former incarnation) a galley slave in a Greek trireme. Trying (not unkindly, I hope) to gain some insight into his lifestyle I once asked him why he never washed his tea mug. He just shrugged his shoulders and said, "I can't be arsed", which neatly sums up his approach to life in general.

Thank you for your most generous birthday gift, sent via S, with which I shall buy something really useful to commemorate my 'big seven-oh' as well as our fifty years of friendship. Taking a leaf, so to speak, out of Prof. Jingles's book, I propose to buy my own copy of the New Oxford Dictionary of English, currently retailing at £39. The appeal of NODE is that it defines every known word in current English usage, including proper nouns, from Aachen to Zyrian, plus variants (e.g. 'ballock' for 'bollock'!) and foreign usages such as 'bakkie' (S. African for pick-up truck) and 'prepone' (Indian English for bringing something forward – geddit?) It also includes brief biographies of notable people such as George Best, Attila the Hun and Margaret Thatcher and descriptions of places of interest. A mine of information for us un-Googled prisoners. One word not yet included is 'woke', except in the traditional sense of 'awakened'. (Perhaps that is the derivation? Nobody seems to know.) As you will have noted, even *The Times* now uses it without explanation, much to the chagrin of fuddy-duddy correspondents on the letters page. I asked an amiable officer to check out 'woke' online and decided that it pretty accurately describes... me! (She agreed).

S came in last week with former colleague John in tow. What a lot of reminiscences and laughs we shared – it was a real tonic to see him. (We kept off the Brexit topic as, inexplicably, he is of a different persuasion.) John has set himself the task of learning one poem by heart every month as a way of warding off dementia and has challenged me to do the same. He intends to send me monthly poems and proposes a contest, post-release, with the penalty for failure being paid in pints of beer. Were I to accept the challenge, I fear John would be drunk as a skunk well before we finished as I am, and always have been, totally incapable of learning anything by heart. If this is dementia it must be the early-onset type as, in my case, it began in the cradle. John has already sent me the first poem, *Keys to the Doors* by Robin Robertson. It is a lovely poem recalling the wonderment of a small child such as Harry as I first remember him. I have been grappling with it all weekend and still cannot recall even the first line!

Chapel yesterday was enlivened by a pigeon joining our meagre congregation during the first hymn. After getting the measure of the place while cooing from the safety of the rafters, it then proceeded to dive bomb the altar in a series of well-targeted swoops throughout the sermon. When first heard, I had imagined it as an emissary from the Holy Spirit doing a recce ahead of Pentecost. However, when it finally revealed itself in full flight it turned out to be merely a dishevelled grey feral pigeon (the sort farmers are no longer supposed to shoot) and not a pure and wholly white dove. Our accompanying prison officer this week was the ever-charming and aptly named Miss Hope. She went for a rummage in the kitchen, coming back with bowls of water and breakfast cereal to feed and water the poor bird pending the arrival of pest control with, doubtless, more toxic sustenance. Our church used to have problems with pigeons and bats crapping on the pews and altar cloths. Incense was said to be a deterrent, but I think that was merely an excuse for the sacristan to burn even more of the stuff. I may not win over our Anglican Rev to that idea, but could try a quiet word with the Catholic lady.

I am finishing this letter after a break over the week-end when there were so many newspapers to attend to, plus latest issues of *The Oldie, Private Eye* and *National Geographic* which all arrived together from the post room on Saturday. Terry was ready with a birthday card first thing this morning and I received several others in the post including a homemade one from local friend Eleanor showing a (carpenter's) file – a picture, not the real thing. There are no visits on Mondays so S's birthday visit is deferred until tomorrow morning. Today will be like any other, but celebrated with a McVitie's ginger cake but no candles, not even a single one, let alone seventy. Candles are allowed, but only on the chapel altar. Otherwise they are on the banned list, along with jam jars, chewing gum, spiral binders, smart watches and clothing with offensive logos. (List not exhaustive, as they say. Thinks: should have asked my little egg-shaped arsonist friend if he could source a candle). I know you'll soon catch up with my age but, for the record, being 'old' seems finally to have arrived at 70 in a way I never felt at 60. Perhaps it's being thrown into the company of so many younger men who address me as 'Pops'. I have a thick skin in this regard. In Tanzania I was addressed as Mzee – old man – even though I was a mere 50 at the time.

However, I do have a genuine cause for celebration. I have been doing the numbers and find that today is the very day on which I pass the half-way point of my confinement. Another milestone!

Old lags who have been in and out of prison for most of their lives (we have several such) tell me that the second half of a sentence always seems to go faster than the first. Here's hoping it is true. Sometimes 'all day' can seem a very long time indeed.

36. Monday 22 May, 2019

This is a little daunting as I now have three of your letters in front of me to respond to. The first crossed with mine. Its diminutive handwriting on blue paper must have had the censor reaching for his magnifying glass! It brought news of M's scary mishap with the over-tight hospital garment and J's wheezing fit in the dentist's chair following your five-mile hike to the Heights of Abraham. That'll teach you! I never cease to marvel at your energy, especially now I spend so long lolling horizontally on my sagging iron-framed bed, or hunched over the tiny prison-issue desk, as now. S and I took Harry to the Heights when he was about seven and remember his excitement at the swaying cable car ride and some engaging activities at the top. I also remember being very stern with the manager of Castleton Youth Hostel, where we stayed, who had messed up our booking. On the drive up I had listened to an 'Assertiveness at Work' course on the car cassette machine and relished this fortuitous first opportunity to put my new skills into practice. The poor man ended up grovelling so basely that he allocated us a superior family room completely free, and I've had a conscience about it ever since.

Reflecting on the above (written yesterday) I think the title of the course may have been 'Negotiating Skills', but the end result is the same. It amounts to 'how to get your own way and yah boo sucks to everyone else!' I wish I had those tapes in here. They could be really useful. It's depressing to acknowledge, and even more so to witness, how the more trouble certain people cause, the more likely they are to get their own way in the end. Prison authorities, like everyone else, want a quiet life. As if on cue, we have today had yet another smashed-up ('flatpacked') cell just as the maintenance men (and their minders) had finished putting the previous ones back together again. How I wish I could report that some of the improvements we have tried to negotiate through the wing council have been achieved. Not so. We are still waiting. We have another meeting scheduled for next Tuesday so I will try and resurrect some of those negotiating skills that proved successful in Castleton. HMPS may be a tougher nut to crack than the YHA, but if we bang on long enough we may 'wear the bastards down', or so some residents suggest.

Thanks again for the New Oxford Dictionary, so heavy it is best lifted with two hands to avoid wrist strain (or 'trigger wrist', perhaps). It is an invaluable companion for the Google-less. S brought it in for me last week but I had to wait for it to be approved and delivered from 'prop'. Had they seen how many rude words it contains they might have thought twice about letting me have it. I don't wish to be accused of impiety and corrupting the young and forced to drink prison tea, or hemlock like Socrates! Along with the dictionary came two surprise books sent by nephew Anthony via Amazon. *How to Read Water* (Tristan Gooley – lovely name!) and *Non-violent Communication* by Marshall B. Rosenberg PhD. Both, in very different ways, are self-improvement manuals. Is Anthony investing in my coming out of here better than I arrived? If so, he may be the only one. The prison authorities apparently have no interest whatsoever in 'reforming' me and I have still heard not a dicky-bird from my 'Offender Supervisor' or anyone else come to that!

N-V Communication, by the way, is the antidote to combative negotiating skills and cell-smashing and should be sub-titled 'How to get your way by being nice.' If only it worked in prison. Here, minor disputes all too often follow a familiar trajectory from raised voices to full-blown confrontation. I might also recommend N-VC it to certain residents, mainly the tribes of Youfs and Innits, who habitually speak in a series of staccato bursts as if they were inflicting stab wounds on a dodgy drug dealer. Maybe our blankets are to blame? A letter in this month's *Jail Mail* states that bright orange blankets 'are well-known to exacerbate violence' and that the Prison Service could save £100k p.a. by switching to pale green. I don't know what research this sum is based on, but someone's had a lot of fun being creative with a calculator.

With half an eye to self-improvement, I browsed round our little landing library last Thursday hoping to find something to help hardened miscreants turn over a new leaf. My attention was immediately drawn to a prominent display on the table headed RECOMMENDED READING. This comprised the following titles: *Capital Crimes, Time to Kill, City of Sin, Death Wish, Parents who Kill, Mile End Murder,* and *Mafia Life,* all conspicuously well-thumbed. Lucy Worsley's *A Very British Murder* was also on the table. Next time Lucy speaks to your alumni group, perhaps you could mention this to her. No, on second thoughts, don't, lest it encourages her to appear on TV clanking keys and dressed as a 'screw'. As for new leaves, if prisons are merely greenhouses for crime, as reformers say, the instructive literature on offer here must add a little fertilizer. The phrase 'criminogenic behaviour' gets bandied around in official literature and seems apt in this context. The librarian tells me (in response to my unofficial 'freedom of information' request) that currently the most-borrowed title is a biography of a South American drug baron.

Last Monday a 'New Regime' (words with authoritarian overtones emphasised by Obligatory Capitalisation) came into force and a revised timetable was pinned up so that we could all see how our daily routines will change. Of course everyone – especially the landing officers – immediately decided that it was a) inoperable, b) unnecessary (old cliché: "Why fix it when it ain't broke"), and c) a typical example of senior management's failure to consult the poor sods who would have to implement it... and so on. This became a self-fulfilling prophecy. Within an hour or so amendments were already being made and by teatime a completely revised version (looking very much like the previous regime) was posted. I wonder if some of our governors (the men in grey) trained with Railtrack? Or British Leyland? We are now into the second week of the not-so-New Regime and there are still tweaks on an almost daily basis. I don't know if anyone kept a copy of the original iteration, but I guess they are selective about what they archive.

The stated (and laudable, were it true) reason for the change is that the new system will enable more out-of-cell time. It's hard to discern if this truly is the case. For me, the only change is that daily outdoor exercise has been brought forward from mid-afternoon to immediately after lunch. However, for some unexplained reason, its duration has been reduced from a max of one hour to barely thirty minutes. While this wouldn't matter much in midwinter, on these warm sunny days it feels like serious deprivation. (The previously-quoted *Expectations* document, signed off by Chief Inspector of Prisons Peter Clarke, stipulates a <u>minimum</u> of one hour!) This will be another agenda item for 'non-violent communication' at our Council meeting next week. In fairness, I can report that my cell door is now normally left unlocked for the remainder of the afternoon, which is a bonus, especially if I can find another old codger to help complete the crossword. The regime document also states that evening association for enhanced prisoners will henceforth be 'guaranteed'. That's an unwisely strong word to use in a prison, where nothing can ever be guaranteed. It is already apparent that evening association is not so much a commitment but an aspiration, entirely dependent on staff availability, etc.

Another 'laudable were it true' development this year is the introduction of Key Workers for all prisoners in 'closed' prisons (like this). You may have read about this scheme in the national press, as have I, and there are notices near the chapel plus a few copies of a colourful explanatory leaflet. According to this, more **prison officers** are being employed to **make prisons safer** and **help people change**. Every prisoner will have a **key worker** whom they will **meet regularly**, every week or two weeks, working with us to **help us progress**. We'll have a **progression plan, set our goals** and record achievements. And so on. I indicate the words that appear in bold. It sounds like a grand and long-overdue reform, but as yet we have heard nothing in here. The wing officers are characteristically dismissive of this non-initiative, no additional officers have been appointed and the inevitable training for existing staff has yet to be 'rolled out', as they say. There is a faint whiff of decay about the place, of good intentions not materialising and established routines falling apart. Even the motivational slogans stuck on the walls are taking a tumble. The one outside the Meds dispensary upstairs now reads ' F YOU NY INO IS POSS '. I hesitate to pass on this, but also on the walls outside the dispensary is scratched 'Jake Wills [not real name] sucks old mens cocks'. Somehow, I doubt this. He is not the type, and his jagged prehensile teeth would surely deter all but the most desperate customers. Anyway, I duly reported this to Ms S, the duty landing officer, in the expectation that she would remove the offensive graffiti without delay. Not a bit of it. She just shrugged her shoulders and said, 'oh that's been there for ages.'

I'm glad to hear that your newly-seeded lawn is now sprouting to justify your labours and expense. A neighbour writes with a similar tale of lawn woes, at least I think that's what it's about but he's a retired surgeon so his handwriting is almost completely undecipherable (at least it gets past the prison censor). The grassy patches here are lusciously green just now but full of daisies and dandelions. The sound of the mower is heard in the land, albeit only occasionally. It is music to my ears, a reminder of normality. One of my regular companions – a trio of old blokes on a bench – was enthusing recently about the National Lawnmower Museum in Southport. Do you know it? Apparently it displays every model of Atco known to man as well as early pony-drawn models made by Ransomes of Ipswich (the ponies wore soft leather shoes so as not to damage the grass).

37. Friday 7 June, 2019

Thanks for your letter with hilarious account of gas men at work, reminiscent of Flanders and Swan *The Gas Man Cometh* (punch line: 'It all makes work for the working man to do.') As for your 'total lack of communication at every level', you must realise that this is the *modus operandi* of most large organisations, especially those in public ownership like HM Prison Service. That said, the attempted privatisation of probation services and some prisons seems to be a dismal failure according to shock-horror articles in almost every issue of *Inside Time*. I note that Justice Secretary Gauke says that his latest new panacea 'will build on the successes of the current scheme'. What successes? He should read the parable of the foolish man 'who built his house on sand'. (It fell with a great crash.)

I often wonder at the state of our welfare, rather than our Welfare State. I have just spotted a colourful new poster on the wing board that, without any intended irony, announces. "We are very happy to be launching an exciting new project to assist those who will be homeless on release." This – it gushes – is the availability (but only if booked at least one month in advance) of a FREE URBAN SURVIVAL PACK comprising of fifteen 'essentials for life on the streets.' These include: a warm hat and waterproof mac, a blanket, a water bottle, a toothbrush and paste, a nutritious biscuit and a £5 supermarket voucher. This remarkable generosity is in addition to the Statutory Release Grant of £46, an amount unchanged since it was introduced in the 1980s. I guess you'll be as shocked to read this as I am. How can prison ever 'work' (as the old mantra maintains) if people get chucked out at the end of their sentence like so much garbage, taking their chance on the streets with a little more than a mac, a blanket and hat? Who are these do-gooders who are 'happy' at such degradation, lauding it as if it was like winning the jackpot at Bingo? Is it any wonder that 48% of prisoners re-offend within 12 months of release? Bah!

Here's another enterprising release idea, from this month's *Jail Mail*. Apparently if you contrive to leave prison wearing a prison-issue blue and white striped shirt, you may be able to flog it on Ebay for upwards of £60. There is a steady demand for them from TV companies making those dramas about prison life (aka Prison Porn) that are currently in vogue. However, *Jail Mail* goes on to say that so many shirts have been 'ganked' that they are no longer readily available to prisoners. I don't possess one myself, though I have seen a few. They are currently unavailable from stores (I have tried). In case you wondered, shirts printed with arrows (a signifier of government property) have long gone, though Primark used to sell arrow-patterned T-shirts and pyjamas. I may invest in one after my release as a remembrance of times past.

Thanks for the latest additions to my burgeoning postcard collection, especially those of places I actually know such as Kyle of Lochalsh and St Helier. No, I haven't been to Bergerac's cottage. It was his burgundy-coloured 1949 Triumph Roadster that took my fancy. I have met several classic car enthusiasts in here, including one owner of a vintage Rolls. (Most of my earlier cars would now be 'classics' if I hadn't run them into the ground.) *Classic Car* is on the approved list of magazines and at least one guy on this landing is a subscriber. No, I don't know anyone who takes *Razzle* (tits-and-bums soft porn; I doubt you are regular readers) or indeed most of the others on the official list. I forgot to tell you that *Yachting Monthly* was embargoed, so I submitted a Comp 1 form to query why. Maybe they think I'm planning to escape downriver to the sea? I've had no response (no surprise there) so must now escalate it to a Comp 1a, if it's worth the hassle. How easy it is to slip into prison attitudes and prison-speak!

In which context, a notice was pinned up last week headed TELEPHONY, informing us of new ways of contacting the Prisons and Probation Ombudsman. I wonder if they meant TELEPATHY? It might be more effective. One paragraph referenced the authorities' recognition of the need to communicate with prisoners in plain English. But it was worded in such a tortuous, convoluted and opaque style that I began to suspect that the author had consciously modelled it on that great exemplar of lucidity, the King James Bible (written by committee – and it shows). Or that he (it sounded like a he) was just taking the piss. Either way, I doubt if many prisoners, or indeed some officers, would have had a clue what it was supposed to mean. One lengthy paragraph consisted of a single sentence with two semi-colons, multiple subordinations and the odd misplaced apostrophe for good measure. Indeed, quite enough to provoke me into subordination. I thought of writing to the Guv'nor about it, but the notice has now disappeared, so the moment has passed. There may be more important issues to get worked up about.

I'm glad you were both able to cast your postal votes in last month's elections for the European Parliament. All a bit of a charade in the circumstances – flogging a dead donkey you might say – but important to make your mark as a matter of principle. Happily the wretched Farage's Brexit Party lost the Peterborough by-election, albeit narrowly. Terry and I seem to be almost the only residents who show the least flicker of interest in politics (apart from Hopalong, who is a Faragist!) Otherwise we have one self-professed Anarchist and a few more crypto-Fascists, but the almost instinctive reaction at the mere mention of Brexit is to poke fingers in the ears and scream. The plain fact is that, for most prisoners, what goes on beyond these walls is another world that barely impinges on our daily routines and concerns. The most prevalent attitude here seems to be that our governments, even Tory ones, are dominated by namby-pamby fairies or foreigners with funny names and accents who haven't a clue what they're doing. My contention that the Brexit campaign was an elaborate game of deception and dissimulation foisted on a gullible electorate by self-serving fantasists has little currency within these walls. All we really need is to restore the Empire, and all will be well.

The young guy in the adjacent cell is a case in point. He is a proto-fascist (EDL member) and spouter of casual racist tropes if only because, as he admits, he 'was brought up that way'. He's a decent sort at heart, though, and Terry and I are working on him. He's recently formed an unlikely friendship with Vijay, the charming Bengali on the landing above, and has now joined our Scrabble group. He lacks the necessary vocabulary so we're all (I hope not too obviously) letting him win, occasionally. I'd like to think that when he is released (soon) he will be one of those rare characters for whom prison has been a genuinely improving experience.

Another potentially divisive issue is religion, though only Mr Fundament ruffles a few feathers from time to time and even he is learning to keep his Protestant prejudices to himself. We have a small contingent of Muslims on the wing, more visible than usual now that the Holy Month of Ramadan is here, so they must fast between sunrise and sunset. Instead of taking our regular hot evening meal, they are issued with special containers, like those B&Q plastic tool boxes with hinged lids and handles but pre-packed with a halal meal to consume in their cells long after 'bang up' time. On Friday afternoons one of their number, Hussein, likes to sing the call to prayer before they all troop off to the Multi-Faith Room (which I have never seen). Hussein has a melodious baritone voice and, despite mutterings from a few of the faithless, has been complimented on his singing by more than one Infidel. I close my eyes and imagine myself back at the Koutoubia in Marrakech or Al-Azhar in Cairo. Happy days! An unlikely Muslim is Robert – middle class, middle age, middle England – who tells me that he decided to take up religion quite recently, read all he could about the major faiths, and chose Islam on the basis that 'it makes the most sense'. Now he troops off to Friday prayers with the best of them, keeps his Ramadan fast, and looks at one with the world, even the strange world of prison. Good luck to him.

New item on menu this week: 'Morrocan Beef'. It's so delicious that even I can pardon the spelling. Bad news on the Quaker front, though. The well-liked Quaker chaplain has left to become managing chaplain at another prison. You might have thought he would tell us (and maybe bring a farewell cake to Meeting). But no. Prisons seem to practise a cult of secrecy in which nobody gets told anything until it actually happens. So much for 'transparency'.

No further sightings of cockroaches, wasps or even our resident rat. However, another cell a few doors away is currently under attack from columns of ants crawling up the walls and along the windowsill. Old Pete, its sole occupant, is most put out. He is in his mid-eighties and steadily declining to a state of dribbling senescence. He spends almost all day propped up on his bed, his face a graven image, listening to Radio 4 or reading James Patterson or Lee Child. (He can't get up the stairs to the library, so I change books for him every week.) As fast as he wipes away one troop of ants, the next battalion appears. Unfortunately ant powder is a banned substance in HMPs. I guess most white powders are suspect except those for essential cleaning or culinary purposes, like flour, Vim and salt. Pete has complained to the landing officers who are sympathetic but say that the Pest Control Dept is short staffed and too busy to come. I guess Pete may just have to wait for winter to disperse the ants, if he survives that long. Meanwhile he seems surprisingly cheerful and content with his current lot in life, which is, I suppose, preferable to many a care home. At least the company here is relatively youthful and much more lively.

38. Friday 21 June, 2019

Many thanks for your card of lowering thunderclouds over Newark Castle and letters including updates on monstrous cruise ships, flatulence and misdiagnosed dementia. You ask about the emailaprisoner.com system. It's worth a try if you ever need a quick response from me as most emails are delivered the following day, except over weekends when the office is closed. If you'd like an emailed reply you must pre-pay it on my behalf (sorry). Bear in mind, though, that I only get a single reply sheet, part of which is taken up by the header and large QR code. I'm quite adept at writing really small, but even so, don't expect a discursive response. On balance it's best to run with Royal Mail as we have done so far.

Between us, and a lot of less regular correspondents too, we certainly keep the prison post room on their toes. According to my tally, I have received or sent some 662 letters since last May, or fifty per month. Apparently they are all recorded in special ledgers, something I only know because they print these books here. All letters are opened and may be read, which doesn't necessarily mean that they are. They must also be checked for illegal substances (I wonder if the Palace of Westminster post room checks Mr Gove's mail following his recent admissions?) By the way, my current commodious accommodation is numbered C1-01 and it may save some lowly-paid clerk the bother of looking it up if you write this on the envelope, though I guess they probably know it by now.

Some letters escape scrutiny if they come under Rule 39 and are marked as such on the envelope. This Rule covers confidential correspondence between prisoners and their lawyers – or 'legal team' as many prefer to say, as if to suggest proprietorship of a premier league outfit or, at very least, a whole cohort of willing hacks constantly at their beck and call. The procedure for Rule 39 mail is slightly bizarre. We are supposed to write 'Rule 39' on the envelope, but hand it to an officer unsealed. He or she then takes out the letter and, without reading it, shakes it to check for dodgy powders, then replaces it and seals the envelope, signing it across the seal. Why would anyone be posting drugs out of prison? There's something I don't understand here. I could, of course, post my letters to you under Rule 39 on the basis that you are, or were, both solicitors and that John used to handle my conveyancing in the 80s. But that would be stretching a point.

I'm glad that you have also read, and been horrified by, *The Secret Barrister*. In our present predicament I can't see any government having the political will or the funds to commit to overhauling the justice system, let alone prisons. They are not vote winners. Our mutual friend P, wrote, 'I cannot bear to mention Brexit or the nauseating Tory leadership contest…' Quite so. I guess he knew all the candidates. It was disappointing that Rory Stewart failed to make the final round. Terry and I avidly followed the televised hustings, the courteous ITV one and the scrap that passed for debate on the BBC. Terry has a relative (his mother's cousin) who is a prominent Tory peer and Terry is even more ashamed that, despite his best endeavours, both his parents voted for the Brexit Party. Aargh! I risked a straw poll of fellow prisoners re. Tory leadership, only to wish I had not bothered. Mostly they favoured Boris. God help us (Boris certainly won't!) As a classicist, he must be familiar with Plato's adverse critique of democracy and he seems determined to prove that stale old philosopher right.

From politics to religion. As you have gleaned, I do occasionally get to attend the Saturday RC service in chapel despite being banned some months ago. I'm not sure if the Rev has relented or just not bothered to check current attendance sheets. There is now a visiting Catholic priest, Fr Nick, who comes in to celebrate Mass on alternate Saturdays. On the other weeks the lady lay chaplain holds a sort of Mass-lite. Attendance at either is poor and the same may sometimes be said of behaviour. Fr N is an ex-Anglican (as is their local Bishop) and tells me that he was for some fifteen years chaplain and A-level theology tutor at Winchester College. This may explain why his sermons are so well crafted, scholarly and engaging (attributes that rarely hang together in the pulpit), unlike his Anglican counterpart's tedious rambles. Last week Fr N apologised for not sticking around for a chat after Mass, said he had 'a quick confession' to hear, then disappeared into the vestry with one of our troupe. Why did he think it would be quick? He doesn't know the penitent as well as I do. While being escorted over to the chapel earlier, the penitent was asking around, "Is it a sin to punch someone?" As one wag said, "only if it's an officer."

Thanks for the reminder about the Wing Council and my proposal for an Over-50s club with visiting speakers. I passed on the contact details for the local U3A branch (obtained via my brother who was secretary of his branch in Hants) and made sure I included them in the minutes. But that is as far as it has got. There is obviously little appetite for innovation within these walls. However, we have been offered an over-50s gym club instead. It may not appeal to me (surprise, surprise) but I hope we 'may be able to roll it out soon' (prison jargon for 'chuck it on the back burner and forget it mate').

For the first time since my arrival we have had a 'major incident' on the wing. After 'tea' one day last week, a wild-eyed screaming ingrate on the landing above had a confrontation with an officer, refused to go back into his cell and embarked on a two-hour rampage. Seized with a seismic energy in a predatory raid, he systematically smashed up everything he could lay his hands on, broke off cell door flaps and demolished the table-football game. This gave him the weapons he needed. Brandishing its tubular rods as swords, he danced near-naked on the netting like a Roman gladiator, a sweaty *retiarius* lunging his weapons at a *secutor* (any officer foolhardy enough to approach). All this, of course, accompanied by incoherent yelling and swearing. In ancient Rome we'd all have been out there cheering him on and braying for blood. In reality we were safely locked in our cells from which it was just possible to catch glimpses of the mayhem upstairs through gaps in our door flaps. Eventually the riot squad was called in. A troupe of officers, known as Ninja Turtles or 'hats and bats' from their protective helmets and shields, advanced in Roman 'tortoise' formation, cornered and handcuffed the combatant and led him away, presumably to 'Seg'. I guess 'spice' may have played a part, but I've no idea what petty grievance triggered the incident. It left most of us shell shocked. The governor – No. 1, I believe – came round later in the evening to check that everyone was OK, which was considerate of him. Phew.

I was interested to read of the Scouts' project in Tanzania though I don't know the region. Just occasionally I meet people in here with East African connections. Our recently-departed Quaker chaplain had worked as a theology lecturer in Dodoma and a fellow Listener here was brought up in Blantyre, Malawi. It was, to him if not to most Malawians, a demi-paradise and he becomes quite dewy-eyed at the very mention of the place. We have a Congolese prisoner, a musician-cum-lyricist, whose second language, after his tribal language, is French, but also speaks Swahili and English. I have made the mistake of trying to address him in my pidgin French and Swahili. It makes him laugh, but then sets him off on long discourses in those languages that I completely fail to follow. Otherwise, Romanian and Bengali are currently the most widely spoken foreign languages on the wing.

After nearly fifteen months I am now one of the longest-serving residents on the wing and thus no longer the clueless ingénue overwhelmed by the uncertainties of this sometimes-baffling existence. As you know, this is classified as a B-Cat local prison and houses mainly remand and short-term prisoners or others awaiting dispatch to more permanent accommodation. My longevity is not the norm. As a white-haired Listener, Shannon Trust mentor and Council Rep I quite frequently get asked for advice or help. I couldn't do much about old Pete's ants, but fared better with someone's cell-mate's smelly feet problem. Medicated hand-wash (available from canteen, a snip at £1) also works on feet, at least it did on Arthur's. Coping with other people's foot rot, snoring and worse (WC in cell, turbulent bowels – say no more) can call for super-human forbearance. Incredibly, as recently as twenty years ago some of these same-sized cells were occupied by <u>three</u> prisoners. They were definitely not the 'good old days'. In fact, even double occupancy contravenes EU minimum standards legislation. No wonder certain politicians of questionable humanitarian instincts were so keen to get us out (of the EU, I mean, not the cells, where they'd probably rather keep us permanently).

My luck is in. I picked Stradivarius, the favourite in yesterday's Ascot Gold Cup sweepstake. I am now awash with milk, having won eight cartons, and can afford a Weetabix every night before bed as well as for breakfast. I suspect gambling may contravene some PSO (Prison Service Order) but nobody seems to care.

39. Sunday 7 July, 2019

Thanks for your letters and cards of Abbot Hall, Sizergh and baa-coded sheep cartoons. I have shown them round 'the lads' to a chorus of chuckles and bleats.

It's unusual for me to start my letter on a Sunday, but the days seem to have skipped by recently with meetings (Council and Listeners), visits, Buddhists discussions and even a Bible study. This is an innovation led by a lady minister (indeterminate denomination) who looks and talks like a clone of the Vicar of

Dibley. I felt duty bound to attend *pour encourager les autres*, but found I rather enjoyed the session. The other attendees were a mixed bag. The sanctimonious Mr Fundament was there, of course. He is 'born again' and doesn't accept the ministry of women, saying (none too diplomatically in this company) that they should stay home, obey their husbands and definitely not speak in church! Mr F himself is divorced, hardly surprising. Then there's Paddy, an ex-boxer who nowadays looks more like a boxer's punch-bag after years of prison food and is known as Pregnant Paddy. He proudly shows off photos of himself with Mohammed Ali and tells me of his longstanding personal friendship with luminaries from Reggie Kray to Mother Teresa, with whom he worked in Calcutta. Or so he claims. I attempted to swap notes on that intriguing city, but his knowledge of its geography and attractions is vanishingly slight! Finally there's stubbly Eric who says little and knows less but comes along for the ride. Our lady leader didn't seem fazed by this motley crew and had come well prepared with Bibles to thumb, note pads to scribble on and hand-outs to reflect on later. It resembled an undergraduate seminar.

Why do I bother? I guess talks, seminars, formal discussions and meetings are just wired into my psyche, and engaging with others with such different outlooks and lifestyles can make for a refreshingly heady brew. I respect the other guys even when I don't agree with them, which is most of the time. You're so lucky with your Dante Society. Here we don't need to discuss Dante: we live our own daily version of the *Divine Comedy* in a perpetual *Inferno*, or at best *Purgatorio*. Almost every topic of serious discussion inevitably gets filtered through a prison lens. What I didn't reveal to our study group was that I am awaiting a copy of John Barton's *History of the Bible*, well reviewed in the press and endorsed by my brother Mike who has sent it as a belated birthday present.

Snippet: Mr F tells me that Donald Trump is God's Anointed whose presidency was foretold some years ago by a 'modern day prophet'. Mr F, by the way, was released recently to a bail hostel only to reappear a few days later on a recall wearing a very hang-dog look. His fanciful explanation is that he bought cheap SIM and memory cards for his 'phone. When later checked by probation staff at the hostel, they turned out to be stuffed with dodgy images explicit enough to breach his licence conditions. He could hardly have found a surer way to set himself up for a pratfall and we now suspect that he's just a po-faced Portnoy after all! Since his return, Mr F has had a major fall-out with the cleaners (motto 'Wash me throughly' – Psalm 51, KJB), for persistently and deliberately walking across their freshly-mopped floors.

There is now talk of a possible Creative Writing course run under the auspices of the County Library Service. It may only be six weeks or so long, but I could do with learning a few tricks of the trade. It will be a challenge, though, as creativity is not my natural *metier*. Meanwhile Terry is determined that I should join the monthly Book Club. Until now I've had the sound excuse that I can't get to any activity that is 'off the wing' (e.g. Equalities Strands meeting, of which I have heard no more). The bibliophiles meet over at VTC (workshops – I've no idea what the abbreviation stands for). However, recent regime changes mean that I now go over there for outdoor exercise, shared with the workers during their lunch break. Maybe I could be allowed to stay on for the book group if I promise not to cause trouble? Terry can be very assertive, so he may just get his way and I will have to fall into line. On the other hand, I doubt the system will be able to cope with an unexpected extra body on site, necessitating endless roll-calls and recounts. That won't be my problem. Yes, I'd like to go along. Reading yet another book won't be much of a chore. As well as their set books (chosen from a national list ranging from 'graphic' novels to – currently – Stephen Fry's *Heroes*) they also read short poems of their choice, or in Terry's case, mine.

We've not had many Listener call-outs recently, a good thing. On the other hand, owing to releases and transfers, our crop of Listeners on this wing has withered from eight to a mere four. We have made a surprising discovery. In all the wing telephone booths is a card advertising the number of a free-to-call Samaritans service for anyone in distress who, for whatever reason, may not wish to talk to a fellow prisoner. Well guess what – when we tried it, we found that it didn't work. Apparently the number is years out of date. As an alternative, prisoners can request a portable 'phone that connects directly to the Samaritans. Again we checked, only to find that its batteries have been nicked and, according to the landing officer, it is probably broken anyway. (Did it not occur to anyone to report it?) It's very unwise in prison to make assumptions about anything – or anybody.

Our Listener who was transferred last week strangely seemed as relieved to be on the move as we were sad to see him go. Strangely, that is, until we discovered that he had got himself into debt with certain other inmates who were about to enforce repayment in a variety of ways, none of them pleasant. Sam, my first pad-mate here, advised me never to lend or borrow anything in jail. It invariably ends in grief. For debts of a less reputable sort, interest may be 100% <u>per week</u>, which makes Wonga look like a charity. Even with innocent cartons of milk, I prefer to give (if I have a surplus) rather than lend, and it has proved a sound policy. Vape 'caps' are the most common currency for loans/debts, but as I never use them I can't get caught up in scams.

A governor came round recently and asked to show a group of visitors (don't know who) into my cell. It's not the sort of request to turn down. He probably chose my cell because of its air of spaciousness (see before) or homely decoration/clutter (which impressed the visitors). He did not choose it, I think, for its tidiness or sparkling cleanliness (also, see before, *passim*). I try not to look too hard and hope the visitors didn't either. Prison socks moult strands of grey cotton that congeal into long grey swags under the bed. My drab but welcome bedside rug – a gift from another departing Listener – is almost permanently flecked with fluff and hair despite weekly brushings.

Recently I tried to order a new bedside carpet runner from the Argos catalogue, choosing the same size and faux-oriental design as that of Darren Trimmer the induction orderly. It gives his cell (which is always immaculate) a gentrified aura. My order was denied, returned by some mean minion, or office boy dress'd in a little brief authority. The grounds for refusal were that the rug was 7 inches longer than HMPS regulations allow, even though it was some inches narrower and thus, I calculate, of lesser overall area. The snotty tone of Office Boy's response brooked no argument, though I now wish that I'd submitted a Comp 1, offering to cut 3 ½ inches off each end, just for a wind-up.

On the subject of orders, I am pleased to report (at last) a minor success at Wing Council. Try to picture me on the lower mattress of bunk beds – railway couchettes make a good comparator, the size of the compartment also being similar. The (still unoccupied) upper berth casts a long shadow and after dark it blocks much of the light from the ceiling lamp. Railway compartments (including Indian ones above AC3 class) usually provide reading lights; not so prisons, and reading in bed would be a strain even without my wonky eye and incipient cataracts. The obvious answer should be a bedside light (also available via Argos) but these are not permitted. As with the rug, I've tried but been denied. Torches are also on the contraband list – they could be used for signalling. Seemingly that's the official reason, though why I should wish to signal out of my window across to the hideous reprobates in B-Wing I cannot imagine. Happily we have now persuaded the authorities to allow those little battery-powered LED lights usually sold for use in small spaces such as cupboards, engine compartments, wardrobes and so forth. We can now purchase these via the canteen sheet for a modest £1.99, and worth every penny. I feel very cosy with my little LEDs stuck above my head and the top light off, almost like being in a narrow four-poster with a low tester and no curtains. I just need a feather bolster and Jeeves (the fictional valet, not the prison governor of that name!) to bring my nightly hot choc on a silver salver and, while he's in attendance, squeeze my toothpaste, hang up my socks and pick up my trousers from the floor.

One of the gardeners recently presented me with a whole punnet of shiny scarlet strawberries freshly picked from the poly-tunnels. Things are looking up. Last year, you may recall, I received but a single fruit, the only one I ate all year. Currently Cells 01 and 02 are as deliciously aromatic as a pesto factory thanks to the gift of a fistful of basil leaves that Terry is now drying on his windowsill. We have both also been given bulbs of fresh garlic though, on my insistence, we're keeping these in sealed containers. We could hang them up to ward off witches but, on balance, I'd rather risk the odd evil spirit than put up with even more pungent odours. Some pongs are inescapable.

There are no questions about smelly cells (or smelly cell-mates) in the Prisoner Survey we've been given this week. Most of the questions are anodyne and inconsequential and the survey seems to be a mere box-ticking exercise is every sense. I doubt if much will come of it. Which is a shame, a lost opportunity. Had they thought to discuss it first with the Wing Council, I'm sure we (intelligent, reasonable, sensible people) could have had a constructive input. It sounds cynical, but maybe that is exactly what they didn't want in case it forced them to look critically at how the place is run. In the event, neither we nor the regular officers were consulted or forewarned and there were not enough questionnaires to go round anyway. The screws didn't know what to do with the completed papers and binned most of them. Several blokes ripped them up claiming (erroneously) that the results were not anonymous and could lead to recriminations. I have since spotted a bundle of completed papers stacked in the SO's office, but I don't think he's bothered to look at them *. There are, of course, no questions about strawberries (lack of), just a single chance to rate prison food from VERY GOOD (you must be joking!) to VERY BAD (which would be grossly unfair.)

* *I doubt if anyone did – there was never any feedback.*

Nor were there any survey questions about pests. To everyone's consternation, a notice has today been pinned outside the servery headed BED BUGS, regarding 'recent concerns of the alleged infestation of bed bugs on A and C wing.' I quote: 'The Works Departments have carried out extensive periods of monitoring on suspected contaminated cells and kit being returned to the CES' [What's that?] 'This has concluded that THERE ARE NO BED BUGS.' It continues, 'If you have any concerns please speak with Healthcare, however, please rest assured that this issue is now concluded at this time.' The last time I came across 'bed bugs' was in the 18th century, in Parson Woodforde's diaries. Nasty little blighters, the constant scourge of feather beds in coaching inns. I read somewhere that a Parisian doctor once attended a patient who complained of deafness only to find a nest of bed bugs in his ear. Yuk. I have conducted a thorough inspection of my ears, mattress, bedding and the dustier corners of C1-01, but the only little nippers I can vouch for on C Wing are the YOs on remand. Perhaps I should order some insecticide just in case?

40. Wednesday 24 July, 2019

Another week underway and I have now well and truly passed the 'one year to go' milestone. Not yet the final strait, but 11+ months feels more comfortable than a whole year. Commiserations re. your updates on roadworks and health issues. If only the latter were as easy to mend as the former. I have pressed into service your lovely cards of Levens as bookmarks for current reading, e.g. John Julius Norwich's *Travel* anthology and Terry Waite's account of his captivity. Both arrived recently from mystery donors, and I am trying to discern from whom and what oblique messages they may convey – e.g. my current captivity could be a whole lot worse (Waite – true) and I should escape as far away as possible at the earliest opportunity (John Julius – improbable). Possibly to the Antarctic – another donor has sent me Michael Palin's *Erebus*. Unfortunately the post room delivers books minus packaging or any enclosed messages, but at least it saves stamps for thank-you letters.

I can only envy, and admire, your breadth of reading and enjoyed your quote from Anne Clifford about coach travels in pre-turnpike days. 'Sweaty, smelly and filthy' describes pretty well the toothless vagrant who came this morning to ask me to write some letters for him. His marinated and wrinkly face looked like TS Eliot (of whom Hockney memorably said, 'If that's his face, whatever are his balls like?') but otherwise his appearance brought to mind the 'casuals' who used to tramp round circuits of rural workhouses a century ago. They were able to claim two nights' free accommodation in return for a day's manual labour and (unlike regular inmates) were not even obliged to take a bath. Besides, many of them wrapped themselves up in layer upon layer of brown paper in the autumn to keep them warm and dry until the following spring. Some of our regulars here seem to treat prison in much the same way, though without the brown paper which has possibly been replaced by bubble-wrap. Our current vagrant tells me he usually beds down in a tent by the seaside and isn't even a blip on the Social Services radar. A politician might claim it's a lifestyle choice. He seems stoical about his lot in life, which is just as well. He is genuinely grateful for a hot shower. His short stay in prison also comes with a complete change of free clothes, even if the starchy blue boxers have previously been worn by hundreds of other inmates, something the more fastidious among us balk at.

My App about the proposed Creative Writing course has finally elicited a response: "Courses are run on an occasional basis and we hope to run another one in the autum." So there's just time to slip in a spelling course for staff in the meantime, then. (I have read out the above to Terry, but he says I'm being pedantic. Old habits die hard, I fear. *) The course, if it runs, will be organised through the Library Service who are known for their helpfulness. Meek and tentative librarians of the popular imagination, with prim uniforms and horn-rimmed specs, might find the idea of working in a prison daunting, though there is little to fear here. Ours are well-liked though not especially robust physically. With local libraries closing by the day it may soon be Hobson's choice.

I read an article recently about semi-colons; apparently they are nowadays used mainly to demonstrate that the writer has had a college education.

I now have John Barton's book on the Bible and *The Lost Art of Scripture* by Karen Armstrong (from the library) on the go and shall be all scriptured out by the time I leave. Sad to report, the lady minister who started leading the study course has now gone on long-term sick leave. I hope it wasn't anything I (or Mr Fundament) said, but we have sent a card to her via our Anglican chaplain. Cheekily, I took the opportunity to suggest to the Rev that his sermons are way too long for the attention span of his audience. I nearly quoted (Churchill?) that they should be like a girl's dress – 'long enough to cover the essentials but short enough to be interesting'. I then thought better of it and stopped myself just in time. Anyway, the Rev took my observation in the good-natured way I had intended, and we had a laugh about it. But I don't think he'll take a blind bit of notice when he starts composing next Sunday's ramble!

You may imagine how much I am enjoying the current heat wave, though concerned about what climate change may portend for future generations. I have unpicked the J-Cloth draught excluder from my window which now hangs wide open day and night. The cell is become a slow cooker, or even a fast one while in the direct glare of the afternoon sun. There are no cooling through draughts during bang-up! Battery-operated fans were available from canteen throughout the winter but were inexplicably withdrawn as soon as anybody might actually need one. I spend all day in my cheap Primark shorts and many inmates have improvised their own by simply razoring off the lower halves of their prison-issue joggers. Rules on 'decency' don't permit the wearing of shorts, or indeed flip-flops and bare chests, in the meal queue and servery. Anyone appearing *déshabillé* for dinner may be sent back to change, though this depends on how observant the screws choose to be, and who the miscreant is. Some officers don't give a flying fuck, as the saying goes (see how I'm picking up the lingo?)

Thanks to the heat, we are getting a little longer outdoor exercise than the prescribed thirty minutes (ref. previous complaint) probably because the officers don't want to be stuck indoors either. Our yard, with its high fences and razor wire, could hardly look less like a beach, but the youngsters among us do their best to give it a holiday feel of health and efficiency, fresh air and fun. The young Adonises lay their threadbare blue prison towels on the tarmac and strip down to pose in shorts or boxers, displaying their abs and pecs suggestively in the sun as if just back from a fruity modelling session in Caravaggio's studio. It's not exactly a beauty pageant on our older cons' bench, though, but as soon as I reach the yard I too whip off my T-shirt hoping to absorb a little Vit-D to supplement the pills that I now know almost all prisoners are prescribed. Allowing oneself to get sunburned is classified as self-harm and is officially an offence. One day last week we even had an impromptu sports day with sprinting races (for the young and lissom) up and down the yard. Great fun until one lad slipped and slid along the tarmac, grazing his arms and legs badly enough for the supervising screw to blow the whistle on the event. Fun while it lasted.

The prison gardens, what little we see of them, still look fresh and green thanks to a timely thunderstorm or two. Exotica in the beds on the south side include hibiscus, canna lily and bottle brush shrubs that flourish in our micro-climate (boosted by hot air exhaled by disconsolate inmates). The house martins, who nest under the workshop eaves, are busy feeding their new broods, but the usual gaggle of cackling gulls have deserted us, lured to the seaside by the promise of free pasties and chips. However, Terry and I were disturbed last week by the mysterious affair of the duck in the night, a mallard that engaged in choruses of strident quacking outside our windows just before dawn. It had disappeared by breakfast time having realised its error. Bare tarmac yards hold few attractions for web-footed visitors, though one of our garden workers tells me that a pond is under construction in another hidden part of the gardens. Someone else is constructing a windmill, about 8 ft tall and currently smelling strongly of creosote (does this induce a 'high'?), so maybe they are planning an ornamental scheme inspired by Dutch landscapes.

Our weekly menu sheets have recently appeared in revised format with most, but not all, of the spelling errors corrected. So-called 'healthy options' are now marked as such. Broadly speaking, anything containing meat is classified as unhealthy (or rather, by omission, not healthy). Unless the meat happens to be chicken, in which case it's apparently OK. 'Breaded fish' is now listed as healthy, though its grey colouration and flabby texture suggest otherwise. In any case, I have long abandoned it in favour of the jumbo sausage (unhealthy) or beef-burger ('contains beef'). I do like the 'curried eggs (contains chicken)' but have never yet found the chicken. It's a chicken and egg conundrum. Just now we are getting regular salads including lettuce, tomatoes and cucumber all grown on site. These too are officially healthy options.

The Samaritans contact issue has at last been resolved, though not until I submitted a Comp 1 form. Credit has been put on the free-to-use PIN number and a new portable 'phone provided to enable prisoners to make confidential calls direct to the Samaritans. Such has been the recent turnover of prisoners that I am now the longest-serving Listener on the wing, so responsibility for drawing up rotas, etc. falls to me. We have put notices up on all three landings (I am also the self-appointed notice board monitor) and are hoping to recruit more candidates for another training course starting in September.

One of our Listeners, a most likeable young (former) teacher, recently lost his mother to cancer and applied through the chaplaincy to attend her funeral (on Tyneside), as is his right. What a horrendous ordeal that proved to be. Because of the distance involved, he had to spend a night at HMP Leeds en route. He found it rowdy and dirty with peeling paint, and he was given no food. He was handcuffed throughout the car journey there and back, with lavatory stops only at designated police stations. He was chained up during the funeral to the great distress of his father and family. It was a relief to be back, he said, though the prison strap line 'we see the person not the prisoner' now has a hollow ring.

SECTION TWO
A Divine Comedy – *Paradiso*

---

41. Tuesday 6 August, 2019
HMP North Sea Camp, Boston, Lincolnshire

Well, what a surprise! Please note my new address, above. I was warned long ago never to count on anything in prison until it actually happens, and how true that turns out to be!

As you know, I was initially told that I'd be moved to a C-category prison and, for a time, awaited this expectantly on an almost daily basis. After a year of such waiting, I was then re-classified as D-cat, but confidently told that I would *never* get moved to an open prison for a variety of administrative (no sentence plan) and practical (no available places) reasons. I was persuaded that it would be pointless even to put in a formal request. Actually, this was a relief. The prospect of being moved further from home, where visits from S and H and my loyal team of local friends and supporters would be so much more difficult, was a source of some anxiety.

In the event I am the victim of doubly unlikely circumstances at my previous abode. First, an electrical fault put the emergency bell system out of action on the ground floor. (Not that certain officers were ever in much of a rush to answer it!) Thus forty-four or so prisoners had to be decanted (that bibulous HMP term again), some to distant prisons up and down the land from Durham to Dartmoor, others just shuffled around internally. I was initially in the latter cohort and got moved to a single cell upstairs. I was told it was a purely temporary move 'for the duration' so I left most of my books down in C1-01.

No sooner had these moves been accomplished when the wretched bed bugs (those pests that didn't officially exist, remember?) raised their nipping little heads once more with a full-blown infestation on another wing. * This led to a further round of decantations and, sure enough, an officer showed up at my door (and those of two others) at 8 a.m. yesterday morning. He handed over three big bags for me to fill with as much as they could carry (the 'volumetric allowance') to the waiting 'sweat box' prison van. They were clearly anxious to see the back of me (the feeling was mutual) and rushed me through a hurried discharge procedure at Reception. This included inevitable form-filling and a hand-over from 'Prop' of various impounded magazines and other debarred items such as my razor, clock (still ticking) and freshly-crumpled court suit. As we were about to leave, with me already wedged into the Serco van cubicle (more truly a 'sweat-box' in August than that Arctic February day of my arrival) an officer rushed up with one final item – my bedside rug! It would have been an ill omen to leave that behind.

* I read somewhere that bed bugs were often found in Victorian ice-cream, along with human hair, straw and snot, so it's not so surprising that they should also pop up in prisons.

So here I am at my new (almost) seaside home. I am also, as you may realise, back in the county of my birth though I have not laid down my head in Lincs since 1965, long before most of the staff here were born. It certainly feels deliciously liberating not to have any perimeter walls and to be free to wander round the site at almost any time. Initial impressions are mostly positive. The gardens are colourful, expertly tended and accessible and I've already identified some sunny or shady spots for sitting out. There is a prison farm complete with rare breed Lincoln long-wool sheep, black pigs and (allegedly, though I haven't seen it), a llama. Also a meadow/field fringed with trees and big enough to accommodate two football pitches and allotments for budding horticulturalists. (There is a prison football team who play in a local league, but I shall not offer my services. I value my life, they wouldn't want me, and practices clash with Sunday chapel.)

Bizarrely a public footpath cuts right through the prison site between the living/office area and the farm/field. This track leads to an RSPB nature reserve extending onto the marshes at the edge of the Wash – but that's out of bounds, of course, as a big sign warns. It used not to be, but provided cover for prisoners enjoying trysts with local ladies of the night, so they put a stop to that. Spoil sports.

Beyond the farm fields are open easterly vistas towards the sea banks of the Wash so the air is pure, with a salty tang, and I can almost hear the sea. Inland, the River Witham and canal lead towards Boston and after dark the navigation lights of fishing boats and small cargo ships appear to slide across the fields. The distinctive tower of St Botolph's Church – aka Boston Stump – is the most prominent landmark a few miles to the east. These verdant surroundings are already filling me with interior sunshine. On site I'm gradually finding my way round and discovering such facilities as the dining hall, health centre (resembling a small NHS surgery), chapel and library, all freely open at most times.

Almost all the prison buildings here are prefabricated single-story structures, functional rather than beautiful, more like an army camp than a prison. The big downside for residents is that there are so few single rooms (never referred to as cells) for which the waiting list is at least a year long. I shall be a fully free man before I reach the top of that list. However, like all new arrivals, I am initially accommodated in a six-bed 'dorm'. It's reminiscent of fourth form accommodation at school, and just as noisy, or of youth hostels in the days before the YHA upgraded to accommodate less active ramblers who rolled up in cars. The other lads in my dorm (sounds like a Jennings story from the fifties, eh what?) are all friendly types with an easy-going familiarity, but so much younger than me that they have already christened me 'Gramps'. I suspect this may stick, though I preferred 'Colonel', which at least had rank.

The biggest problem for me now – and the reason I had tried so hard <u>not</u> to be sent here – will be visits. The drive from home will take at least two hours and S doesn't feel up to it, certainly not on a regular basis. It's much further for Harry, too. Boston is also possible by rail, but only at great expense and with three changes. From there to the Camp was a bone-shaker of a ride in the prison van, about twenty minutes up a narrow country road between fenland dykes and flat fields of cabbages. I guess that was always a part of the plan – no prison walls, but make it as hard as possible to evade capture should you decide to abscond.

The rest of this week is taken up mainly with induction presentations by staff and residents, visits to different departments, issue of kit, a whole sheaf of Welcome booklets and hand-outs to read (they've even learned to use computer spell-checkers here!) and so on. They are nothing if not thorough, a very different kettle of fish from my previous brief induction with Darren the Orderly, a trusty prisoner who'd been in long enough to know the ropes. (Oops! Not the ropes in the long-drop chamber. They were last used in the 50s.) Every new admission here must sit English and Maths Levels 1 & 2 tests, irrespective of previous educational attainments, and it felt weird being back in an exam room almost fifty years on. I passed. Apparently in due course we are also obliged to attend a Health and Safety at Work course (with certificate) and another on 'Employability'. They do seem serious here about preparing people for life after prison, unlike elsewhere where life after prison so often means…. just more prison.

On our visit to the library I picked up a free butterfly identification chart, then spotted a flutter of colourful specimens indulging themselves in the buddleia bushes (named after botanist Rev Adam Buddle – great scope for a Limerick) in the Garden of Remembrance. Later, during one of our induction sessions, a wren flew into the pre-fab and tamely hopped around between our legs. I start to experience a certain sense of dreamy liberation and re-connection with my long-ago Lincolnshire country childhood. It fills me with interior sunshine after my long confinement.

Further good news is that within a couple of months I should be able to apply for 'Rottles', as they are known. ROTL = Release On Temporary Licence. This is a system of day or longer release to enable NSC residents to go into Boston and perhaps further afield to 'practise' freedom (most residents have been in closed prisons for many, many years) or undertake voluntary work in the community. I will investigate this more thoroughly and report back, meanwhile all ideas welcome. Eventually I may even be allowed occasional visits home for up to four nights at a time, but there are lots of hoops to jump through first. This level of trust has to be earned and not everyone passes the test. Someone has just been caught breaking the rules and summarily dispatched back to an enclosed prison. His offence? 'Shagging on a shopping trip'. The mind boggles.

42. Monday 19 August, 2019

Thanks for both your letters. HMPS have been unusually efficient at forwarding mail and even emails, though unfortunately there is no facility here for sending email replies. It's the only prison in the country that will not do this. I don't know why. A pity, especially now I have perfected the art of microscopic handwriting. On the positive side, delivery of mail here is prompt unlike before, when it was sometimes held up in the office for several days. I'm glad that my birthday cards arrived on time for both your birthdays even if the images were a little inappropriate. We must order cards unseen and never know what will arrive. Thinks: must buy a selection for all occasions. The canteen system here is also much more speedy; order Mon for delivery Wed unlike Sun for Fri as before.

It's hard to believe that I have already been here two weeks and all the inductions are finally over. Phew! I have never had to sign my name so many times to acknowledge receipt of contracts, 'compacts' (not the sort my Mum used to carry in her handbag!), appointments and information packs. I have already had appointments with mental health, doctor and two nurses (blood tests, pressure and falls assessment.) It is a novel experience to be able to book medical appointments within four days and for them to be on time. My BP appointment was scheduled for 8 am and I was out by 8.03. You'll be pleased to know that I passed the falls assessment by answering 'yes' to the question "If you fell over would you be able to get up again?" Did I say thorough? If only all exams were that easy.

I'm still accommodated in a six-bed 'dorm' (but a different one from on first arrival), and I have had three changes of bed so far. I can't really complain about the other lads I share with as they are decent enough and, in their way, considerate if one overlooks their raucous voices, salacious banter and practical jokery. We share a TV, a big-screened and noisy machine, with an old sofa for viewing. The TV is almost always on until about 10.30 pm, which is when one of the lads named Daniel falls into a deep sleep, snoring with rasping stridulations, a singular performance that lasts all night. The others all started work this week, either on the prison farm, in the kitchens or the lobster-pot manufactory. Unfortunately their differing hours of work mean that I very rarely have the room to myself. To write this (para. 3 onwards) I have borrowed the key to a portacabin that serves as a quiet space for writing or study when not in use for meetings.

The least laddish of my dorm-mates is William (aka Wilting Willie), an overgrown 40-year old mummy's boy who is painfully withdrawn and secretive. He is also obsessively neat and lays out his personal belongings such as cutlery, wash things and biscuits in orderly rows graded by size, function and colour. It is an open invitation for the rude boys to rearrange them while he is out of the room so that he must sort them back into their established categories on his return, which he does without comment or complaint. (I have now persuaded them to desist from this little game. They are not unkind, just sometimes keep their kindness concealed.) I had managed a few amiable conversations with WW until last week when he sheepishly sidled up to me and said, "Please don't speak to me for the next three days because I won't answer but I don't want to seem rude." Happily he relented after day two, but it was weird sharing a dorm with a ghost in the adjacent bed.

Until I can settle into a longer-term room I am still living out of bags - bin bags, that is. This means that all my clothes are permanently creased (unlike William's, that he so carefully smoothes and folds) and documents, books and other possessions are almost impossible to find quickly. I wonder how Jeffrey Archer coped with the communal living arrangements when he first arrived here twenty years ago? I must see if they have his prison diaries in the library. I'm told that he would spend two two-hour periods every day writing, then post his scribblings off to his secretary for her to sort and type up. On our initial tour of the site, a high wire fence was pointed out to us. This was apparently erected adjacent to a public footpath, not to keep prisoners in but to keep journalists and photographers out! The noble Lord Archer is still remembered by one or two of the more long-in-the-tooth staff. He was not popular with either lags or screws – too 'up himself', or so it is said.

Despite the drawbacks chronicled above, it's definitely a better life here. The buildings (since you ask) are mainly single storey pre-fabricated units, but not unpleasing to look at being set amongst trees and colourful gardens. As well as the previously-mentioned butterflies, the gardens bustle with bird life, with nesting boxes and feeding tables to attract tits, robins and blackbirds; house martins have built well-secured mud nests under the eaves and out on the field I have spotted several goldfinches as well as wagtails, wrens and murmurating starlings. Lots of pesky pigeons, of course, and great gangs of predatory gulls who use the sports field as an assembly point before setting out on raids.

On my second night here I was awakened by a loud snap around midnight. On investigation the next morning this turned out to be a mousetrap catching its victim behind a cupboard. I guess, with giant combines at work nearby, some small creatures take a chance on prison life in preference to the perils of the open fields. Bad move. I have also discovered a surprising fact about my fellow residents – that the younger and noisier they are, the more they are scared of spiders, of which whole families lurk in every shady nook. Meanwhile I have earned the accolade of dorm fly-swatter in chief. In this role I spotted a slightly larger creature scuttling across the floor and demolished it so completely that it wasn't possible to determine whether it lived and died as a beetle – or a cockroach.

You also ask about the library. I'm pleased to report that this is in a separate building with the look and feel of many a small public library. Unlike most of those, this one opens mornings, afternoons and evenings seven days a week. It has a comprehensive selection of books (lots in religion and philosophy, history and science plus the inevitable shelf groaning with 'true crime' of the *Lives of the Great Poisoners* genre) as well as audio-books and films on DVD. There are several pre-bookable computers and laptops, though (for obvious reasons) they don't connect to the internet. They may be used for typing up anything from correspondence to memoirs (J. Archer could have sacked his secretary), which the librarian will print off selectively if he has time.

Being here feels like a step forward (or a giant leap for some) towards normal life – which is, of course, its purpose. I enjoy eating cafeteria-style instead of cooped up in a locked cell next to the loo. The library and chapel act as social hubs and there are 'association rooms' with comfy sofas and pool tables etc. There's also a degree of openness between staff and residents, symbolised by Suggestions boxes on every wing.

One of my old C-Wing mates who was decanted here with me has just started work on the farm, digging carrots for delivery straight to the veg-prep team in the kitchens. But I was wrong about having a llama; they actually have two alpacas who live outside with the chickens and are skilled at scaring off foxes. Just over the fence from the field there are several bulky sows – Gloucesters, I think – housed in arks along with their litters of squeaking piglets, all looking very contented. The prison is said to be 70% self-sufficient in food including eggs, pork, occasional lamb, and most fruit and vegetables including salad stuff grown in poly-tunnels, or 'pollies' as they are known. The menu choices here are more imaginative including, once a month, speciality evenings featuring 'international cuisine' – next one: Caribbean.

43. Tuesday 3 September, 2019

Glad to hear that you are both improving day by day and that No 38 makes such a comforting convalescent home. How about you submit a grant application to Boris from his new-found largesse? That £350m saving from EU payments won't last for ever (if indeed it exists at all outside of his imagination).

The weather pattern here is frustratingly similar to other North Sea shores and I now understand why nearby Skegness was so famously advertised as 'bracing'. It was a two-edged compliment. While inland may be bathed in brilliant sunshine, the immediate coastline is often shrouded in mist. In this regard, 'immediate coastline' includes the entire North Sea Camp site! The converse may occasionally also be the case, and here we seem to lurch between two extremes of hot and steamy or wet and wild. The latter lasted throughout the whole of my second week here and I was more than glad of the green waterproof cagoule issued as part of our basic kit. From the minutes of a recent Age Forum meeting

I note concerns were raised about the need for 'worm clothing and terminal underwear.' Different prison, same old spelling! (The underwear is a pair of long-johns. I thought they were intended as a life saver, but maybe the opposite is the case?)

At first glance the site bears more than a passing resemblance to a downmarket Pontins minus the Hi-di-Hi's and knobbly knees contests. Or alternatively, one of those government-run safari lodges in Zimbabwe but without the passing elephants or hippos honking at the water hole (here it's a muddy Lincolnshire dyke with the odd vole or frog). While the sun was shining one day last week I briefly shed my shirt to sit at a picnic table on a lawn outside the chapel. Big mistake. Such displays are only allowed on the field, not around the residential areas, and I earned a sharp rebuke from a passing officer. I must remember to read the rules, of which there are a great number. Suncream is not available, and getting sunburnt is classified as self-harm and may lead to disciplinary measures.

Despite superficial appearances to the contrary, this place is very definitely run as a prison. One of the people I arrived with has already been sent back to a closed establishment for breaching the rules. Taking all due care, I have begun tanning myself by small doses out on the field, have discarded the Vitamin D supplements, and now sport a brown ring round my neck and a white one round my wrist when I remove my watch. I have identified several sheltered sunning spots, some with brightly-coloured park benches made out of recycled plastics, where I can sit alone and enjoy the whisper of the wind in the willows, of which there are a great number. The novelty may already be wearing thin, but these freedoms still feel like a rare privilege after 18 months trapped within high walls with not a tree, willow or otherwise, in sight.

Good news – I have finally been moved out of the dorms. Talk about Cox and Box, I was in and out, up and down (top or bottom bunks) all over the place. No sooner had I staked my claim to a quietish corner of the dorm, laid out my cups and jars and re-folded my clothes than I would be shunted elsewhere. It didn't help being so hot outside and in. The SW facing open windows looked directly onto a field of wheat where a great red combine harvester was hard at work and, aided by a steady westerly breeze, enrobing all our kit in a fine coating of dust and chaff. Well now I have been moved from the South Unit dorms (down south?) to a shared room 'up north', i.e. in North Unit. My companion here, Keith, is an unassuming man of few words and of about my own age, which suits me fine on both scores. Keith has been in prison for thirteen years and is a wheelchair user, the consequence of childhood polio, something for which the minimal floor area of most NSC rooms is ill suited. But hey – I keep pinching myself as a reminder of how lucky I am to be here at all. Thanks bugs!

Sara and Harry came over for a joint visit last Saturday. She met him off the train at Boston and he later drove her home before catching the train back to Lewisham on Sunday. It was a memorable visit with lots of laughs, so much more relaxed here than in the overcrowded visiting halls we previously had to endure. (In fairness they did their best to make it congenial, but the otherwise punitive surroundings inevitably cast a long shadow over the experience.) H was very tired and briefly fell asleep on the sofa, though no one seemed to notice. S and I were able to sit next to each other on comfy sofas (instead of opposite, as was the rule under the previous regime) with cakes made on the premises and genuine ground coffee. We even held hands, rather coyly, like on a first date. Had it been warm enough, we could have sat outside at picnic tables in the garden.

The visitor centre doubles as a residents' cafe on non-visit days and is another welcome little return to near-normality. S has spread the word around my followers and various more mobile friends have promised to come over this way for a day out embracing a prison visit as a bonus attraction (Boston Stump being higher up the list, I suspect). I think S may have painted a rather rosy picture of life here at NSC as a couple of friends have asked if they can book in for a week to sample the sea air and award-winning prison food.

Like (probably) all prisons, this place is PC to a fault. They actually hold Equalities Strands' meetings with an open door policy, as I think it's called. Despite being what used to be described as an all-male establishment in pre-non-binary days, a notice in the dining hall reads 'No shorts, skirts or dresses above the knee allowed' (also, for the record, no bare torsos, work boots, green trousers, sandals, flip flops, slippers or vests) and a cubicle in one of our washrooms is labelled 'Female only shower.' And not without some justification. The occupant of the adjacent room was called Cheryl, 6 ft tall with tattoos, gruff voice and a rather manly gait. Unfortunately she had a fall-out with her roommate Kirsty and punched her rather too hard, bruising her arm and fracturing her pride. Cheryl was promptly escorted off the premises to be shipped back to 'closed conditions' elsewhere. Here, retribution for infringement of rules is swift and decisive and invariably results in expulsion rather than merely being sent to stew for a while in the naughty corner ('Seg'), as usually happened at the previous place. Kirsty has done rather well out of the altercation and now has the room to herself.

Coincidentally one of the prisoner newspapers recently reported that HM Chief Inspector of Prisons claims that some 1,500 current prisoners are transgender, ten times more than official government estimates.   According to the same article, one in fifty male prisoners 'self-identify as ladies, though not always in the most convincing of manners.' The writer recommends transitioning before conviction as women are less likely to be jailed, and their prisons are more congenial. He (or she or they?) goes on, 'Some reports suggest that almost no women should go to prison because they're basically nice and didn't mean it, unlike men who are foul and should probably be in prison whether they break the law or not.' I'm not sure how much of this is tongue in cheek but warm to the style of reportage.

Our librarian (how quickly I feel assimilated!) runs a Book Club that I hope to join at their next monthly meeting. No (supposed) logistical excuses here as residents are free to move around the site without escort. As you may remember, my former cell-mate Terry was a Book Club stalwart. During his final month inside he was chosen to attend a meeting of peers and prison governors at the House of Lords to discuss prisoner reading. I don't know if Terry was nominated by the prison or by his cousin, a Tory life peer, but they may have got more than they bargained for – especially if regulations required him to be chained up (like the poor bloke who attended his mother's funeral). Terry can be very assertive when he gets his teeth into some issue or other, though he is sufficiently self-restrained to stay just shy of confrontational. He is due for release next week and has written to me.

As well as Book Club there is a fortnightly Shared Reading Group run by an outside facilitator – a volunteer, I think – called Jenny. Jenny brings along copies of a short story for us (max. 6) to read aloud in turns, pausing every page or so to discuss content. It's like reading round the class at school, and potentially just as embarrassing for hesitant readers, which is why the practice largely died out in schools years ago. Last week we had a Jeffrey Archer short story, though not about his prison experiences here. I don't think he has ever written about prisons in avowedly fictional form, though I'm sure he must have embroidered some of his published diaries. We all enjoyed the story, but I felt for one man who read haltingly and mispronounced almost all the many places and artists' names mentioned. All credit to him for keeping on going, or was he oblivious of his errors?

As I've commented before, prisoners are mostly supportive and tolerant of each other's shortcomings. By the way, I had my magazines redirected and now keep abreast of the news (mostly bad as usual) in the library where they take several dailies. There's often a queue for *The Times*, so I aim to arrive early. I still order my own weekend papers so I can refer to them during the coming week.

Motivational slogans and aphorisms must be a nationwide prison tradition. You may recall 'If you can dream it you can do it' about which one inmate commented ruefully, 'I dreamt it, then I did it, which is why I'm here.' There are some similarly wise saws in the corridors here including, on the wall outside my room, 'Take care of your elf.' I guess it may have been seasonally adjusted last Christmas. More thought-provoking, however, are the 'Thoughts for the Day' that appear on a white board outside the chapel. Examples of cod wisdom: 'Far better to remain silent and appear a fool than to speak and remove all doubt,' 'Old age is not total experience – misery helps,' and 'Speak happiness – the world is sad enough without your woes. No path is wholly rough.' I don't know where they come from, or who writes them up, but I do notice that a lot of residents pause to read them. I dared the chapel orderly to write 'Life is a shit sandwich and every day you take another bite', which more aptly describes the prisoner experience. He declined, declaring it disrespectful to his calling.

44. Thursday 19 September, 2019

Both your letters arrived on schedule, so I apologise for my own tardiness. I'm still trying to catch up following the hiatus of my transfer here. It's a relief to have left the dorms (and those noisy young tykes) behind and to be here in North where mostly older residents are housed. It's much quieter here despite the internal walls being thin and the snorers and sleep prattlers along the corridor quite voluble! Keith is an agreeable sort, an archetypal 'Essex man' unlike the mainly northern prison population here. Our paths may have crossed before as I was a regular visitor to his former workplace and knew his boss well. Otherwise I know nothing of Keith's background (only that he once owned a Cortina), family or criminal record. 'Don't ask, don't tell' is the motto drummed into us here. It's on just about every page of the induction handbook and seems to be a wise policy. Sometimes it's better not to know. Keith and I have no arguments over TV usage, which is sparing (news and documentaries OK, but no old films or soaps) and we are therefore, in that essential at least, well-matched. Some of the other 'oldies' in the unit spend almost all their time with curtains stuffily closed watching daytime TV, a sort of death-in-life by my reckoning.

Since my last letter we have been moved down to what is probably the largest room in the block (13ft x 9ft) in order to accommodate Keith's wheelchair. A further bonus is that it faces south and looks out onto a small courtyard with overgrown grass and bright-red fuchsia bushes. The north-facing rooms opposite are very gloomy. Note 'rooms', not 'cells'. No window bars and we have keys to lock/unlock our doors. Right down to the lino on the floor it could be a cheap doss at the YMCA (or OMCA over here, the YMs being mainly in other units). My pin board and cupboard walls are already well covered with scenic pictures and personal mementos of the 'real world' beyond these walls boundaries. In other words, I have re-created my usual domestic muddle and begin to feel at home, well almost.

I'm impressed, John, by your mental gymnastics and list-learning and have always envied you your super-power memory. I have struggled but failed to learn the poems sent in monthly by my former colleague, another John. They were not exactly *The Ancient Mariner* or *Faerie Queene*, just short and already familiar offerings such as *Ozymandias* and *When you are Old*. While I enjoy his every choice, I have proved frustratingly incapable of memorising more than a few lines. This may explain why I never appeared in school plays apart from once (blacked up!!! Very non-PC nowadays) as the Third Priest of Klesh in *A Night at an Inn* by Lord Dunsany, for which I only had to utter one exclamation, albeit three times. People imagine that being in prison means we have endless time for thinking, reading, writing and so forth. I have never found it so as I spend so much time engaged in a general – and really rather satisfying – mental torpor.

What I do enjoy here, as respite from the above, is time out of doors. I walk round the field several times every day and it always presents new delights. Yesterday found me sitting careless under a shady tree with my book when a dragonfly hovered in front of my face then, sensing that I was no threat, settled on my wrist. He was soon joined by another who perched on top of the page and swayed his little head looking at me while his long abdomen quivered. The field is just starting to smell of autumn though only a few trees are as yet yellowing. I rather hope my colleague will send Keats' *Ode to Autumn*, not least because I did once have to recite it at school, which would give me a head start. Through the hedge I can glimpse the farm's orchard and can confirm its 'mellow fruitfulness', some of which has started to appear in our diet, e.g. apple crumble on Sundays. The farm pigs snort and munch away blissfully unaware that, before long, they too will be butchered on site to reappear in the dining hall as sausages, strangely misshapen chops or roast pork. Some of the rare breed black pigs were parked up in a trailer (awaiting dispatch to the Boston abattoir) and I was able to reach through the slats and scratch their bristly backs, which they seemed to appreciate. I did not tell them how much better they taste with apple sauce, something that did not feature on the menu at the previous place.

I have just returned from a brisk pre-lunch mile-long (two full circuits) walk round the field. I like to keep an eye on the goldfinches who live in the corner where a Buddhist grotto is under construction. Also the wagtails, pied and yellow, that hop around the field rummaging for grubs in their socially segregated sectors, like occupants of different wings in a prison. Behind the Harrison accommodation unit (named after the first governor in 1935) live a whole family of tiny field mice in a nest just above ground level under a dense bush. This I know from a Harrison resident who feeds them popcorn twice a day (he buys it specially from the canteen order sheet), which I have watched him do. They seem to respond to his voice and he claims to recognise each one. He has named the largest male 'Jingles', the same as my former cell-mate, the Scrabble-ace fascist Pagan also known as Hopalong, but there the similarity ends.

A bonus of being in North is that it is close enough to the dining hall for us to get near the head of the food queue once 'roll correct' has been called over the tannoy. Lest anyone should consider bunking off by legging it over the fields (and a few do, though they are invariably caught within a day or two and dispatched back to a closed prison) we still have several roll checks every day starting with one at 6.30 am, after which I return to bed. The tannoy is in frequent use for summoning people etc. but some officers' announcements are so garbled as to be incomprehensible. They must have trained with Ryanair.

My current room is just two minutes' walk from the chapel which, as well as services, hosts a variety of secular events. On Monday this week there was something of a ruckus over there that has led to the temporary suspension of evening activities. Once a month the chapel has hosted bingo evenings for over-50s. This is classified as a cultural (in the loosest sense) event that I have yet to sample. I may not now get the chance. It seems that an about-to-be-released prisoner (50+) decided to turn bingo into an altogether different sort of cultural offering. A bottle of vodka (contraband, obvs.) was produced and a noisy knees-up ensued, so noisy that it drew the attention of the authorities (not the chaplain, who lives well out of earshot in faraway Peterborough). The following day the participant revellers all had saggy eyes and woebegone expressions as they faced the prospect of 'nickings' and possible return to the restricted regimes of the 'closed estate'. A notice was pinned to the chapel door announcing the suspension *pro tem* (rare Latin usage by our Evangelical chaplain) of <u>all</u> evening events – even Bible Study! Sounds like the parson's nose cut off to spite his face.

On the positive side, my prayers for a choir to be formed have been answered with the arrival of a new inmate who was formerly a music teacher / cathedral organist with an MA in choral conducting. He and the existing amazingly talented pianist (confusingly they are both called Jim) are working together on repertoire and obtaining copies of religious and secular works. We may be only five strong so far, but it's a start. Rehearsals had been scheduled for Thursday evenings but, in the wake of Monday's illicit jolly, it will be on Saturday mornings instead, which suits me better as Thursdays would clash with Buddhist meditation. It was great at last Sunday's service (weekly Communion, quite well attended) to be able to sing hymns and a short anthem in parts. Some notices are now up in the units to advertise for new members of the North Sea Singers, a name adopted in preference to The Camp Choir, which may have been open to misinterpretation.

45. Tuesday 1 October, 2019

Great to note how much more positive your letters sound now that improving health enables you to resume at least some of your normal activities. I hope the same may also be said of mine! I still feel like a caged lion released to a safari park – more Woburn than the Serengeti plains, but still a leap in the right direction. I hope you won't be tempted to walk too far too soon. S and I were often aghast at the walking distances you mentioned as if they were but nothing. The highest number of circumambulations of the prison field (aka The Park, which is a bit silly, though it does have 117 deciduous trees round the perimeter) I have so far notched up is a mere five, which equates to 2 ½ miles. If the view changed with each one I could be lured into attempting more. However, there is usually something new to observe, especially now autumn is really here. I am starting a collection of leaves, pressing them between the pages of the big New Oxford Dictionary you so kindly sent – leaves within leaves – and attach a sample herewith.

S, on the other hand, complains of almost constantly aching legs and I so wish I could cosset and encourage her. I've no idea if, or how soon, I'll be able to apply for my first home leave. Definitely not until after Christmas as there are so many hoops to jump through and the process hasn't even started yet. The information booklet we were given on arrival said we <u>should</u> have an initial interview within two weeks or <u>definitely</u> by the fourth week. Well I'm now in week 9 and still haven't heard a whisper. Not for want of trying on my part! I have put in an App (same process, different form, same non-response), spoken twice to my 'personal officer' (yes, I actually have one here! Nice chap - he came to introduce himself in week 2). I have been three times to the relevant department (as before, it's known as OMU, or Offender Management Unit), but all to no avail. It's the same old excuse we always had before – staff shortages. If only the initial information were more realistic, it would reduce expectations and the attendant frustrations when targets are not achieved.

At my third attempt I gained a brief audience with the manager of OMU who was quite candid in admitting that the paperwork about my case sent on by the previous prison was wholly inadequate and that they had written to complain. It is hard to see how my so-called Offender Supervisors there (three different ones in succession, as you may remember) could have written anything meaningful as we never even met. As entitled, I asked for a copy of the paperwork (known as Oasys) which was sent, marked 'confidential', a few days later. Most of the form had been left blank, and the parts that had been hastily filled in on the eve of my departure were demonstrably wrong in matters of fact. It does not inspire confidence in the system. Only nine months to go!

I'm glad you have been able to get out to a few of the Heritage Open Day events in your area. I picked up a leaflet in the library advertising the many attractions in Lincs, far more now than in the days of my Lincolnshire childhood. I note that St Mary's RC Church, which saw my baptism and my Dad's funeral, is now listed as 'Grimsby's hidden Victorian gem'. Well I never! In anticipation of days out in Boston I went to our library for a little local history research only to find... nothing! Well, almost. There is a book of historic photos of Old Boston. I must ask if they can get hold of a guidebook to St Botolph's Church whose famous Stump (tower) stands so tantalisingly in the middle distance across the flat fields from here. My schoolboy album has a home-printed black and white photo I took of it in 1962 during my early career as a church-crawler. I could hardly have imagined the circumstances in which I would live nearby in later life! The Stump is one of the grandest parish churches in all England and must surely have a guidebook – if not, that could be a little project for me to work on. Dave, the Librarian, tells me that they ordered a guide to Boston for the library but prisoners who went there on visits were disappointed not to find all the skyscrapers shown in the book.

I'm delighted to report that Rev Terry, who has been 'covering' pending a permanent appointment, has now been appointed Managing Chaplain here. He seems to be very well liked and is uncompromisingly supportive of prisoners of all religious persuasions or none. Terry's title Rev is more than usually apt because of his much-admired and powerful motor bike on which he commutes daily from Peterborough. He is truly a man of the cloth, having started work as a motorcycle mechanic before swapping his oily rags for clerical cloths in his 30s. There are several other part-time or occasional chaplains including the Imam (who comes in weekly all the way from Bradford), Buddhist, Hindu, RC priest and visiting deacon, Salvation Army and a local Baptist minister who takes fortnightly Sunday evening services. No Quaker – they can't find anyone suitable. There may be others, but these are the ones I have met so far.

Chaplains are a much more visible and welcome presence here and all faiths are respected. A calendar in the chapel lists all their festivals, including 23 September, when the Pagans had the day off work to celebrate the Autumn Equinox. They were permitted to meet at the farm pond (normally out of bounds except for farm workers) to celebrate with 'Pagan food', which turned out to be nothing more unconventional than chocolate muffins. Given the location, I had envisioned them slaughtering a duck and studying its entrails to divine when they would get their first home leave. It might have been more reliable than the official estimates.

Today it is raining heavily with daggers of wet stuff blowing horizontally across the fens. Old hands warn that NSC in winter can be as miserable and shivery as a fit of ague. Last winter it was cut off from the outside world by heavy snow. This morning's regional TV news threatened floods in the Boston area at around 8.30 a.m. caused by a tidal surge. I wondered if I might step out onto a waterlogged floor (I didn't) so maybe Boston, where a flood barrier scheme is still under construction, also escaped. The North Sea Camp site is below sea level, I think, but protected by two high banks. The inner one of these was raised as part of a land reclamation process in the late 1930s when the camp was established, initially for borstal boys who provided much of the manual labour. It truly was a 'camp' then as they lived under canvas for the first summer until more permanent lodgings were constructed. The inner protective bank interestingly incorporates an air raid shelter, now sadly blocked up (apart from a stove pipe for ventilation) so not open for public inspection, even on Heritage Open Days. Pity.

I did briefly venture out of doors after breakfast, but turned back at the farm buildings where some very bedraggled sheep were penned up, possibly awaiting transport to begin the process of conversion into shepherd's pies by the kitchen workers. The Lincs Long Wool breed are very shaggy, as overburdened with long woollies as a bag lady emerging from a jumble sale. Instead of communing with nature, or sharing pleasantries with the sheep, I have spent all morning at the little shared desk. Keith is asleep on his bed at the other end of the room. I have never known anyone sleep quite so much. His morning sleep is only briefly punctuated by the arrival of his lunchtime filled bread roll before his afternoon sleep commences. Because Keith uses a wheelchair, his food is brought to him in the room as the narrow gangways between rows of fixed four-seat tables in the dining hall can't accommodate wheelchairs. A system of 'buddies', i.e. fellow prisoners who help those in need of practical support, provides this service. There are also Listeners, of course, and I could enrol to join the team without any further training. However, I declined the offer when first admitted on the basis that they already have a surplus of numbers but very few call-outs. I may change my mind later on.

46. Wednesday 16 October, 2019

Your letters arrived on schedule and I begin to wonder if you have a special arrangement with Royal Mail. My outgoing mail, as before, can be more erratic though most letters seem to arrive at their destinations sooner rather than later. But not all. I had a letter from someone at the previous prison – nice chap, college art lecturer with family associations with East Africa – but my reply to him was intercepted and returned to me a week later. My letter, like his, was of course entirely innocuous but apparently breached some rule banning serving prisoners from writing to each other. Oops! I didn't know, as they acknowledged, so the breach has been noted but not as an actual black mark on my record, just gently slapped wrists. Every item of incoming and outgoing post is recorded which, in my case, now exceeds 1,000 items. I calculate this as representing about four weeks' clerical time (to allow for opening and at least skimming content). No wonder it costs so much to keep people in prison, currently about £45,000 a year each, on a par with the fees at Eton. (I'd opt for Eton any day, even if I had to be top-hatted and tailed). Accommodation in open prisons is about £10,000 cheaper, so I am now saving taxpayers money. Just think how much more they could save by releasing me early!

The weather here has been unremittingly gloomy and wet. The surrounding fields and fens are waterlogged in places, despite which gangs of orange-coated prisoners have been out cutting cabbages and sprouts on contract to local farmers. Most residents have decently warm and waterproof anoraks (or whatever we can call them now that 'anorak' has such nerdy connotations) to wear around the site, and all over-50s have recently been issued with a new pair of long johns! Unfortunately we are allowed only one 'personal' coat (something loosely governed by the so-called volumetric allowance). On her last visit, S brought in my splendidly thick and heavy sheepskin coat, so warm that even the sheep look at it with envy. It's a bit OTT for October, but will come into its own during the winter. For now, I'm relying mostly on a non-waterproof, shapeless grey and orange prison coat (a sort of donkey jacket without the donkey) with a prison-issue green cagoule thrown over the top on wet days. I may look like a bell tent, but at least I'm dry.

The so-called covered walkway round the site is only partially covered, like an elongated bus shelter, its open side cheerfully hung with baskets of still-flowering petunias, fuchsias and pendulous geraniums. The inner side is less cheerfully decorated with dire notices about STDs, HIV, hepatitis and 'Ten Signs of Dementia', almost all of the latter which I have exhibited since childhood! Unfortunately one end of the walkway stops short (by the chapel) and doesn't reach the residential units, while the other end fails to extend as far as the dining hall. Soakings are thus unavoidable on monsoon days. Truly 'it never rains but it pours' here.

I still manage to enjoy fresh air and walks every day, but keep to the concrete roadway (dodging the puddles) down one side of the field rather than taking to the wet grass. My shoes have been squelching in protest and, though not actually leaking yet, the soles are split and won't last the winter. They could be difficult to replace. If the worst happens, I've been advised to sweet talk the guys who man the stores department into issuing me with a pair of so-called work boots. They may take pity as long as, a) I don't let on that I'm retired, so don't actually work; and b) I claim that I had to throw away a leaking previous pair. So, with a little dissimulation, I may yet end up with something like miners once wore down t'pit, with waterproof soles and reinforced toecaps. It would be good to resume my perambulations round the field edge.

I'm glad you appreciated my pressed leaves. I made a card for S, in lieu of a bunch of flowers. It lacked her artistry, but she liked it well enough. Next week she has booked to visit with church friends Barbara and Brian, so at least she won't have to drive. This evening she's invited a friend to supper with the ulterior motive that the downstairs loo is dripping and he may be able to fix it. Having a husband in prison may save on basic housekeeping but costs a lot in incidentals. I have also heard from my brother who has asked me to deliver the eulogy at his funeral. Poor Michael is 84 and fading, but he hopes to outlive my release next July.

Last week there was a celebration of 'Lincs Day', an annual event when the County Flag (a recent confection of brilliant red, yellow, orange and green like that of some newly-independent former colony) was flown in the library along with a small display of books of local interest. I told the man at the desk (not the librarian) how proud I was to be a 'Yellowbelly' (Lincolnshire born and bred), at which he gave me a most disparaging look as if I'd just slithered out of a swamp. I had to explain the term to him. Obviously not one himself. In fact, as a true native of the county (plus 3xgreat-uncle, William Henry Adams, who was mayor and then MP for Boston in the 1850s), I'm a rare species at North Sea Camp. I doubt if many of the staff are Yellowbellies either. I suspect many have migrated here for an easy life and cheap housing.

Last Thursday's Mental Health Awareness Day was also marked with events and displays in the library, chapel and gym (first time I've been there since our induction preview, the heartiness of which quite put me off). An assortment of organisations and charities came in for the day, set up displays and stalls and sat around to chat to prisoners about how they may be able to support them whilst here and after release. I was impressed, not least by how many of our residents went along to participate. The therapy dog was available for stroking. He's an Alsatian lookalike called Scout, though, given the reason some people are here, his name may be a tad unfortunate. By the end of the afternoon Scout looked very fed up at having to deliver so many licks and tail wags on demand. I gave him a scratch on his doggy G-spot (just above the tail) and was rewarded with a liberal covering of sandy hairs all down my arms and trouser legs and came out looking like a Gruffalo. Scout visits us once a month to provide solace and cheer to older residents, though I have not yet consulted him professionally, so to speak. Better a live dog than a synthetic 'Joy for All Companion Cat with Vibra-purr' recently advertised.

From gym to chapel for a talk about autism. But I was more impressed by the governor (longstanding – he was here in Archer's day) who, rather bravely, I thought, spoke of his own diagnosis of autism and how it had impacted on his life. The talks were followed by the prison band performing sixties 'covers'. Was this a cue for reminiscence therapy? Maybe, but if so it was far from soothing being shouty, twangy and bangy on the voice, guitars and drums respectively. I stayed just long enough to show support and applaud ostentatiously, but left before my aural agony became too apparent.

Last Sunday, 13 October, saw the canonisation at an open air mass in Rome of St John Henry Newman (who once visited my old school, long before my time of course). Here we marked this event by singing his hymn *Lead Kindly Light* at the Anglican Communion service. I hope he looked down with approval at this ecumenical gesture. Jim the Choir is a demanding taskmaster but also an experienced teacher whose instinctive wit, determination and optimism are already knocking our little band of singers into shape. I anticipate a more musical Christmas than last year.

I'm sorry to report that my application for day and home leave 'Rottles' has taken a step backwards, partly as a result of the incomplete and incorrect paperwork previously mentioned. OMU here are now awaiting further papers – which should at least set the record straight – from the Probation Service. It could be a long wait. Meanwhile I have had two meetings with my OS (Offender Supervisor) here, who I like well enough, and who is tasked with completing the necessary forms. He is a good listener, and supportive, but vague to say the least, especially as to when I may get my first 'away day' in Boston. It does not help that the OS is also an SO (how confusing is that?) and is about to start a period of night duties followed by a couple of weeks' leave. So the earliest date for the ROTL Board (Release On Temporary Licence) is now mid-December, not 7 October as originally stated. Thus, taking the most optimistic view, it looks like late-December for an initial accompanied day release and home leave not before March. 'Home for Christmas' was a carrot dangled before us at induction. Isn't that what the troops were told at the outbreak of the Great War?

47. Wednesday 30 October, 2019

You seem to be back on form as far as theatre is concerned. The Edward Albee play sounds like a niche offering but it's a shame they lost money on it. The acting was slicker than the writing, by your account. I'm not aware of any Am Dram activities here at NSC, though nothing would surprise me. Yesterday afternoon we had another special event, this time for Black History Month. There were readings, presentations, reminiscences, information panels and packs of background materials so I could not fault the preparation. The whole event was well-organised and thought-provoking. While one prisoner was talking disparagingly about prison 'equalities' (or lack of), somebody in the audience scribbled and held up a note for him saying 'GOVERNOR IS IN FRONT ROW !!!' And indeed she was, the first time I have set eyes on her. She gave a heartfelt vote of thanks at the end, which was well received. If only the 'top brass' were more consistently visible…(Can you imagine a school where the pupils never saw the head teacher? You must be sick of my little gripes by now.)

I now know that we have two bands (of musicians, maybe others of outlaws!) and the second one is incomparably better than the first. I especially enjoyed all their Bob Marley numbers that brought back fond memories of Aswan where Bob Marley is a cult figure amongst dreadlocked young Nubians. Our band rounded off with some Jimi Hendrix pieces and sounded every bit as convincing and professional as the various touring tribute bands S and I have heard over the years. What talent! It's a good job the embargo on guitar strings is not enforced here.

Britain Behind Bars – ITV's latest excursion into 'prison porn' – made for depressing viewing, as you say. So depressing that most people here didn't care to watch and I switched off before the end. But I hope the programmes opened viewers' eyes to the realities of our cash-strapped, under-staffed and demoralised Prison Service – though it may not help the current recruitment drive. Of course it was edited to focus on particular issues (and individuals) deemed to make compelling television viewing. A more balanced view of the humdrum tedium of daily life would soon have had people reaching for the off button. As an older inmate on a VP wing, I rarely saw the sort of aggression or drug-fuelled conflict that featured so prominently in the programmes. But we did hear frequent alarms go off on B-Wing, the signal for officers immediately to drop whatever they were doing and run (some more enthusiastically than others) to the Bs.

Those who had been in the system for a long time claimed that ours was one of the worst B-Cat prisons in the country, though I didn't believe them then, and even less now after watching these TV documentaries. Undoubtedly we were chronically understaffed and inefficient, the regular staff seemed to be permanently at loggerheads with the management, healthcare – especially mental health - provision was patchy, and everyone was locked up far longer than they should have been. Gang warfare sometimes spilled from outside into the other wings where young 'hoods' were housed. But at least the place was clean and reasonably orderly, food was OK, relations between regular officers and prisoners were generally respectful and, up to a point, friendly, and most inmates felt safe most of the time.

Also, I was lucky to share a certain camaraderie with other older and like-minded individuals, in truth rather more than here at NSC, and there was a genuine sense of community on C-Wing which I came to value. I shall always retain fond memories of the place and (some of) the people I met, though I am very glad now to be enjoying the relative freedom and much better facilities of North Sea Camp. You ask about canteen. As featured in the first programme, my own experience is much as depicted on TV. The officers hate being on canteen delivery duty as there are so many errors and defects – e.g. fresh fruit turning up mouldy, a regular occurrence. Some prisoners get quite stroppy, demanding refunds or replacements involving time-consuming form filling in duplicate. The problem is that orders are processed and packed by inmates at another prison so errors can rarely be rectified on the spot and refunds take a month or more to come through – if indeed they do, which it is almost impossible to check.

Something I have always needed is a proper desk/bedside light. Terry and I campaigned via the Wing Council and IMB (Independent Monitoring Board) to be allowed to purchase lamps through the Argos catalogue, but every request was denied without explanation or regret. Decisions are rarely justified with reasons – "it is as it is" is the best response you get. Eventually we were permitted little battery lights, though they were barely bright enough. Well I now have a proper lamp at last thanks to a tip-off from my roommate Keith. He said I needed an F35. It seemed an extreme measure to call in a multi-million pound American fighter jet to secure a £15 table lamp. However it turned out he meant a Prison Service medical exemption form with the same designation, which I applied for and was granted. With cataracts forming in both eyes and the vision in my right eye distorted following/despite my 2017 macular hole operation, this was a doddle. How come none of the officers, even the SO, had ever suggested this option? I guess they just couldn't be arsed, as they say. Now the lamp has arrived and been PAT-tested, and what a difference it makes! I can now read without eye strain, either at the desk or in bed, illuminated by a snazzy angled halogen lamp with three brightness settings.

Last week's relentless downpours have left the surrounding farmland part-waterlogged and host to gangs of gulls, hundreds of them. Pity the poor cabbage pickers in their high-vis orange jackets whose only respite from the rain is provided by a solitary blue portaloo perched precariously mid-field. I was forced to temporarily suspend walks round the sodden field but have now persuaded the stores dept to issue me with a pair of brown work boots. They are no fashion statement, being clunky enough to make Doc Martins look like ballet pointes, but they are rugged, waterproof, fleecy lined and unexpectedly comfortable. Also, according to the label, they have oil-resistant soles, reinforced toes, and heels with integral shock absorbers, indeed they are a veritable Land-Rover of footwear and I now feel protected against every eventuality.

Today however is crisp and sunny and some of the smaller trees are as bedecked in gold as a Persian satrap. Sara has sent me a tree-spotter's guide that just fits in my coat pocket and has become my companion on walks. She also brought in some blank cards for me to decorate with dried leaves to make cards to send at Christmas. At least that was the plan. However, when she posted me a sample of her own creative card-work along with some surplus ready-pressed claret coloured Virginia creeper leaves, they were intercepted at Reception and I was summoned (by tannoy) to face a stern-faced 'Miss', the duty officer. "How do you explain this?" she demanded peremptorily. Apparently the sending-in of flora is contrary to HMPS national rules, i.e. that hodgepodge of arcana known as PSOs and PSIs. It could be cannabis or worse, or impregnated with the dreaded 'spice' (you'll know all about that from the TV). With a dramatic flourish she scrunched up and tipped the entire contents of the envelope into the bin before my very eyes, then handed over S's card, now pruned of all its verdure. Whether or not I shall be allowed to send any leaf cards <u>out</u> is a moot point. Technically, leaves from prison trees are HMPS property and to send them out, i.e. permanently deprive the prison of them, would constitute theft. I await resolution and hope common sense will prevail, though it can be an elusive commodity in HMPS.

Further rules for the record – and a couple of differences between prisons. A ban on the smoking of tobacco ('burn' in prison slang) came into force at the start of last year in all closed (i.e. Cats A, B & C) prisons. Since then only vapes (or electronic cigarettes) are allowed. What a relief. There must have been a stupendous fug with two inmates puffing away within the confines of a tiny cell. However, here at North Sea Camp real tobacco is still permitted, but only out of doors, as applies to other public buildings 'on the out'. I don't think ready-made cigarettes are still available, but in any case, all prisoners make roll-ups with loose tobacco and Rizla papers; shaping them between the fingers is an essential part of the ritual and potentially allows for the insertion of other substances. Despite the above rules, the toilets here invariably stink of smoke in the early mornings!

On the other hand, NSC-specific rules (there's a regularly-updated sheaf of them for reference in a bulging folder outside the wing office) prissily ban all sexual activity between prisoners. This is not national policy, which is calculatedly evasive on the topic but states that 'prophylactics' *may* (but not necessarily *should*) be provided on request. However, anyone at NSC who is caught *in flagrante delictu* will immediately be sent back to a closed prison. (The above is not something of direct concern to me, as I hope you realise!) So you may imagine my surprise when, on going to the loo in the early hours a few days ago, I found a used condom floating vertically in the lavatory and staring up at me like an accusatory eye. Since then I can't walk down the corridors without wondering who among my 94 companions on North Unit are the Secret Shaggers who go hump in the night. They must be desperate, so I hope they don't get caught.

My little diary is starting to fill up with regular engagements, a further reminder of normal life. These include fortnightly chapel discussion groups, twice-weekly choir practices, meetings of various 'forums' (Age, Disability, Faith), book and reading groups in the library, and now also the newly-launched monthly creative writing course. There were just five of us at the inaugural meeting last Thursday, but that was OK. We'd all had some experience of writing, either at university or for work, recreation as a self-styled poet or, in one case, a rapper (who 'rapped' during our meeting, more for his benefit than ours). The ever-resourceful librarian came prepared with discussion points, then gave us little snippet-writing tasks to get our creative juices flowing. Homework for next time is to write a short story (500-1000 words) inspired or loosely based on random Wikipedia entries he handed out. Everyone took away something different. Mine is about the flora and fauna of the uninhabited sub-polar Auckland Islands, not exactly a promising topic for an historian, but I'll think of something!

Another highlight is the Thursday evening meditation session with Jeremy, the Buddhist chaplain. Actually, 'lowlight' would be more fitting. It is a subdued session, held in the peaceful multi-faith room, where we are surrounded by trees and serenaded by birdsong as the shadows lengthen, the evening comes and the busy world is hushed. There are usually half a dozen or so attendees, mostly older residents who have over perhaps many years in prison found solace in Buddhist teachings and practice (or just like the charming chaplain). As before, we start and finish with discussion, sometimes of prison or personal issues, sometimes of Buddhist principles. During the hour-long guided meditation, Jeremy lights a candle and incense sticks and sounds the beginning and end with the hum of a ringing bowl and chanting *sotto voce*. It is very soporific and usually at least one of us falls asleep and has to be prodded.

Last Thursday we celebrated Sangha Day, honouring the worldwide Buddhist community, with an all-day event in the chapel. It was open to all, though attendees were expected to book in advance. The kitchen staff prepared a simple but delicious vegetarian lunch (not mushroom-mush), and it was remarkable just how many people who hadn't previously attended suddenly decided, around lunchtime, that they too were Buddhists and joined us for the 'nosh'. The morning had consisted of various guided meditations and sessions led by Jeremy on Buddhist teaching, and after lunch we re-convened for a documentary film about a remote monastery in the mountains of Tibet. It was moving, slow, and slow-moving and I eventually fell deeply asleep, waking with a bit of a start just in time for the tea and cakes.

I passed our evangelical Anglican chaplain this morning outside the chapel and cheekily saluted him with "Hello, Father." Almost immediately a pigeon crapped on my head. God has a sense of humour after all.

48. Tuesday 12 November, 2019

Thanks for yours and further updates. My room-mate Keith also has medical issues which, in his case, progressed last week to the stage of an urgent-ish appointment for a biopsy at Lincoln Hospital. Unfortunately he became anxious at the possible side effects treatment might involve; at the last moment he took fright and cancelled the appointment. I tried gently to persuade him, but got nowhere. Silly man. One particular issue (I can't remember what) was rated as $> 0.1\%$ likelihood. I explained to him that this meant only one in a thousand chance max, but he is utterly convinced that he will get whatever is potentially on offer. I hope the nurses here took account of his anxieties and possible lack of comprehension. By the way, I agree about leaving 'Dr Google' outside the consulting room. I wonder how much time GPs waste allaying fears caused by patients' internet searches of symptoms?

My own health seems stable at present – the better for country air – but I could probably identify a few things wrong if I had the internet to help. The arthritic pains and swollen ankles have subsided thanks to more exercise since moving here and (though I'm loath to admit it) the firm, flat NSC beds. Here I sleep on a wooden/MDF bed assembled from a flat pack, not unlike King Tutankhamun's but without the gilded lions' feet. It is less immediately comfortable than the old and dippy iron-framed jobs that held me as tight as the arms of a bosomy woman, but it may be a lot better for the spine. I've now invested in a second soft pillow - £9.99 (canteen) is a small price to pay for eight months of slumber. However I am troubled by recurrent dreams about being late for appointments. While browsing in the library I found a couple of books on dream interpretation (more practical, I hope, than those endless 'true crime' stories). Both suggest that 'lateness' dreams have something to do with anxieties about under-achievement. They may be onto something. I've never lived up to Kipling's "fill the unforgiving minute with sixty seconds' worth of distance run". I wonder if I shall dream of prison once I leave?

Mention of lateness brings me on to clocks. Clocks aren't much in evidence here, though the tannoy PA system is very intrusive, e.g. "Attention! Attention! Will Mr So-and so report immediately to Reception!" (Whole message then repeated.) From this there is little escape except out on the field – good excuse for another walk – and in the chapel where it is turned off, but only during religious services. There were no clocks at all at the previous prison, though one would have been very useful in the Visits Hall to gauge how long we had left with our loved ones. Watches (for those who had them) had to be handed in before visits lest they were used as vehicles for smuggling in drugs. I was told that there was once a clock on the wall, but it got stolen. What? In a prison! Very few prisoners seem to have wrist watches, one possible explanation being the near-impossibility of replacing batteries, as one of my former cell-mates found. He gave up in the end. Foreseeing this difficulty I put a new battery in my own watch shortly before arrival. It continues to tick and I hope will last out until July.

I have continued refining my short (1017 words) story for the creative writing course. Happily I was allowed to use one of the library computers to type it up as a word doc – and surprised, as I expected to be told to attend a computing skills course and pass Level One before being let loose on an actual machine. (I may yet have to take a 6-week Employability course before being eligible for voluntary work outside.) It was gratifying to find how quickly all the computer basics came back to me after twenty months' absence from a keyboard and I have requested a couple of print-offs so that I can send one to S. Unfortunately, and for obvious reasons, computer usage does not extend to internet access, so I will need to re-learn how to send emails and Google my symptoms after release. Otherwise, I don't really miss the computer and certainly not mobile 'phones, not that I ever made much use of them except when abroad. The police took my mobile and plugged it into their tell-all machine, but it found... nothing! Nothing incriminating anyway. 'Phones with Facebook, Snapchat, Twitter, Instagram and the like must be a real Achilles heel for the criminally inclined.

I was amused by your description of your new opera-groupie friends, especially the one who is 'very posh, despite coming from Mansfield'. More at home in Mansfield Park, as you might have said. Most people would think that anyone who watches Janáček, even in Llandudno, to be pretty posh! I'd never heard of the opera, but I am a mere rude mechanical in such company. If there are any 'poshos' here, I have yet to meet them. There are a few graduate sophisticates (e.g. our choirmaster) but the general mode of communication is of working class mateyness which I don't even try to emulate. That said, I've not experienced any overt prejudice or hostility from anyone in either prison.

Choir is a proving great success thanks largely to the advanced musical and social skills of our director. We now have nine regular choristers, five with good voices who can read music (not essential, but it helps), two more who can sing in tune, plus two who sing weird approximations of the melodies or harmonies of their own invention. Practices are split in two, the first half singing secular pieces and the second (smaller group) learning something new for Sunday chapel at which we sing the Gloria, hymns with harmonies, and an anthem during communion. It's a sort of Sung Eucharist-lite so I'm on familiar territory. We're also practising several carols for Christmas. No need of a 'boom box' with two first rate accompanists to play the electronic piano/organ. Our secular offerings are challenging in a jazzy way and include the likes of *I'm Walkin'* (Fats Domino), *Let it Be* (Lennon & McCartney, 3-part arrangement), *Lean on Me* (Bill Withers) and *Redemption Song* (Bob Marley). We will perform the above at a yet to be decided future event. Choir practices are highlights of my week.

Last Sunday we observed Remembrance Day with a modified chapel service followed by an outdoor gathering and wreath laying in the Garden of Remembrance (behind chapel, with goldfish pools). Chapel attendance was about fifty, twice the usual number, and they obviously enjoyed singing *I Vow to Thee my Country, Jerusalem, Fight the Good Fight* and (inevitably) *Onward Christian Soldiers*. Like all HMPs, NSC contains a disproportionate number of HM's former armed forces. I offered to read a war poem (as last year) but here this role is always – and rightly – performed by Veterans. The 'Vet' who read *In Flanders Fields* did so in such a thick Geordie accent that I was glad to be already familiar with the words. There's another Geordie in this corridor who regularly exchanges pleasantries with me – at least I hope they're pleasantries, though I can barely understand a word he says. Over the years I have attended a great many Remembrance services, but this was the one I shall never forget. It was strangely moving, especially as we stood outside to lay wreaths and hear the bugler (recorded; no bugling residents at present) sound The Last Post. He had stiff competition from the shrill trilling of a robin who joined in from the top branch of a silver birch tree. The robin won.

49. Monday 25 November, 2019

What good news of your expedited hospital appointment. Also the latest political promise of a further 50,000 nurses coming on stream, as if they could just flick a switch and make it happen. Not to mention sixty brand new hospitals – or is it six refurbished old ones? They take us all for mugs. But you do seem to be well served by your local NHS when speed is of the essence. Keep me posted. Meanwhile you are in my thoughts – 'and prayers', as even the least prayerful of politicians feels obliged to add these days for fear of losing the faith vote.

Last week I had my own brush with the NHS, or my teeth did, with a visit to the dentist's van. Yes, van. I have never before had my teeth examined in the back of a white LWB Transit, but it was a weirdly surreal experience. The young female dentist (Australian) and assisting nurse (ditto) were charm itself and in no rush. I have heard them described by some residents as 'chicks', and appointments with their facility are surprisingly popular, for a dentist. I suspect any flirtatiousness on their part is in the imagination, or safely reserved only for the severely senile or obviously gay. My room-mate, by the way, is fully-dentured having had all his teeth taken out some years ago. 'The best decision of my life,' he said. The young lady gave me a most thorough explanation of the horrors she saw in the battlefield that is my mouth, with all its gaps, cracks and half-filled craters. She flattered me by declaring my oral hygiene 'good' ('better than most' would be nearer the awful truth of prisoner dentition), then outlined the operations she proposes to inflict during two follow-up appointments early next year. Sadly the NHS will not run to implanting a porcelain molar in my most visible gap, a vastly expensive procedure if privately funded. Look on the bright side. As a prisoner there are no charges to pay, a good reason for having work done before next July.

I had assumed that this well-equipped dental facility would spend the remainder of each week touring the outlying rural areas of the county; but no, it is currently retained (with dedicated driver) solely for the use of North Sea Camp. Where else in the country would one find an entire surgery serving a mere 435 people? Mind you, the need is dire. Most older and many younger prisoners have terrible teeth – blackened, broken and often missing fangs that must severely restrict their chewable options on the weekly menu. Several prisoners have commented that I have amazingly good teeth 'for my age' (compliments in prison are rarely unconditional), and not a denture in sight!

Mention of cell-mates brings me to my main news item, which is that I have yet again been obliged to move rooms. So I now reside in my fifth location, and sixth bed, at NSC. The reason this time is the arrival of a new wheelchair user who must be accommodated in a room that is a) large enough to manoeuvre in, and b) accessible by ramp. So I have relocated to a similar room but slightly larger at 7'6" x 13' (hurray!). I'm still in North Unit but on the dark side and gloomy with no view (boo!). Poor old Keith is very put out. I don't think he has much in common with his new companion and dreads juggling two wheelchairs round their narrow shared space..

My latest – and I hope last – companion is Len. Len is what you might call 'a character' and comes with a health warning from several sources, both official and unofficial, that he can be irascible and 'difficult' and invariably falls out with his padmates sooner rather than later. Len is staunchly Old Labour, and old – 81 next week, though he looks younger despite a pickled walnut of a face. He still sports a generous head of salt-and-pepper hair, albeit slicked back with Brylcreem, 1950s style. He is eager to impress on me at the earliest opportunity that he does his exercises and is stronger than most men half his age, which I can well believe. Despite this, though he would never admit it, he is moderately deaf in both ears. On principal he won't wear hearing aids (sign of weakness), but prefers to turn up the volume on the TV while hectoring me from the other side of the room with all the decibels (and tone) of S summoning me from the bottom of the garden when I've ignored two previous calls. Pity the poor guys in the next room who have taken to thumping on the partition wall to silence him when in full flood.

Politically, Len favours a cod-Marxist conflict-based interpretation of events and buys into the most loony of conspiracy theories, e.g. that the moon landings were fake and 9/11 was a set-up by the US government. Malign forces are ubiquitous in his fevered imagination. He is immune to reason so I am working on an alternative strategy to de-ridiculize him. Len's (saner) political heroes were Nye Bevan and Tony Benn rather than Jeremy Corbyn (I have some sympathy with him there). Just now, Len says he wants the Tories to win the General Election as they are sure to bring conflict and ruin, cause a revolution and thus usher in a socialist utopia. Len subscribes to a great many '-isms', e.g. nationalism, sexism, covert racism, classis, atheism and nihilism, but realism is not among them. Needless to say, he despises religion, which he regards as mere hocus-pocus and 'the cause of just about every war in history'. As I said, Len is a 'character'. He likes chewing on raw onions (for his health - we could try it?), is tone deaf to satire and doesn't do humour. But otherwise we get on just fine. I like him.

Len has already told me a great deal about himself, probably more than I need or want to know just now, especially on the medical front. He was given an IPP sentence – one of David Blunkett's iniquitous 'Imprisonment for Public Protection' sentences that merely specified a minimum term, the actual release date being left up to the Parole Board years later. Blunkett intended IPPs only for exceptional use, but they were widely used as a cop out by judges who couldn't immediately decide a fixed tariff. Though IPP sentences were abolished in 2012 (they contravene Human Rights legislation) and many such prisoners have since been released, there are still about 2,500 prisoners languishing in jail unsure of when, if ever, they will be released despite already having served years longer than their original minimum terms. Len was sentenced (I think) to 10 years, but keeps getting knocked back by parole boards and has now been inside for seventeen years. Len is understandably bitter at his treatment, but I don't see him as dangerous to anyone except possibly himself. I suspect his forthright and sometimes confrontational manner may have a lot to do with it.

You may have read that another of our IPP prisoners absconded from here last week. He was caught (they almost always are). You must think 'silly man – it won't help his case for release', which would be true on both counts. But it underlines just how desperate such people become once they suspect that they are forever trapped in the system and may never be released. This is no Colditz, but that doesn't diminish the urge to escape.

Len has an interesting political pedigree. He was brought up in the East End of London during the war and post-war period. His uncle was a radical Tyneside Labour MP who lived with Len's family while attending parliament in London and his ideas shaped Len's during his formative years. So, for the second time in less than two years of prison life, I find myself sharing with a close relative of a member of parliament (though Terry's cousin is a Tory, and now in the Lords). Statistically what chance is there of that? Vanishingly small, I suspect. I can see that Len and I will be having heated debates with the General Election only four weeks off. We tend to shout at each other quite late at night until the blokes in the next room thump on the partition wall to shut us up, but we are still friends the next morning. For now, Len spends most of his waking hours doing parquetry (making patterns, not pictures as in marquetry), at which he is very skilled. At least it keeps him quiet.

We have now had our second creative writing session and participation has shrunk from six to four students. Despite being twice the prescribed minimum length, my story went down well and raised a smile. Two of the other offerings were very good. We had all found it much easier to come up with original ideas when presented with a specific scenario, however daunting it seemed at first. My story, related to Wikipedia pages on the Auckland Islands, was set in a UK museum diorama. Familiar territory there! Another participant's pages were on a painting by Pieter de Hooch, for which he created an ingenious and colourful back-story. The other wrote a reminiscence as if by a 1930s Italian footballer. Nobody incorporated prisons into their story. Thank goodness for that! Our next task is to write a first person narrative presented as one side of a wrong-number telephone call. I'm going for black comedy.

In my short story, I managed to reference your Dante Society (my lead character was a stalwart!) and I would have enjoyed the Italian Gardens talk with ref to Ravello and Ischia. I haven't seen either of these, though have been (twice) to the other one, the Villa San Michele on Capri. I love its cool vibe, as Harry might say. Currently our gardens here are buzzing with gangs of captive gardeners completing the late autumn clearance and bedding out wallflowers for next spring. Just think, by the time they have finished flowering I shall be preparing to leave. I am now almost ¾ of the way through my 'time', though still unsure what my costly detention was supposed to achieve. I may be a little wiser in the worldly-wise sense, which is no bad thing, but at what price to the state?

Popped into chapel today for a catch-up with the orderlies and picked up a free booklet, title: 'Jesus Loves Prisoners', written by a former prison chaplain. I'm not sure all Christians would agree. From what I hear, some church communities can be very particular about whom they welcome.

S and Harry came in for a joint visit on Saturday and I shall not see either of them again until just after Christmas. S stayed again at the £36 B&B she has found in Boston where Harry joined her, having found no available train connections linking Boston to the main line for London. To return that evening would have required a long bus ride to Peterborough and a train from there. I can understand why open prisons are usually remotely located (to discourage residents from legging it), but it does make visiting difficult and expensive for their long-suffering families. Anyway, they enjoyed whiling away their unplanned evening together at an Italian restaurant down by the river. H will be off on his travels again soon, first to Essouira (Morocco) with his girlfriend before Christmas, then another work project in Tanzania in January. My own wanderlust is severely curbed; even the library is a bit short on travel, though I have spotted a few guidebooks, Bill Brysons and *Britain's 100 Best Bus Journeys* to whet my appetite.

50. Monday 9 December, 2019

I was much amused to receive your copy of Boris Johnson's election communication and can only observe that you, Maggie, made much better use of the blank reverse of the sheet than he did of the front. Research on readability suggests that sentences over seven words long are not readily understood by children of primary school age. Johnson's first 100 words contain no fewer than fifteen sentences… What does this tell you about his estimation of the electorate of Rushcliffe constituency? Let's hope their political understanding is more advanced than their reading age! (According to *Inside Time*, prisoners have an average reading age of eleven and a third have a learning disability. At least here they are guaranteed some support, which is more than can be said for some prisons.)

Thursday's general election will be the first since 1970 when I haven't been able to vote. Denying prisoners the vote was contrary to EU Human Rights law, not that our governments ever paid more than lip service to that, unless dictated by political expediency. A notice in the library here informs residents that those on remand may apply for a postal vote, rather superfluous, as there are no remand prisoners here. This week my room-mate Len is away on a 'home' leave, in practice to a probation hostel as he no longer has a home to go to. The upside of this is that I can watch TV election broadcasts without a constant barrage of anti-Tory rhetoric from the other end of the room. Loosely speaking Len and I are on the same side, but I don't accept that all Conservative-leaning voters are total idiots or wicked capitalists leeching on the poor. That said, the election seems unnecessary and absurd – BoJo's vanity project – and I shall be glad when it is over.

Urgent announcement over the tannoy, Saturday mid-afternoon: "Will all farm workers report to the farm <u>immediately</u>, repeat <u>immediately</u>. The sheep have escaped!" This may explain why the Moroccan (note correct spelling, a first) lamb tagine was dropped from the menu at short notice. The urgency of the announcement was for once matched by the clarity of its delivery. This varies greatly according to which officer is on microphone duty. The last few days have been even worse than usual with rapid, garbled delivery and an almost total absence of consonants. This morning I heard, "ah-oh-or-eye-or" reminiscent of the French station announcements at the start of Jacques Tati's classic farce, *Les Vacances de M. Hulot*. My brain eventually unscrambled our message as "last call for dining hall" but only because the same message is delivered every day at around 7.50 a.m. (Despite the excellence of NSC's home-made sausages, I do not, of course, attend breakfast, it being far too early as John will understand.)

The issue of garbled tannoy announcements is a regular on the agenda of the monthly Age Forum meetings and I brought it up again this morning. It may not have any effect as the governor who was scheduled to chair the meeting failed to show up. The twelve attendees carried on regardless, one of our number taking notes in lieu of formal minutes. I plucked up courage to speak to the governor in her office later (only the second time in 22 months that I have spoken to an actual prison governor, apart from the chaplain who is *ex officio*). Her explanation for her absence was reasonable enough – she hadn't been told of the meeting by her predecessor. Also, she hadn't heard any of this morning's tannoy announcements calling her by name. Perhaps they were turned off in the officers' quarters or just too garbled? I was able to get a few other issues off my chest for good measure. It's a shame there are so few opportunities to communicate directly with the management. They might learn something to their advantage (and so might we).

Our third creative writing session has been and gone. We were joined for the session by the regional overseer of prison libraries who professed herself amazed at the standard here. She told our librarian that she'd spoken to the Lincoln Prison writing group about sentence length and syllables (see above re. Johnson) but was greeted by several blank stares. Most of them didn't know what a syllable was. Maybe they thought she was offering them a whipped cream dessert? Our next task is to write a character profile, then a short story or extract from a longer work featuring that character. My working title is *The Christmas Market* and will be loosely based on the eccentricities of a lady vicar of my acquaintance. It should be a tragedy but may end up as a farce.

I may not win any awards as a writer, but at least I can now describe myself as an 'award winning prisoner'. Tomorrow I'll attend a special ceremony in the chapel to receive my 'Three Month Award' certificate for surviving my time here (so far) without any negatives. There are no prizes, but rumour has it that after six unblemished months prisoners are presented with a Wagon Wheel or Twix.

My current bedside reading, Jeffrey Archer's Prison Diaries Vol 3, *Heaven*, provides an entertaining and sometimes amusing take on this place, revelatory for anyone who has not shared the experience. I'm almost at the end when he is transferred to Hollesley Bay, his fourth prison, at which point he discontinues the diary having exhausted every possible angle in the previous volumes, *Heaven* and *Purgatory*. Last night I made a mental note of this apt comment: "As so often in prison, someone will look for a reason for not doing something rather than find a way of making a good idea work." You may remember how, at an earlier Age Forum meeting, I suggested having occasional talks by visiting (or resident) speakers. Today the reply came: the idea is completely impossible as there is no budget to pay speakers. Who said anything about payment? I had thought that the local U3A branch or similar (Dante Society? – joke) might find some generous-hearted individuals who would be more than willing to speak to groups of older prisoners *sans* fee. Obviously I was wrong.

Christmas cheer has already arrived here, but still slightly too soon to my Scroogean way of thinking. There are now two fake Christmas trees down the long corridor in North Unit along with dangly things like tribal dancing skirts but suspended from the ceiling, just low enough to brush the hair of our taller residents. Most of our regular officers are short in stature, and sometimes in manner too, and escape unscathed. Not to be outdone, the chapel has sprouted three artificial trees in ascending height from a squat mini-tree on the welcome desk to medium height in the meeting area and a tall model near what passes for the sanctuary. All have multi-coloured flashing lights and impressive baubles. A long straggle of mauve-coloured lights now hangs above the mural on the wall behind the altar (or Holy Table, as the Rev prefers) from where they flashed throughout last Sunday's Holy Communion service. If the chaplain were of a different theological persuasion he could perhaps programme them to flash only at the *Sanctus*, Consecration and *Agnus Dei*. This might offend his Protestant sensibilities, but I could point out that flashing lights are not specifically proscribed by the 39 Articles, only 'gazing upon and carrying about' of the Sacrament. The orderlies have also assembled a crib in front of the altar with handsome wooden figures and concealed interior lighting, a feature unknown in first century Palestine. The Three Kings/Wise Men/Magi (black, brown and white-skinned in accordance with HMPS equalities policy) are still some way off, on the window sills, but will doubtless arrive in time for Epiphany. It's all reassuringly traditional.

The above reminds me that I may not have described the chapel to you in any detail, apart from outlining its layout. While it is just another plain pre-fabricated building, it is a warm, welcoming and comforting space, usually open during daylight hours and manned (this being a largely male establishment) by a rota of orderlies. These 'chaps' (the chaplain's favoured term) welcome all comers and dispense worldly wisdom and occasionally biscuits and cups of coffee. Only one seems to be a committed Christian (an Evangelical of the very best sort), the others are not conspicuously well-informed on religious doctrine and practice. They are worryingly vague, for example, about the niceties of denominational differences and might easily semantically confuse angels with Anglicans. The business end of the chapel, with the altar, lectern and so forth is mostly curtained off to make a quiet area during the week when not in use for services (RC on Friday evenings, C of E on Sunday mornings).

The most striking feature of the chapel is its mural that extends right across the end wall behind the altar. This was painted by an inmate about twenty years ago and depicts the Last Supper with life-sized figures, surrounded by smaller-scale representations of other biblical events including Adam and Eve (plus serpent), the Nativity and Baptism of Jesus, the Crucifixion and Resurrection. The artist was an ex-paratrooper and, if you know where to look, you may spot a tiny parachute and Chieftain tank. Intriguingly, he based the faces of Jesus and the Disciples on the inmates and officers he knew. (A well-established custom, as you'll know. One of the best-known examples is Zoffany's *Last Supper* in St John's Church, Calcutta. His modelling of Judas on the unpopular city auctioneer landed him in court for defamation. He won the case, but his come-uppance came on the return voyage to England in 1789 when his vessel was shipwrecked and the crew staved off starvation by cannibalising the cabin boy, chosen by lot.) I find our chapel mural inspiring and I keep discovering new and intriguing details. Apparently it was nearly 'lost' a few years ago when a previous chaplain wanted to paint it over on the grounds that it was 'disrespectful'. Bah! Luckily he was overruled and this minor masterpiece was saved.

Sorry your trip to the Troy exhibition was underwhelming and a hassle on the train. Conversation overheard while standing in the dinner queue. Long term prisoner on his first home leave 'Rottle' travels by train. It's crowded. He sits down in first available seat. Irate woman passenger approaches, taps him on shoulder and berates him saying "I've reserved that seat". Uncomprehending, he replies, "Tough luck, Mrs. I got here first" or words to that effect. She points to little reservation slip on back of seat. Oops – he'd never seen one of those before! (Anecdotally, some prisoners have been so long inside that they have never seen a pound coin.)

This may be my last letter before Christmas, so I hope you will enjoy a cheerful and sociable time with family and friends. Please pass on my greetings to anyone who might like to receive them. I had imagined that many of our residents who are approved home leave would be away over Christmas. Not so. Christmas leave is not prohibited, but is very rarely allowed as the authorities are jittery that the lure of parties, booze and screws might get the better of some men. So we shall have a full house for Christmas. I wonder how many will turn up for our choir-led candle-lit carol service?

51. Monday 23 December, 2019

I'm putting pen to paper according to my regular schedule in the hope, rather than expectation, that you may receive this before 2020 dawns. A slightly confusing notice has appeared outside the unit office advising residents that mail may not get 'processed' this week. It doesn't state if that means incoming or outgoing post, or both. None was delivered on Saturday but there was a bumper crop on Sunday. Most inward mail is at least a day late to allow for opening and checking anything suspicious, for the reasons you now know well.

One of the ancillary duties of the officers on night duty in the wings (there's always someone either in the office or wandering round – sniffing out illicit smokers, perhaps) is to read that day's outgoing mail. "So you know all my secrets?" I ventured to one such. "Yes," she said, with a smirk verging on grimace. I found this slightly unnerving! Incoming mail must be checked for drugs, especially the now notorious spice plus, as we now know, Virginia Creeper leaves and tuning devices (see below). At the other place, where drug use was rampant on some wings, it was said (though I don't know on what evidence) that a blind eye (+ stopped nose!) was sometimes turned, as spice in small doses helped keep some of the more frisky 'incarcerateds' docile. (BTW, I like your new word!) Even North Sea Camp is not immune. Recently someone from this unit was shipped back to a more restrictive regime elsewhere after being found in the lavatories 'off his head' with the stuff. What an idiot. He was due for release quite soon after but will now have to serve up to two additional years in a closed prison.

The festive season here begins to live up to its name and I have already described the proliferation of decorations even in the most incongruous of settings. Last week's candlelit carol service was a resounding success, well-attended (70+), every seat in the chapel taken, lusty singing by one and all, mince pies * specially baked in the kitchens and gleefully consumed (with tea, not mulled wine), the Governing Governor herself exuding bonhomie and echoing Tiny Tim verbally if not physically, "A Merry Christmas to us all; God bless us, everyone!" The order of service followed the traditional pattern of lessons and carols, albeit five instead of nine.

I delivered the first reading – Adam and Eve walking in the garden in the cool of the day – and gave it all the 'welly' I could to get proceedings off to a confident start. We North Sea Singers were thoroughly rehearsed and in good voice for our items. The Gov herself read the final lesson, thanked us fulsomely and declared herself gobsmacked to find such talent at NSC, though, apart from chaplains, no other governors or officers bothered to turn up. It's not often you get an ex-cathedral organist directing a rag-tag assortment of reprobates, but it shows what can be done. Watch out, Gareth Malone!

* Mince pie tale from December's *Jail Mail*: "The governor at HMP Wymott believes that foil pie cases can be used to smoke drugs and the fruit can be used to produce hooch.... DHL will sell them at every *other* prison (having) passed them as no threat to security." Is there no end to prisoner ingenuity – or official credulity?

I can't quite bring myself to comment on the general election result. What I find alarming is the near adulation, even here, of Boris Johnson. A member of staff within my hearing swooned at his very name – "Boris... How I love that man!" Yuk. Most prisoners here seem happy enough with the result despite all the rot Johnson spouts about the justice system and prisons in particular (like 'Laura Norder' aka Mrs T of old?) Are they crazy? Or maybe they're canny enough to understand that BoJo's populist policies on increasing prisoner numbers and lengthening sentences are just so much hot air, completely undeliverable with the service already at breaking point, or broken. You will have read reports of riots at my previous prison *alma mater*. I'm not surprised. They are dangerously short-staffed and find it almost impossible to recruit and retain staff.

A goodly number of cards have now arrived and are strung on three sides round my end of the room. As you observe, robins are 'in' this year with 5, plus 2 more at Len's end. Robins are notoriously aggressive birds so I hope they will not come to blows before the Christmastide season of peace and joy is over. Also a redwing, helpfully captioned for the non-twitcher. As you will know, I did send out just a few homemade leaf cards, more in hope than expectation. They seem to have arrived OK. Both the card designs available from canteen are, like last year's, heavily bedecked with glitter and feature a ruddy-faced Santa who is clearly three sheets to the wind after a booze-up with the elves in the pub. However, I was able to buy a pack of 'superior' cards from the HIS (a church-based national charity) shop on site. This opens once a month mainly to sell end-of-range clothing at knock down prices. I have also set myself up with a pair of new leather shoes for £5.

My superior cards also depict Father Christmas, parked up in a present-laden sleigh, reading a list on a long scroll. I have captioned it "Santa checks the prison facilities list only to discover that <u>none</u> of the gifts he has brought for residents of North Sea Camp are permitted." The inspiration for this comes from the gift of a 'singer's chromatic pitch pipe' from nephew Anthony. (A little chrome instrument for a singer to blow into to get the pitch of a given note). The reception officer's response? "Sorry, mate. You can't 'ave it. It ain't on the list." It will now become a late birthday present rather than an early Christmas one. I'm not sure what <u>is</u> on the list of allowable gifts, but get the impression that it wouldn't take long to read. Books are usually permitted here, as long as they are not obviously pornographic or with titles like *The Dummies Guide to Escapology*.

Unlike the outside world, no one here need go hungry this Christmas, except possibly the lad (Wilting Willie – who asked me not to speak to him) who only eats tomato-flavoured noodles, on which he spends almost all his weekly earnings from the lobster pot manufactory. The Christmas menu is a cornucopia of challenging choices. As a creature of traditional tastes, I have pre-selected for Christmas Day the roast turkey and stuffing, though the salmon *en croute* came a temptingly close second. I have gone for the baked gammon on Boxing Day and roast beef and Yorkshire pudding on New Year's Day. Otherwise the menu is little different from the usual Week 4 (of a 5-week cycle). Thus Christmas Eve choices include 'pilchard bap' and 'chips with onion gravy' for lunch, both of which also featured on Jeffrey Archer's 2001 menu. The latter has a strong following but to me looks as unappetisingly soggy as it sounds. As to the former, I wonder if HMPS bought up a trawler-load of pilchards around the turn of the century and is still trying to palm then off on prisoners? Other delicacies that featured in Lord

Archer's day (twenty years ago) and are still consumed here are 'chicken balls' and 'faggots in gravy', the cause of hilarity to some prisoners in a 'nudge nudge, wink wink' sort of way. Archer helpfully provides a weekly menu sheet in his NSC diary. I've compared notes and find two thirds of the choices in his day are still on offer in 2019. No *nouvelle cuisine* here!

I note from today's 'I' Newspaper that the number of older people (that's us) who are malnourished has trebled over the past ten years. One suggested remedy is to get them to eat off blue crockery, which apparently helps them (us) to see what (we) are eating. The science behind this revelation is far too complex for my little brain, but I observe that all prisons use blue (albeit plastic) plates. Could this possibly explain the high proportion of older prisoners who are obese or pot-bellied? There may be a Lancet article or a PhD in that one. Remember, you read it here first.

My hopes of a pre-Christmas haircut are dashed as the NSC barber has been on a home-leave ROTL all week. As he's a Muslim, I'm not sure if he celebrates Christmas. In fact he doesn't celebrate much at all being a real sour grapes Mr Grumpy. He's a competent enough haircutter, but lacks the barber's customary gift of the gab. With captive customers, he doesn't really need to try; nor can he earn tips for small talk. Unlike regular prisoner barbers who work on the landings and get paid in Vosene, he has a proper little barber's shop, advertised with a stripy pole outside and featuring an adjustable-height chair within. He is fully equipped with everything – even scissors, a significant concession reflecting the D category of this prison.

With love and best wishes for a truly festive and jolly Christmas!

P.S. I have had my hair cut after all! A chap on my corridor, who was a barber professionally before landing in prison, offers a scissor-less service with a smile in return for a small gratuity. To avoid detection by prowling staff we have to hide round a corner. I am 'well pleased' with the result, all achieved with a rather fancy electric beard trimmer.

52. Epiphany, Monday 6 January 2020

Heading this sheet with the magic number 2020 feels more than usually like a new leaf as well as a new year as I enter the final straight of my imprisonment. I hope, in your case, it will be much less troubled by health scares and hospital appointments, and for all of us a more joyous year ahead.

I've headed this letter Epiphany to make a point. I kept all my cards up in my room until this morning. In the end there were 33 of them, more than most people here but well short of the 1,704 Jeffrey Archer received (in this very room, I think!) for Christmas 2001. His diary notes that most were from mere well-wishers and that he 'only' sent 200 that year. A pretty poor show I'd say. Sad to report, however, that our dapper Three North Sea Kings figures never reached the chapel crib. Inexplicably, on Saturday the orderlies swaddled them in tissue paper, boxed them up and returned them to the store as part of a general post-Christmas tidy-up. The whole Christian narrative may need to be rewritten, even TS Eliot's famous poem, *The Journey of the Magi who Never Arrived*.

I can report however that our seasonal menu was just as anticipated, and much appreciated by all. Even the plum pudding tasted authentic despite its lubrication with custard (unadulterated) rather than rum sauce or brandy butter. Would crime statistics improve if we were given gruel, as misanthropic readers of the red-tops might prefer? I doubt it. A postscript to the carol service (re-branded as a Festival of Carols lest non-believers were put off attending by the thought of a 'service'!) came in the plaudits from the Governor in the weekly staff briefing. She has since floated the idea that we might go out to perform in the local community, though I doubt if this will come to anything given the amount of official paperwork involved. Singing *a capella* with all male voices produces a rather strangulated effect, less pure than King's College Choir (in every sense). Neither do we have the numbers or strength of voice - or the beer - to mimic a Welsh male voice choir. Our renderings of old favourites such as *Gabriel's Message* and The Coventry Carol had a distinctly barbershop timbre - not necessarily unpleasing, just different.

You ask how S and Harry's visit went on the day after Boxing Day. I'm sorry to relate that it was only 50% successful. H forgot to bring his wallet (containing driving licence) so had no photo ID to show. A mere bank card or two wouldn't suffice. S was very cross with Harry and we can only hope that their next planned visit on 15th will be more successful. S stopped short of blaming me for passing on the absent-mindedness gene, but must have lurked at the back of her mind. Given the generally more relaxed regime here, it is tempting to forget that most general HMPS rules still apply. In some respects (leaves and pitch-pipes come to mind) they are more rigorously applied here *, even contrary to common sense. (Wow. Sticking me neck out there. Must be demob happy!)

* BUT… Christine has sent me a 2020 Yorkshire Dales calendar. I didn't tell her, but last year's had the spiral binding cut loose and removed in the post room and was delivered to me as twelve separate sheets (plus cover). This year's has remained unmolested and now hangs as intended from a hook on the wall (yes, we have those too!)

In other respects the family had a good Christmas over at Grandpa's, though he has now turned 99 and was content to observe rather than participate in the usual games such as charades and up-Jenkins. Harry's girlfriend also visited, but found our house a little intimidating with its tribal masks, creaky floorboards and old pictures at every turn. H says her family home is 'north London minimalist' so ours must have seemed like Dracula's castle by comparison. Incidentally, Len and I tried watching the latest Dracula on TV but turned it off half way through the first episode. We were both too squeamish to watch worms wriggling out of eye-sockets and worse. Not something to see in prison – I preferred the old Christopher Lee versions they showed at that fleapit cinema in Cambridge. Len, by the way, sincerely believes that Arthur Scargill should have become Prime Minister. Now that might have been a real-life horror story, though maybe we should reserve judgement until we see what sort of job BoJo makes of it.

I expected to defer writing to you until later in the week as today I was scheduled to attend a two-day City and Guilds Level 2 Health and Safety at Work course. I duly rose earlier than usual to be ready for the fray at 8.30 this morning and sat through the first session without disgracing myself or breaking down with a coughing fit (bad sore throat last night). However, on presenting with the other eleven students for the afternoon 1.30 – 4.30 session, we were informed without explanation that it had been cancelled, and tomorrow's too. This was a complete surprise. Nothing untoward had happened during the morning. Everyone behaved impeccably. I do hope that our tutor did not overbalance a fork lift truck, have a lorry reverse into him or a pallet of bricks drop on him from a high crane, or suffer a spinal injury from trying to lift a too heavy object in an non-approved manner. These were the principal examples of avoidable work accidents that we studied during the morning.

What I did discover is that the tutor is very easily discomfited and, entirely unwittingly, I managed to embarrass him at least twice by asking the wrong sort of questions. He blushes bright red when put on the spot, not an ideal look for a tutor, though in other respects I thought him pretty good. Exactly what relevance this course has for a long-retired pensioner I'm not sure, but I'm happy to go along with it, earn about £4 a day for attending, and collect another certificate at the end. We still get paid despite the cancellation so I shall be able to buy a little extra chocolate on next week's canteen.

More seriously, I have been handed the Oasys Report prepared about me by my OS (Offender Supervisor) and am therefore in correspondence with the prison/probation authorities. I'm not sure in what sense it is an oasis *, but it is neither green and pleasant nor fertile. First the good/bad news – using some obscure algorithm *, it computes that there is a 2% risk of me committing an offence of violence within one year of release. Not sure how that is calculated (I've never been accused of violence in all my life!), but I'll let it lie (unintended pun). What concerns me more is that it states as fact that I had committed offences of which I was acquitted or was never even accused. Also that I 'accept responsibility for' the offences which I 'regret'. Nice of him to add that, but I have to wonder if he was even listening when I unequivocally and unambiguously said that I am <u>not</u> guilty and maintain my innocence, as I always have.

* I now know it's an **O**ffender **A**ssessment **SYS**tem.
* Confession time – I had to look up the spelling of algorithm having initially assumed it was a 'rhythm'. The word has one of the longest multi-lingual derivations in the dictionary, including Greek, Arabic, Med. Latin, Mid. English and O. French and is ultimately related to al Kwarismi, 'the cognomen of the 9th century mathematician Abu Ja'far Muhammad ibn Musa, author of works on algebra. So now you know!

Unfortunately the OS is now on leave (yet again) for a couple of weeks, so I have tried to put the record straight with the Senior Probation Officer. Initially she looked at me witheringly, like a bowl of chips she hadn't ordered, but eventually she capitulated on the basis that the facts (not necessarily the assessment) may be in error, which they are. She will ask him to revise the report. In case I need back-up, and on advice from someone I trust, I have been in touch with a solicitor who specialises in prison law. I'm sure you have read recent press reports on how the judicial system is crumbling – well that's just the tip of the iceberg (mixed metaphor – icebergs melt – sorry). Grrr…. The downside of all this is that, yet again, my assessment for ROTL release has been put back to February at the earliest, i.e. four months behind schedule. Will I ever get day release? This could drag on and on…

Notice on board outside unit office: "PLEASE ADHERE TO THIS NOTICE". (Nothing more – just that.) I have visions of all 94 residents of this block firmly stuck to a single A4 sheet of paper. A feat fit for the Guinness Book of Records?

Happy New Year!

53. Tuesday 21 January 2020

I have just returned from the best walk of the year so far. No great distance, just a couple of circuits of the 'park' field, once in each direction for a change of scene. But today it was white with a heavy frost, spiky and scrunchy underfoot with only the peaks of the mole hills poking out above the grass. Warm socks advised, but I have yet to try on the free-issue long-johns. I used to have a pair that had belonged to my Dad. They were cream coloured, all wool and labelled with the CC41 utility mark, which dates them. They were scratchy to wear and tended to unroll from the waist down so I was not a fan except in the most severe climatic conditions. Also, no need today for the multiple-reinforced work boots. This means that I can go straight from field to library for a glance at the day's newspapers. But, as a 'colleague' (a former RC priest, I suspect) remarked as he passed me *The Times*, "Yet again, no good news!" Yesterday we were both rather naughtily amused by a brief item in the 'T' about an automatic translation system. Translating from Burmese to English this repeatedly rendered the name of President Chi of China as 'President Shithole'. I hope that hasn't made you choke on your breakfast muesli.

President Chi (or Shi.....) is much in the news just now because of some mystery new virus called Coronavirus or Covid emerging in the Chinese city of Wuhan, now locked down to prevent further spread. I'm not one to get alarmed about such things, evidently nor is 'our Boris', as one of our healthcare ladies affectionately calls the PM. Nor indeed is room-mate Len, whose take on it is that, like the moon landings, it is probably just a hoax. So that's OK then. My hacking cough/cold is no worse and may be on the mend (so not 'the Chinese virus' after all). I saw the Doc last Friday who suggested a course of Doxycycline but said there was only a 50:50 chance of success but did I want to try it? Of course I said yes, never one to be shy of any free pills on offer - I'd have made a compliant guinea pig or laboratory rat. I'm familiar with Doxycycline from East African days as it's an antibiotic used as a malaria prophylactic and safer over long periods than, say, Lariam, that can have such embarrassing side-effects (think loosely President Chi in translation). While I doubt if the Doxy will do much for my cough at this stage, at least I won't get malaria, as poor old Oliver Cromwell did. It was prevalent is his day in the 'unwholesome fens' hereabouts.

Luckily, Len was away on home release from Mon to Fri last week so he escaped the worst of my coughing bouts that were exploding like cluster bombs. Despite his reputation as a cantankerous, stubborn and confrontational old misanthrope, Len is tolerant of health issues, even coughing and snoring. Deafness helps. I am sure that Len benefits from getting away from prison life, but he candidly admits that he has to work hard to stay on his best behaviour especially when negotiating with his moronic (according to Len) probation officer. The probation hostel is very restrictive and requires checking in several times a day. This is a chore for poor old Len and makes it all but impossible for him to meet up with his 'support network', most of whom live several bus rides away, unreachable within the available time frames. He is due for a parole hearing in a few months' time and is moderately optimistic of release this time. I very much hope so.

I have enjoyed having a few days with the room to myself, able to listen to Radio 3 without headphones and with uncontested control of the TV remote. Luckily Len and I enjoy many of the same programmes, mainly (in his case) of the documentary or technical genre. His current no. 1 favourite is *The Repair Shop* during which he maintains a constant running commentary, either endorsing the presenters' craftsmanship or (more frequently) loudly advising them (and me) where they are going wrong. But in Len's eyes Fred Dibnah, his role model, was a true saint who could do no wrong. Len still has one leg in the Great Age of Steam and tells me he used to shunt a pug engine round the steelworks. Them wuz the days, to borrow a Dibnahism!

Though Len may be short on interpersonal skills, I have nothing but admiration for his practical ones. Building, decorating, carpentry and joinery, motor mechanics and light engineering, he is multi-talented. That's not just on his word, but is supported by photos of some of his workmanship and verified by those who have known him elsewhere and still turn to him for practical advice. Len is the go-to Mr Fix-it here for prisoners with faulty or broken possessions and the prison could probably save a lot of money by employing him on the maintenance team. Also, of course, I cannot but admire the beautiful precision of the parquetry he works on as his prison hobby. Sadly, Len is now a man out of time as there is so little call for his skills in the 21st century, though he plans to set up a workshop in a friend's garden if/when he leaves here. To his credit, he noted an obvious gap in his skill-set and enrolled for a computer course here at NSC. He soon came to grief. Computers don't work like steam engines, he found.

Your letters are full of their usual crop of outings, talks, concerts, etc. Thanks for the PC of the Bromley House Subscription Library. It sounds quaint and charming, especially the garden. However – in the light of my recent H&S non-course – I wonder if they have done a thorough risk assessment on use of the portable ladder? As you will remember from office days, there are strict guidelines on how many steps employees/customers may climb without hand-holds and assisting personages. I was banned from storing stuff on the top shelf of my office cupboard, so the boxes of redundant materials ended up as a trip hazard rather than a falling one. Happily the Prison Service has a more relaxed attitude. I keep many little-used items on top of my wall cupboard with neither handholds nor ladder for assistance. I confess to being an inveterate hoarder, not a good fit with our minimalist prison lifestyle.

During his sermon last Sunday, the Rev referred in passing to the Holy Spirit's appearance in the form of a dove at the baptism of Christ in the Jordan. For a visual reference, I checked the wall painting behind the altar to discover that, in the section devoted to this scene, the dove had been thoughtlessly obscured by a notice saying OUT OF BOUNDS TO PRISONERS. Since then I have sneaked in and, when no one was watching, moved the offending notice. I have now re-pinned it onto a cloud just above Eve's head (see below) though she is probably too focused on plucking that apple (a Cox, I think) to notice. To explain, the reason for the notice is that a door at this point leads through the wall into the cloakroom (there's a corresponding door to the vestry on the opposite side). The rest of the door's surface features a Garden of Eden scene and it struck me how apt (and perhaps a joke by the prisoner-artist) that a naked Eve, only partly obscured by a leafed stem of papyrus plucked from the river bank, should be shown emerging from the lavatory. Truly, a call of nature. I was pleased to be able to share the joke with my former vicar who recently drove all the way over to see me here, well beyond the call of duty. We were allowed to meet in the chapel rather than the visitor centre and the chaplain even produced tea and biscuits for the occasion.

I have now made a further visit to the OMU department about my wretched Oasys report. This time I met the Head of Department, the boss of the one I saw last time. My OS (Offender Supervisor) is due back at work today and, though I wish him no ill, I hope he may be feeling just a little chastened. I understand that I am by no means the only complainant. Some sections of the report need a re-write and the boss lady is adamant that I must participate in a formal 'planning board' meeting along with the outside Probation Service. A date and names relating to this had been entered on the form, but were pure fiction. How do they get away with it? My experience is by no means unique.

Today we have all been presented with a *Hygiene and Decency Compact* to sign. We must agree not only to keep our rooms tidy, but also to shower daily. Daily! Who pays the water bill? That condition must be in hope rather than expectation as I can't see officers standing round all day with clip boards checking showerers. The facilities here, by the way, are excellent in this respect – decent changing rooms, curtained cubicles, oodles of hot water – the perfect relaxation at the beginning or end of the day. There is even a separate and lockable shower for use by the critically infirm, users of colostomy bags and our (currently) two trans-female residents. Every want catered for. If only all prisons were as well appointed.

54. Candlemas - Sunday 02.02.2020

I'm starting this early as an excuse to write the palindromic date above, a rare opportunity to use only zero and a single digit. After 22.02.2022 the next will be 30.03.3003, if any human beings are left alive to notice.

My little pleasure in the palindrome has already been upended by a feeling of general dischuffment with the establishment. First I found a 'celebratory' Brexit poster on display in the library. I told the librarian that I found it offensive and politely asked for it to be removed. No joy, despite the poster's overtly political triumphalism that surely contravenes prison rules? He (librarian) feebly excused the poster on the grounds that there were 450 other prisoners who had not complained. So that makes it OK does it? I could dance naked on the roof with similar response, but that wouldn't make it acceptable. (Actually I think they would complain, unless they enjoyed a laugh at my expense).

Later, on returning to my room, I was confronted by my Personal (if not Personable) Officer who quite curtly ordered me to take down from my walls all my larger photos and posters apart from the little ones squeezed onto the pin board. The room now looks decidedly bare and unwelcoming. How bizarre that the same or similar pictures have been tolerated, and sometimes approvingly commented on, in all my previous cells/rooms for the best part of two years - until now. Some arcane rule apparently exists and, for reasons best known to themselves, governors/officers have only now dredged it up to enforce. Oh well… only five months to go!

Also, it has been windy and bone-numbingly cold of late, just as we were warned at induction. I've still not succumbed to the thermal long-johns, but that day may soon come. There are two doors into the long corridor in this unit (North), one at each end. Many fellow residents seem to delight in striding through these, leaving them wide open deliberately (it seems) so that icy winds can blast along the corridor from one end to the other. Len and I fight a rear-guard action on this (it's one of the issues that we actually agree on) firmly and loudly slamming the doors shut after other people while they're still near enough to notice. Not that they care. It is a losing battle. Likewise on water waste. Some people turn taps on full to clean their teeth and leave them gushing throughout the operation thus using a bathful of water when a mouthful would suffice. It's ridiculous. There is one particular culprit with whom I've remonstrated more than once, but my complaints completely wash over him, so to speak. Has he never had to pay a water bill? Perhaps he thinks drinking water is free? Bah! There, I've vented my spleen.

The most noteworthy, and thoroughly laudable, happening here since my last letter was Monday's Holocaust Memorial Day event with the title theme 'We All Stand Together'. This has long been an annual fixture in the NSC calendar with talks, readings, music and a writing competition judged by the No 1 Governor herself. In this I won third prize (a handsome box of Fox's chocolate biscuits – it didn't last long) for a letter to an imaginary long-lost gay uncle who perished at Auschwitz. The first two prizes went to well-researched if rather graphic poems by members of the Level 2 English class –

both original and thoroughly deserving of their rankings with barely a contrived metaphor or duff rhyme between them. Some of the music too was really professional, especially our resident choirmaster playing haunting melodies on the saxophone with piano and guitar accompaniment. Our small choir also 'showcased' (I think that's the buzz word) several of our secular pieces to general acclaim, and the whole day was judged to be both moving and uplifting as well as instructive. We reconvened in the visits centre/café for the afternoon session where I read out some pithy poems (as well as my award-winning letter), but the item I shall never forget was an impromptu singing by a Jewish guy (about our age) of a mournful lament his mother had taught him as a child. A real tear-jerker.

Just one little grouse. A huge amount of work must have gone into preparing resources and organising the Holocaust Day events, but most of our residents were unable to attend on the day. Work and education almost always take priority so in practice the only people able to attend and benefit from these events are contributors or retirees, such as myself (on both counts).

I wandered back to the unit after the event chatting to a couple of the other contributors. One seemed very knowledgeable about Yad Vashem, the Jewish Holocaust Museum on the edge of Jerusalem which S and I visited a few years back. I assumed he must have been there. No, he said, and went on to tell me that he has been in prison for all but two years out of 39 since the age of 13. As his mate said, "That's some fucking bird!" He has never in his life seen the sea, ridden a bicycle or been on a train. How lucky I am by comparison to have only a short and fixed-term sentence (not subject to the whims of parole boards), though I do worry about some of the rhetoric we're hearing from our new political masters (and mistresses).

From the chapel (outdoor) notice board:

10.a.m. Gender Re-assignment
BLEST ARE THEY THAT PUT THEIR TRUST
IN THE LORD
I really haven't a clue about what went on at 10 a.m. but hope that

their TRUST was not misplaced! However I can report that the phantom speller has struck again, inside the chapel this time, with a reference to the 'Chaplian' and a reminder for people to attend the 'Prole Board'. There could be a long queue of candidates for that one.

No progress yet on the wretched Oasys. I may be mistaken, but it appears that prison officers here can work 3 x 12 hour shifts over three days which then counts as their full 36 hour working week. This would explain why some of them have so much time off work. They can work six days on the trot, then take a whole week of leave. My OS has not been in since Monday having already been absent for the first half of the month. I don't blame them for working the system to their advantage, but it makes contact time difficult, especially when night shifts are thrown into the equation.

You ask about my reading. By way of homework for the Holocaust Day event I read *The Tattooist of Auschwitz* by Helen Morris, one of those so-called 'Number One Bestsellers'. It's not a work of literature, but a compelling read in its way, though I understand its authenticity has now been questioned. I'm about to start Stephen Fry's *Mythos*, mainly to support S who has chosen it for her ladies' book group and wants ideas for leading the discussion. Have you read it? You'll know that it's not a translation so much as a re-imagining in Fry's inimitable style that I suspect you (M), knowing the myths in the original Greek, would find irritating.

It's quite rare that I get the chance to read books of my own choosing. Partly this is because I don't read as much as I should, and partly because so many kind people assume the opposite and keep on sending me books! Yesterday I had a visit from my distant cousin Andrew who is a Catholic 'perpetual deacon'. He came armed with *The Way of the Sea* (the forgotten history of the Thames Estuary) and *Priests de la Resistance* by Rev. Fergus Butler-Gallie. I'm now reading them in tandem. They make an eccentric pairing, but are all the more enjoyable for that. They will keep me engaged for the month ahead, which rather precludes reading much else, apart from the daily papers, of course. The best books for me are short ones - which both of these are.

55. Monday 2 March, 2020

I am mystified that you never received my last letter, posted into our unit letterbox on 17 February (as you know, I keep a record). I really can't account for it unless it got lost in the post. It could have been embargoed by whatever censorious officer was detailed to read it, but I doubt this was the case as its content was no more libellous, belligerent or obscene than usual. Maybe it was just too long? I've been browsing through the *Prisoners' Handbook,* another sobering tome that is kept in a locked case in the library and available only on request (like the piles of porn allegedly stacked in the tower of Cambridge University Library). I now discover that 'letters of excessive length...' (defined as a modest 4 pp!) '...may not be processed, and not more than two per week.' Cripes. How lucky I've been to get away with 6-pagers, about 560 over the past two years, and counting.

It was good to receive both your letters in quick succession, but not to read of the less than satisfactory throat operation. It must be awful to undergo yet another probing and even the prospect of more of Maggie's egg custards must be little consolation. Our health news is not good either. Father-in-law has barely risen from his bed for ten days or more and spends most of his time asleep. He has all but given up eating anything solid and has stopped taking all his pills as he was having such difficulty swallowing them. The family all fear the end may be near. It's very unlikely that I shall be able to attend the funeral. If only the wretched Oasys and ROTL business had proceeded according to schedule it would have been no problem.

Now to be more cheerful – or not, as the case may be. On Wednesday I shall be having my first outing, but not for a good reason. Healthcare here have finally decided that my longstanding and worsening cough needs proper investigation so I am to have a chest X-ray at the Pilgrim Hospital in Boston. The appointment letter states the reason is "Pneumonia? Lung pathology?" They're hedging their bets, which doesn't sound promising. Anyway, it will be refreshing to get out of here for an hour or two's pilgrimage. What a holy hospital it must be. There's a mural in our dining hall depicting the attempted departure from Boston in 1607 of a band of local Puritans, later celebrated as the Pilgrim Fathers. Like most of our hapless escapees, they were quickly recaptured and briefly imprisoned in the town. They didn't finally make it until 1620 on the Mayflower (from Plymouth). I wonder what they would have made of the religious freedoms we now enjoy? Not much, I suspect. They were all 'Master and Mistress Fundaments'.

In which context, you'll be pleased to hear that I am now officially the C of E Rep on the NSC Faith Forum and attended their monthly meeting last week. The FF acts like a prison version of a PCC (Parochial Church Council) but without the factional in-fighting or the little old ladies in hats knitting in the back row. Instead, we have Reps for many faiths – Hindu and Muslim, dreadlocked Rastafarian, Catholic, Pentecostalist and Pagan, but no Jedi. Jedi-ism is not recognised by HMPS despite aggrieved representations from alleged adherents.

Minutes of the Forum's previous meeting recorded a request to restore the chapel bell (housed in a cage above the entrance). Wonder of wonders, the Elf and Safe Tea Dept have approved the request re. the bell, but not the rope. Haven't we been here before – remember the guitar but no strings conundrum? The chaplain, for whom the bell tolls (so to speak) is all in favour as long as we can find an acceptable alternative method of sounding the thing. The chapel orderly and I have now hit upon a way to clang it with the offending rope removed, 'clang' being a more accurately onomatopoeic verb than 'ring' in this instance. Improvisation involves Henry the Hoover, whose metal extension tube is just long enough to strike the right note if I (or the orderly) stand outside on a chair, though I'd prefer it if H & S don't see. The resulting clang is more than loud enough to be heard across the entire campus. Mission accomplished!

Yet another minor success: I have persuaded a young lady member of staff called Claire (whose oxymoronic title is Head of Equalities) to arrange occasional talks by outside speakers for us oldies. She has provisionally arranged for someone from a mental health charity to come in and, at a later date, a representative from the RSPB who run the Freiston marshes nature reserve adjacent to the prison site. Claire has also undertaken to address that other longstanding issue of inaudible tannoy announcements, e.g. those concerning the 'prole bore' and the 'dying oar'. * *Solutions at end.*

Taking services is of course not part of a Rep's job description, but that is what I was called upon to do on 9th Feb thanks to a 'rushing mighty wind' named Storm Ciara. Did you have any damage? Apart from a lot of tree debris we survived unscathed, but it was pretty hairy at times with intermittent barrages of rain while the wind whistled round the blocks, setting windows and doors clattering like old railway carriages crossing the Barmouth Viaduct. The Rev sent a message around 9.30 to say that the roads across the Fens between Peterborough and here were impassable and would someone please deputise for him. That someone was me, by general acclaim. Luckily the choir had prepared a Lenten anthem, we read the appointed lessons and sang hymns to match, and I led everyone through the earlier sections of the regular service, omitting communion (obviously). It was neither High Church nor Low Church but short church rather than long church, which found favour on all counts. To my surprise everyone stayed and we had 25+ attendees, slightly more than usual. I wonder how many parish clergy welcome such a congregation of murderers, rapists, gangsters and fraudsters and other heinous reprobates? It's quite a privilege! Perhaps I missed my vocation.

Since then we have had Shrove Tuesday (with mass-produced but just recognisable pancakes) and Ash Wednesday, which unfortunately caused a bit of an inter-denominational spat - something of a hot topic, if not a burning issue. At our C of E Ash Wednesday service (including a *Miserere* sung by the choir, though not the famously long and strangulated Allegri version) we were generously 'ashed' on our foreheads by the chaplain, so liberally, in fact, that I began to wonder if he thought we were blacking-up for a minstrel show. Well, by the time he had finished, all the ash had been used up. Much consternation on Friday evening when the RC parish priest from Boston arrived to say Mass with the intention of starting with an 'ashing' in lieu of Wednesday (Ash Friday?). "Where are <u>our</u> ashes?" he demanded. "The Anglicans used them!" he was told. "But they were <u>Catholic</u> ashes, on the <u>Catholic</u> shelf in the vestry!!!" Oh dear. Ecumenism is all very well, but it has its limits.

Until today it has continued stormy here, with bone-chilling blasts sweeping across the fens, and my heavy sheepskin coat has once again come into its own. The sheep, who I regularly encounter on my daily walks, look disconsolate with their fleeces hanging off them in long muddy tresses. They watch me suspiciously, curious to know what breed I might be (like them, I have a Lincs pedigree) and whether I would be up for a tup. I avoid their gaze, not wishing to get their hopes up. The three-legged ewe and the one who hobbles along on her knees have not been around recently, unless they found their way into last week's delicious Lamb Rogan Josh, one of the kitchen lads' more convincing attempts at Indian cuisine. The wretched cough has caused me to curtail my walks and restrict my newspaper reading in the library as it was starting to attract perceptive comments such as "You've got a bad cough there mate." Should I carry a bowl, cover my face with a hood and strike a clapper to warn of my approach?

[Continued Tuesday] A few days ago Corona-virus warning notices suddenly started appearing in all the public areas around the prison site. The wash places and lavatories are now splattered with illustrated instructions, in eight easy stages, on how to wash our hands. Mr Rees-Mogg may think we should sing the National Anthem or *Jerusalem* while so doing to ensure a thorough infection-free clean, though that may not go down well with some of the more anarchic tykes here. Meanwhile clergy have been told to cleanse their hands publicly with anti-bacterial gel (but it's a <u>virus</u>, innit?) before handling communion wafers. Communicants are not to handle the chalice but may either intinct (dip wafer in wine) or 'make a spiritual communion', though unfortunately not with G & T. Isn't this taking it rather too far? Yesterday the Government held a COBRA meeting about the virus threat, but the PM didn't bother to show up. Not sure what that says about Covid or BoJo. Len's response is "Bah! Humbug!"

Last Friday we had a double bill of special events held in the gym. NSC is good at events, though not at publicising them or enabling people to attend. Even participants, if they work or do education courses, need 'movement slips' to authorise attendance. Friday was a SASH (Suicide & Self Harm) event in the morning and 'LGBTQ+ Awareness' in the afternoon. (Both were supportive/therapeutic rather than practical/instructive in purpose!) The entertainment element during both halves included the NSC rock band who were again on top form, and our North Sea Singers performing some of our secular selection – *I'm Walkin'*, *A Twist in the Air*, *Fly me to the Moon*, *Feelin' Good*, and others including (at my suggestion) *The Lincolnshire Poacher*. It seemed appropriate even if I, as the only genuine Yellowbelly, was the only one who knew the tune!

Other activities included mask making, origami and calligraphy, though I didn't actually see anyone doing either. There were some freebies, such as rainbow wristbands and heart-shaped LGBT stickers, booklets of Sudoku puzzles, word searches and patterns (especially rainbows) to colour in. Also we had what the pre-event handbills described as 'REFRESHMEMENTS' and 'TWO GUST SPECKERS'. The first such was Charlene, our current trans resident, from Wales, who talked about her experiences of being born into the wrong gender and growing up as the only trans in the village. The other 'specker' was a lady officer, described by one wit as a 'radico lesbo in denim dungarees' from HMP Lincoln. That prison has an unenviable reputation locally for being a violent rat-infested hellhole, but that aside, we now know it also to be a veritable oasis of gay tolerance, or so she would have us believe. I doubt if anyone will apply for a transfer. (Someone confided in me that he thought she was 'hot' and just needed a good fuck, for which he'd be most happy to oblige. I think he may have missed the whole point of the day.) Our next scheduled drop-in event is to be held on Stephen Lawrence Day, so we'll have to find appropriate songs – any ideas?

Sorry again that you missed my previous missive but I hope this one has given you something to chew on.

* *Solutions: Parole Board and Dining Hall.*

55a. Monday 9 March, 2020

Just a brief note to tell you the sad news that my father-in-law died yesterday, slipping away peacefully in his bed at about 5 a.m. with S at his side. His passing had been anticipated, but it is always a shock when the moment arrives. He had become increasingly frail and took to his bed about two weeks ago, though he made it through to the garden room in his wheelchair last week-end. He was a very special person, a man of many talents and an inspiration to us all. I lit a candle for him in the chapel here and wrote of him in the book of remembrance. R.I.P.

56. Monday 16 March, 2020

Many thanks for your letters and card, and also for sending a condolence card to S. She has decided to stay on at her father's house for the time being with occasional visits home to check on our house and collect mail. S sounds quite positive just now and benefits from shared time with both her sisters. In view of the Corona virus scare and possible restrictions there will be just a small gathering of immediate family for the funeral at the crem. They don't want anyone to travel far and risk importing the virus into the county. Father-in-law would have approved of that - anywhere west of Lynn or south of Diss was mostly *terra incognita* to him! Once all these panics have passed they will organise a memorial service at the parish church (where he was baptised, worshipped all his long life and served as a churchwarden). By then I should be a free man once more!

So, what of this virus that seems to have everyone gripped by fear? (Except the conspiracy theorists who deny its existence, that is, though my room-mate Len is slowly coming round to see sense on that front.) There is much talk about how it could impact on prisons. Should it get a hold, it could quickly infect everyone, however aggressively we wash our hands. I'm not building up any hopes at this stage but one proposal that's been aired is that low risk prisoners of a certain age with existing health conditions ("cough, cough") and only a short time left to serve – e.g. ME !!! – could be released early on licence, perhaps tagged and curfewed. I've read that this is what the French authorities propose, but it may be just too sensible a solution for our obsessively punitive British mentality. Also it would probably be politically unacceptable to Boris and his *Mail*-reading adherents.

Meanwhile, one of the prison houses here has been set aside as an isolation unit where anyone who develops a new cough and a temperature is being sent. The kitchens send food over (left outside like a leper colony?) and no-one is allowed to enter or leave. The rumour-machine put it about that this was really a rather appealing option and at least one guy held his ear against a radiator to boost his temperature. (There's none of that waiting for the mercury to rise here, it's a swift dunk with an ear probe for an instant digital read-out. I've had it done several times recently because of my barking cough.)

That cough, I'm glad to report, is once again on the mend aided this time by a course of Amoxicillin. Will it work where Doxycycline failed? I hope so, even if it notionally exposes me to malaria, though it's too early in the year for pesky mozzies. My chest X-ray at the Pilgrim Hospital revealed nothing nasty other than a possible yeast-related fungal issue now under investigation. What a relief. 'Lung pathology' wasn't an endearing prospect. I almost enjoyed my trip out to Boston in a prison minibus with three other 'chaps' driven by a matey-type officer who raced down the narrow roads into town like a Lewis Hamilton wannabe. Inevitably, this being HMPS, there was a whole sheaf of paperwork to complete, sign and witness in triplicate on the way out. What a malarkey. The papers revealed for the first time the burdensome licence conditions that I'll have to sign up to if/when I eventually get out on ROTL. There are many, but the fruitiest is the following: 'Not to enter the Katmandhu (sic) Fancy Dress Hire Shop or any premises or abode offering massage or other personal services.' This conjures up a vivid mental image of a queue of lecherous lads from NSC kitting themselves out as 'vicars and tarts' for raunchy parties at an 'abode' down the road.

The hospital seemed to be functioning as normal apart from a marquee set up outside for administering Covid tests. Is this standard practice? I guess you're more up to date on hospital procedures. Glad to hear, John, that your throat is on the mend and now passes the toast test so M may soon be able to put away the liquidiser. This calls for a slap-up meal at your favourite hostelry, but you'd better hurry before the government calls time on such celebrations. The same could apply to Mother's Day.

Harry plans to come home for a long weekend, though with new national restrictions introduced almost daily this may be problematic. Currently he's working on a project up in Glasgow staying with his client's family in a rather grand apartment near the city centre. His latest news is that two of his London housemates are self-isolating with coughs and temperatures, so who knows what may happen. His various musical friends have seen their live performances cancelled and his girlfriend's family restaurant has had to shut, though they may still be able to do takeaways. What a pickle, as my Gran would have said.

Last week I had a few solitary days while Len was away on 'home' leave (actually at an 'AP' – Approved Premises, AKA a probation hostel). What a treat, for me at least, though Len found plenty to complain about, mainly the restrictions imposed on him there. I was able to open the window at night, just a crack, and listen to the Today programme in the mornings without headphones. It's not that Len objects to the Today Programme (he doesn't) but rather that I don't want him to assume it would be OK to put on Radio Two, or worse. Now Len is back, I'm subjected to almost constant wittering about nothing of consequence, except that it's mostly about him, of course. Today it's a monologue on his lifelong dry feet problem, yesterday it was a ponderous disquisition on 'cardigans I have owned in the past' (prompted by his purchase of a new one from a market stall while away). He then went on to complain about a prisoner, also called Len, who he'd known in a previous jail and who was always talking about himself. "Len by name, Len by nature?" I proffered. I think he got the point. Anyway, he shut up, for a bit. I <u>very</u> much hope for Len's sake that he is released following his parole hearing next month. I genuinely think that he should be. But I am also troubled that his successor in here could be even less amenable, if my remarkable luck doesn't last. "Keep a tight hold of nurse…" You know the rest.

Thinking of release reminds me that I was recently summoned to meet someone called Ben in Education for a pre-release chat. I know my release day is (unfortunately) not imminent, but with 'only' 20 weeks to go they like to check if there is anything they can help with. We first established that I have no major issues with Maths or English (or do they offer a cryptic crossword solvers

237

course? I quite forgot to ask.) We did discuss, if only to dismiss, the possibility of a rudiments of plumbing course. Ben then asked, "How are you with cooking?" I admitted that, while I can produce a perfectly respectable Christmas dinner, for anything more fancy I have to reach for my Mum's old autographed copy of Fanny Cradock. He was satisfied with that. Ben seemed a reassuringly nice man – shortish, softly spoken, white hair and neatly-trimmed beard, bi-focal glasses – you know the style.

I have also been summoned for the latest round of negotiations over my Oasys assessment – a slightly prickly subject, as you know. This involved a three-way telephone conversation (by speaker-phone) with my OS and OM, the latter being my young female 'outside probation officer' called something like Karly. She has been in the job just long enough to acquire the breezy informality of the species – "Hi Tom! How ya' doin'?" etc. I will probably meet her if I get a home-leave ROTL, though that looks increasingly unlikely and I shall be lucky to get a half day in Boston the way things are looking. I'm less keen now I know that St Botolph's Church, the only place I'm actually interested in visiting, is currently out of bounds to prisoners. So I'll probably end up mooching round the town's many charity and pound shops, which is what most people seem to do. With security clearance I could sign up for voluntary work at the church, but it would probably mean dusting the pews rather than conducting guided tours (or services, with my newly acquired experience).

Since I started writing this, one of the governors has been round with her deputy to outline and explain individually to all residents the latest Covid-related restrictions. They are clearly very anxious. I have not been treated to a personal visit from a governor since the memorable night of the C-Wing stand-off between our near-naked gladiator and the security gang in riot gear. (I never did take up their offer of trauma counselling.) Today the 'Govs' brought the unhappy but not wholly unexpected news that:

1) All visits for everyone over 70, both in and out (ROTLs), are cancelled with immediate effect;
2) We (over-70s) must go to early meal sittings to avoid rubbing shoulders with younger blokes. By implication it doesn't matter

if they get infected. No, they didn't say that.

3) For the present, we may continue freely to take walks outside, visit the library but not the gym, and socialise with each other, but not in large groups.

4) Meetings and gatherings of more than ten persons (e.g. religious services) may be cancelled.

This is a blow, not least because I've been looking forward to a visit by S and Harry on Saturday, which is now off. The way things are heading, I may not see either of them again until my release in July. That event is a fixture! What a shame they can't kick me out a bit sooner. There has never been the least hint of any sort of 'rehabilitation' during my 2+ years of imprisonment, so it's hard to see what a few more weeks of doing nothing will achieve, apart from costing the taxpayer (thank you!) yet more money. They could send me on a world cruise for less. It would keep me well out of the way of Covid, and I'd get a suntan.

All in all, it's a pretty gloomy prospect, compounded by Len's generally 'glass half full' approach to life. But even he is not half as stricken as the poor bloke in the room opposite who wears a permanent mask of abject misery. Even the officers tell him to cheer up. At least his room is on the sunny side. Talking of which, this week's warm weather has provided a little lift to my spirits and I have read the final chapters of *Death in the East* (thanks for recommendation – great pace and style) sitting on a bench in the sun. I'm now reading a self-help book called *Kindness – Change your life and make the world a kinder place*. Hope to pick up a few tips for life after prison!

57. Tuesday 31 March, 2020

What an uncertain world we are now living in, changed even since my last letter, or Maggie's of 19th. Increasingly draconian restrictions are imposed on us here since a 'national lockdown' was declared last week. We are now being almost totally confined to our rooms apart from just one meal a day taken in the dining hall and a daily hour of supervised exercise on the field (voluntary but essential for my sanity). This is taken unit by unit to minimise social contact between residents, though as staff continue to come and go between here and the local community we are not in isolation, splendid or otherwise. For our one hot meal at lunchtime we must queue up with our trays 6 ft apart (the floor has been marked at intervals with masking tape), then sit to eat diagonally opposite each other (i.e. two per four-seat table) a mere 18 ins apart, knees all but knocking. Consistency isn't one of HM Prison's Service's greatest strengths. As we enter the dining hall we are handed a sandwich supper (+ fruit, yoghurt and biscuit) and packed breakfast (cereal, milk) in what is known in prison parlance as a 'grab bag'.

Meanwhile, umpteen times a day, a newly-recruited platoon of prisoner cleaners swab down the loos and wash places, showers etc. Every so often, while holed up in our rooms, we hear the door rattle as a man in a wheelchair patrols the corridor, wiping handles with an anti-bacterial spray that smells like sweaty socks. Before using the telephones we are told to spray and wipe them. We must do this so 'sedulously' (Boris Johnson's current favourite word) that at least one 'phone has already become so gummed up inside that certain buttons have stopped working. As if to torment me, this currently includes button number 3 – not helpful when trying to contact S at her father's house which has FIVE 3s in its number. I guess I shall be returning to the unavoidable Covid topic in future letters. The misery-guts in the press say it will get worse before it gets better, if it ever does. "We're doomed", as Private Frazer would have observed. For now, the pandemic still has a certain novelty value as the biggest crisis we post-war 'boomers' have experienced (if you exclude Suez, the Cuban missile crisis, the miner's strike, 'winter of discontent', Irish 'troubles', Falklands War, Iraq invasion and all other tiddly emergencies and exigencies too).

News from the home front: Father-in-law's funeral at the crematorium was indeed a small affair attended only by the three daughters, vicar and undertaker. It was 'live streamed' on the Internet for other family members from further afield to watch in 'real time' (what other sort is there?) – a novel idea, but effective. Except that some gremlin got into the works and the first ten minutes were not broadcast. The chaplain here said I could watch on his office computer, but unfortunately that didn't happen for reasons of timing and technology. Still, it was a kind offer. S has sent me the printed order of service with colour photos of her Dad at different times of his life, including in the RAF during the war, plus a fulsome obituary from the Eastern Daily Press. In the circumstances, he had a good send-off. He was a man of wisdom throughout his life and had the good sense to depart it when he did, in the nick of time you might say. S's aunt, who is 94 and now in a care home, was understandably upset to be forbidden to attend the funeral on account of Covid and her own fragility. S had planned to take her to the Cathedral in her wheelchair last Sunday, but all church services have now been cancelled – the first time this has happened since the Interdict under King John, 800 years ago. What strange times we are living through.

All religious observances have stopped here too – just as I had learned how to clang the bell (not that it brought in any additional worshippers, but I guess church bell-ringers are used to that!) Instead the Rev has been handing out copies of Psalm 46 for our edification ('God is our refuge and strength, a very help in trouble.') Has it come to this? The poor man has been re-assigned to general governor duties (as managing-chaplain he's a proto-governor, though that's not a recognised title) and this week he has been sent to HMP Lincoln. Maybe he'll meet the 'gust specker' from our LGBTQ+ event? Never one to miss an opportunity for evangelism, last week he also distributed Bible Study Notes to those of his flock whom he recognised in the dining hall. He and another governor were assigned to lunchtime supervision duties, mainly to check that we were all following 'social distancing' guidelines for which 'Wherever two or three are gathered together, they shall be dispersed' might be a better text. To his great credit, the Rev is the only one of our governors to make himself accessible to prisoners on a regular basis. The others are a somewhat invisible entity, very busy no doubt, but office-bound in areas that are out of bounds to normal mortals. The present emergency is smoking them out into the open where, just occasionally, they may be seen engaging in reluctant deliberations with prisoners. Someone asked what the collective noun is for prison governors. The obvious answer, given HMPS's uneasy relationship with spelling, is a Bored of Governors.

On a related topic, you may remember that a governor and her side-kick came round to visit all us aged and infirm inmates in our rooms. As I suspected would be the case, their initial solicitude barely lasted into the second week despite assurances that they would visit daily. That was before our lock-down (partial), so I guess it is no longer deemed necessary, if it ever was. We have not seen them since. What we have received instead is a 100-question *Have FUN trying this QUIZ*! quiz. It was the best quiz ever as, between us, Len and I managed to answer almost all the questions. These catered for all interests, even Geography (e.g. 'What is the only country to share a border with Portugal?'), Music ('Who composed the Marriage of Figaro?'), Religion ('What is the name of the Muslims' Holy Book?') and – a tricky one for non-mathematicians - 'What is the square root of 100?' Altogether a far more reassuring general knowledge quiz than those in the weekend broadsheet newspapers, apart from the one in the *Sun* that Len and I complete together.

The authorities are obviously trying to ensure that none of us succumbs to brain death despite the potential for stultifying boredom during current restrictions. Even I was surprised to receive today (as did everyone else, I think) a large white envelope containing course materials and exam papers (of sorts) for Gateway Level 1 qualifications in Time Management, Alcohol Awareness and 'Introduction to Mental Health'. Len immediately binned his with a great snort of derision. Sensing conspiracies at every twist and turn of events, he is convinced that these papers are a not very subtle way of the prison eliciting personal information that they can later use against us. I am too wet behind the ears to recognise their malicious little ways, he says! I have checked and, in truth, none of the questions relate to our own experiences with the sole exception of Time Management which asks us to identify a situation from our own past experience when we did not manage our time effectively. (Most of it, I would say. Ask my wife.)

Overall I begin to feel like an extra in a blockbuster disaster movie where the director has lost the plot and no one can guess how the story will end. Prisoners don't get much mention in the media apart from a proposal that those nearing the ends of their sentences could be released early on licence. One man on this corridor has already packed his bags and alerted his family of his imminent return. He, however, is a Jehovah's Witness so may have 'form' as far as unfulfilled promises are concerned. He borrowed a King James Bible from me in order to 'check some numbers' (as he said) on the basis of which he confidently computes that all the signs are now in place for the world to end in 2020, quite probably before the summer. Call me a sceptic if you wish, but I'm a tad dubious of his reasoning and fully expect to be here at least until 10 July, come what may. Beyond then – who knows? I begin to wonder just what sort of world I shall return to. S tells me of local supermarket shelves stripped of toilet tissue and pasta, two-hour queues for the pharmacy (dutifully spaced at 2m/6ft intervals), garden centres closed and dumping their bedding plants. Even her 'occasional lady gardener' has declared our street too dangerous to enter. By comparison, life here seems quite cushy.

Our field exercise hour today was glorious with warm sunshine and melodious birdsong (larks ascending, etc.) After walking a couple of circuits with Jack – 70, ex-teacher, cultured but rather deaf, now something of a soul mate – we took a great health risk and sat at opposite ends of the same bench. I ought really to have sat on the next one, but would have had to bellow towards Jack's good ear, not a good look for either of us. Officers delight in telling us to sit at least 6ft apart, but today three of them were seated on the same bench, so they wouldn't have had a leg to stand on, nor a bench to sit on, had they done so. Len, as is his way, did not venture out but stayed gloomily in our sunless room with the light on and window tight shut. He looked utterly woebegone when I returned, an event that did little to lift his spirits. My own spirits are much lifted now that my cough has all but gone.

58. Easter Monday 13 April, 2020

And a happy Easter to you too! Your letters both arrived in record time – more than can be said of mine to you. Is it Royal Mail or HMP/NSC? I suspect the latter as confusion and procrastination are rife here just now. The normal shortage of staff is exacerbated by Covid-led changes to rotas and patterns of working with some staff having to take on extra duties. We are still confined to barracks apart from just one outdoor hour, a time to cherish during the recent warm weather when even our chilly North Sea blasts have been held in check. Confinement is so tiresome that every opportunity to get out of the room is welcome, even if it's only to go to the loo. What in normal circumstances is a necessary nuisance of bodily function becomes an eagerly-awaited minor pleasure – and an incentive to drink far more cups of tea or glasses of water than is strictly necessary. However, we are not to worry about the potential for catching the virus from cell-mates as the MoJ has declared that each sharing pair of prisoners constitutes a separate 'household'. So it's OK then.

Some mystery attached at first to the shrinkage of our exercise area from the entire 'park' to a roped-off area at the further end of the field. Nobody tells us anything until it happens (usual prison story). All became clear this time last week when a procession of lorries started to arrive bearing individual single-room accommodation units that were craned down onto concrete blocks at the nearer end of the field. So now one mystery has been succeeded by another – who are the intended occupants of these blue and white bijou units? No one seems to know or is willing to say, so speculation is rife. Ask an officer and the stock response is, "Dunno, mate. Nobody tells us anything." One theory is that our smaller existing double rooms (a mere 7ft x 9ft) will become single occupancy (to allow for social distancing, as we must oxymoronically now call it) with the displaced persons moved out to these new units, all self-contained with integral WC and shower. As I write, they are being lined up in neat rows on the field like so many portaloos at a country show. There is provision for 48 of them. I attach a sketch. (Who would guess that I once wanted to be an architect before deciding on a career in law? Ha - what a tale of unfulfilled ambition on both counts!)

The other theory doing the rounds is that the new units will house prisoners from here, HMP Lincoln and elsewhere who develop Covid symptoms and need isolating. I very much hope that I won't fall into either category. Being shut in such a confined space would be a cruel parody of 'seg' or 'solitary'. I can imagine that life isn't much fun for you, either, notwithstanding your anecdote about walks and 'that bra'. Maybe you could convert it into a pair of facemasks to impress your friends and neighbours along the road? I can't offer any tips having, as you'll remember, exercised my prerogative as a retired gent of a certain age to opt out of work in prison 'textiles'.

Talking of work, you will have read of the philistine decision by our lamentable government to sanction Reading Gaol's conversion into flats rather than preserved as a museum and arts centre as the local council hoped. Oscar Wilde, the celebrated former occupant of Cell 3.3, probably didn't get the chance to learn tailoring as he was kept in solitary when not working out his 'hard labour' on the tread wheel. Our most famous NSC alumnus and noble writer, JA, had quite a cushy job while he was here, record-keeping in the Healthcare office. There is no blue plaque on the wall and his only (unacknowledged) memorial is the fence put up to stop press photographers poking their cameras through the windows to snap him at work. The closest NSC residents get to hard labour is making lobster pots, which is pretty tough on the hands (as well as the lobsters). But not any more. All work has now ceased apart from cleaning, kitchen work and animal husbandry on the farm. Even the gardeners have been laid off 'for the duration' so I guess they'll have to buy in all the fruit and veg they used to grow on site.

Of course I'm astounded to learn that you have finally succumbed to getting a TV licence, if not (yet) an aerial and actual set. It may be a good companion during these lonely and restrictive times. You probably already watch *Have I Got News For You*, though it's a strangely discombobulated show with the panel 'live-streaming' from their own homes, left to laugh at their own jokes in the absence of a studio audience. You may also enjoy the repeats of *Outnumbered* on Saturday evenings. Poor Len has obligingly agreed to watch these programmes with me, but he does so with incomprehension bordering on stupefaction. He doesn't do humour. His only comment about *Outnumbered* was, "That kid needs a psychiatrist."

What a strange Easter this has been for me with no religious services to attend and none of the rich repertoire of Holy Week music to sing. Our choir had just started learning Lenten anthems (a covert operation behind locked doors as we weren't really supposed to gather in the chapel) when services were embargoed. Regarding services, all was not lost as the Rev distributed advance copies of his would-have-been Easter sermon. I know it was kindly meant, but I must admit that in places it didn't make a lot of sense to me. Even the anecdotes lost their punch without his inimitably engaging delivery. Then, on Easter Sunday morning, the young lady chaplain from the Salvation Army personally visited every regular chapel attendee and greeted us with "Christ is Risen!" (Response, "He is risen indeed!" – though in what sense 'risen' may be a matter of continuing theological debate.) She had also brought copies of a special 'lockdown' version of an Easter hymn. Sung to the tune of *The Church's One Foundation*, it goes:

"This Easter celebration is not like ones we've known.
We pray in isolation, we sing the hymns alone.
We're distant from our neighbours – from worship leaders too.
No flowers grace the chancel to set a festive mood."

"Why don't we sing it?" I suggested. She hadn't anticipated that, but agreed, and we stood together at the end of our corridor and slightly sheepishly sang the first two verses, she on the tune, me on the bass line, or as much of it as I could recall. At this point we stopped, but several doors opened, heads appeared and asked us to carry on – so we did. I don't know if it was our singing they enjoyed, or just the spectacle of us making fools of ourselves, but we serenaded them with the remaining three verses and gained a round of applause at the end.

That may have been the sum of my active Eastertide musical engagement, but I have not been totally deprived. A benefit of our let's-pretend-we're-in-lockdown rule is that I have been listening to much more music on the radio. With headphones for Len's sake – he doesn't 'do' religion either – I had a bacchanalia of Bach on Good Friday with the St John Passion in the afternoon and St Matthew in the evening, using my Bible in lieu of a programme to follow the text . While writing this I have the B-minor Mass on in the background. On the TV (screen angled away from Len's end of the room) I watched *Easter from King's*, then Archbishop Justin's 'kitchen communion' (unfairly mocked in the press, I thought) followed by the Pope's *Urbi et Orbi* address and blessing from the grander setting of St Peter's Basilica in Rome. This even came with a free plenary indulgence, no awkward questions asked. Fr Tetzel, that notoriously avaricious indulgence salesman, would surely have balked at such benevolence.

Here we continue to be exhorted to follow guidelines on everything from 'distancing' to singing the National Anthem while washing hands. The staff have clamped down on over-enthusiastic squirting of the telephones by attaching the anti-bacterial spray bottles to the opposite wall with cable ties and providing J-cloths for wiping. All three 'phones are currently operational. A tall free-standing pop-up panel has now been placed near the 'phone queue with further gratuitous guidance. Quote: "We can take our time when we wash our hands, ensuring that you wash between fingers and all over your hands." Is this just inept use of English, or does it betray a certain lack of joined-up thinking? I especially relish the final sentence: "Just like other types of flu the cornavirus (sic) will go away." I never knew it affected the feet.

Len is engaged on a complex piece of parquetry which keeps him occupied and more or less sweet. (Also, I laid a Cadbury's Easter egg on his shelf for him to find when he woke on Easter Day.) However, as he was reading April's *Inside Time* last week he suddenly snorted in derision. "What's up?" I asked. "Bloody Tory Government," he exploded with a volley of contemptuous spit, "Now they're planning to re-introduce slopping out [use of in-cell bucket rather than WC] and the minister says it's character building." I asked him to show me the article. It reads as follows:

'... Darcy Brassneck MP, the newly appointed Minister of Sanitation, told the media that due to coronavirus the supplies of porcelain are drying up – meaning that damaged toilets and sinks in prison cells cannot be replaced... Rancid Foulstench, the governor in charge of purposeless activity at HMP Laydown, was unimpressed however. "This initiative stinks," he said. "All my efforts to ensure that prisoners have nothing to do will be flushed down the pan." Prisoners in eight trial prisons will be issued with waste pots made from reinforced cardboard, which they will empty into communal sinks whilst singing the first two verses of the National Anthem...'

When I pointed out the date of the article (1ˢᵗ April) to Len, he still failed to see the joke and just responded rather grumpily that it was "just what the Tories would do!"

Not sure what the authorities have up their sleeves but currently we are being deluged with 'freebies' like kids' treats for the cinema – bags of popcorn, hand-cut crisps, Kit-Kat biscuits, bottles of flavoured water with a nasty taste that lingers like herpes, plus extra loo rolls, Ice-Blue antiperspirant (gives me a rash), vegan-friendly body wash, buttermilk soap, 'Sejem' toothpaste and extra moulting-bristle toothbrushes marked HMPS. The concept of waste has little traction in HMPS just now.

Noted your observation about people telling each other to 'stay safe' or 'take care' – as if they'd deliberately run out in front of a bus. The jury is out on whether in the current Emergency we are safer cooped up here or back home. My money is on home.

59. Monday 27 April, 2020

Despite press reports to the contrary, the postal service may be getting a boost from our present predicament, at least between Nottingham and Boston. But do people use their extra stay-at-home time to write long letters, or are they too busy 'Zooming' or video-gaming? Of course I have yet to experience Zoom or indeed any form of online conferencing. Something to look forward to after 10 July. S has tried Zoom but fell foul of the installation instructions and awaits a call from Harry to talk her through the process.

Now for the bad news. The MoJ reports that the virus has now spread to 60 out of 117 prisons nationally. Locally, according to Prof. Tim Spector (*S. Times* p.9) Boston is currently one of seven UK virus hot spots, so please wash your hands thoroughly for ten minutes after reading this letter, then dispose of it responsibly. Or rather, not, if you are keeping my letters. The news of Boston's infection levels is at variance with the official prison line, which is that 'there is very little Covid in the local community so we have nothing to fear.' I'm unsure which report to believe, not least because the prison service may have an interest in talking down the statistics as most of our officers continue to come and go freely between the town and here on a daily basis. So you saw a press report about North Sea Camp's super-preparedness? Sorry I missed that, though it sounds just a teensy bit exaggerated, optimistic or premature, or all three, take your pick. Currently anyone here who develops symptoms is quarantined for two weeks in the Jubilee Houses (just outside the main campus). Those who feigned symptoms hoping for a cushy life have come to regret it. Their symptoms – croaky cough, sore throat, loss of smell and taste - magically vanished even faster than they had appeared, but they were still obliged to sit it out for the full fortnight. It is rumoured to be no fun at all over there – reputedly even worse than 'Life with Len' and his phalanx of fellow misery-guts.

Predictably bad news too on the early release proposal. The French have already released some 10,000 prisoners early out of a total prison population of 72,000, the Italians have let 6,000 go and Turkey plan to let out 90,000, a third of their entire prison population. Here in Britain the MoJ have let out… just 37 out of 87,000 – that's about 0.04%

Meanwhile, back at the Camp, residents identified as being at risk of Covid have, in typically prison-style voluntary-compulsory manner, been sent letters 'encouraging' them to move to Llewellyn block where they will not be allowed out at all, but will be 'shielded'. (What a lot of new Covid vocab we are learning!) Len, at age 81, falls into the most risky category and also suffers 'underlying conditions', something that he acknowledges only when it is to his benefit to do so. But not now. With his habitual cussedness he has refused to move, but been directed to sign a document absolving the prison authorities from any responsibility should he fall ill as a consequence. Despite being 'old' myself – 70 is the age at which UK prisoners officially become old for this purpose – I have so far been left alone, or abandoned to take my chances with the potential ravages of the virus. I too have a cussed streak and, like Len, have no wish to live out on the field.

We now have the full complement of 48 pods out there, lined up in four rows of twelve, all plumbed and wired-in conveniently close (for the aged and infirm) to the Healthcare building. They are known as BUNKABINS, which sounds better stressed as a dactyl (**bunk-**a-bins) than an anapaest (bunk-a-**bins**). The comparison with Portaloos (another dactyl) is unavoidable as they share the same slate grey and sky blue livery. They are classed as a 'junior deluxe sleeper cabin' and measure 2.9m x 3.4 m overall. Apart from Len and a few other malcontents it's still unclear whom these things are intended for, but the rumour machine is on steroids. My initial response was that, if compelled to move, I would join the Resistance. But I am slowly coming round to the idea of moving, especially if I can get one on the sunny side facing the field and farm. They are still shiny new and (it's said) well appointed with WC, integral shower and heated towel rail. Also, they were designed and equipped with construction workers in mind so may have softer mattresses than prison beds (they could hardly be harder!) and expansive boards for racy pin-ups.

Anyway, our new suburb of BUNKABINS has been christened Selby, which I like because it's where my Yorkshire forebears came from. In fact, the name is that of a former governor, as are the existing Llewellyn and Harrison blocks (but not, I think, North and South, which would be an extraordinary coincidence of geographical nomenclature). Are you wondering why they are not named after the current Governor and Deputy? That would be Quirke and Loveley. 'Nuff said! Word is that the Selby units are merely temporary – but they said that about Llewellyn and Harrison fifty years ago, and they're still here.

I'm sorry to learn that you are having such difficulties with provisioning. Maybe you will have to resort to online orders and home deliveries after all. S tells me that our two nearest local supermarkets still offer a relatively well-stocked shopping experience despite controlled numbers on entry and obligatory wearing of facemasks like bank raiders. Nor do we suffer any shortage of toilet rolls here. *Au contraire* - one of the officers brings round a weekly supply which I declined last week saying that I could only use so many of them. The poor woman looked quite cross, as if offended at my rejection of her largesse, and rather sniffily said, "Well most people use them for other purposes." I didn't ask her to elaborate. I can only take so much gratuitous information. In this time of need, HMPS seems to have become immensely profligate. This is especially so with plastics - mini-bottles of juice, sugar-free flavoured water, finger-size tubes of Nescafe, little packs of biscuits, cheap crisps as salty as Lot's wife, soup powder, curry-flavoured noodles... and so forth, all doled out in single-use plastic bags like the ones that fly round the alleys of African shanty towns. Enough to send David Attenborough to his grave. I don't think most people (residents or staff) even notice, let alone care. If I had a hobby horse, I'd be riding it.

Your Thursday evening 'clapathons' sound entertaining and I'm glad Maggie has dug out her triangle for a discreet tinkle behind the hedge. We have an evening 8 p.m. roll-call (to check if anyone has legged it – which one energetic reprobate did last week) and, on the spur of the moment, decided to applaud the officer on her rounds. I'm afraid she looked confused, then embarrassed, as well she might, no doubt suspecting we were taking the proverbial. Under the heading 'News of the Screws' (also the nickname of a now-defunct redtop paper), the current *Private Eye* reports that prison officers are being paid a coronavirus bonus of £500 per month on top of paid overtime, plus an additional £1750 bonus if they agree to stay the course for a full twelve weeks. One of our screws unwisely told prisoners that he expects to earn so much extra money this year that he plans to take the whole of next year off. I hope nurses and care sector workers don't read the *Eye* (no, they're too busy wiping bums and mopping sick).

One of the casualties of The Frightening Present, let alone the future, is hair cutting. It's too intimate. I've not had mine trimmed since Christmas and was about to do so again when restrictions came in last month. The effect is of a thick and bushy white mop-head up top, reminiscent of late Georgian ladies' fashions. I'm reminded of the pregnant Lady Coke of Holkham who awoke one morning to find a mouse had nested in her hair overnight, which discovery gave her such a fright that she miscarried and tragically lost a future Earl. Here on North we have a qualified barber, whose cheery services I have used in the past, but is now banned from practising. He has qualifications but no scissors, unlike the dolorous 'official' prison barber who has scissors but no qualifications. He tells his victims that he is thinking of taking it up after release, but it may not get beyond a thought process. I could of course use my battery-powered beard trimmer to give myself a Number One trim all over, but then I would look like a prisoner (in the popular imagination if not reality), not a good look so close to my release date.

Further casualties of The Emergency are the library, now closed, and group gatherings such as creative writing, music appreciation, religion and football. The library reading group continues to read, however, and I am now well into *The Beekeeper of Aleppo*, a heartrending but ultimately life-affirming tale. Instead of meeting face to face we are to write and exchange reviews. The creative writers are also exchanging stories (working title: *After the Lockdown*) with an ingenious scheme of collaborative writing of stories in three parts (max 2pp of A4 each section). I have so far written a farcical opening section of one, and pity the poor bloke who will have to continue it. I enjoyed writing the middle section of another story too. What arrived was a touching tale of an elderly couple, she with dementia, he her carer trying to cope despite Covid restrictions. Rather naughtily, I completely turned the story round to reveal that he is the one with dementia and she is his carer from an agency. I wonder how writer 3 will end it.

My name may now be mud in the Officers' Mess (yes, it really is called that). Last Friday I was ambling along the corridor when a couple of officers, m & f, came up behind me chatting loudly. *A propos* of nothing in particular she was spouting forth a torrent of obscenities. I turned round to see who this foul-mouthed woman was when she caught my eye and said, "I hope you don't mind my language." Without thinking through the consequences I retorted, "Yes, I do mind. You're a public servant, as I was in local government. If I'd spoken like that in the hearing of clients it would have been a disciplinary matter. I'm surprised the same standards don't apply in the Prison Service." Her companion appeared open-mouthed with shock at my audacity and arrogance; she flushed red and apologised. Good sense got the better of pomposity and I stopped myself saying "Don't do it again!" – still, I must be getting demob happy.

North Unit are on the early shift for exercise this week, which is a drag, especially as the warm sunshine of the past few days has been replaced by haze with a saline tang, a reminder that the Wash is only 300 yds or so beyond the field. We've had almost no rain all month and in places the grass is become hard and cracked like the Serengeti savannah at the end of the dry season. Despite the drought, I've never known a spring to have sprung so suddenly. Perhaps it's just that I've had the time to observe the same line of trees day by day. I've got my Tree ID Guide out again and also the Sunday Times 'trill of a lifetime' guide to birdsong. I'm not having much success, or maybe the birds are mocking me.

Enjoy your walks and garden – there ain't much else to do!

60. Monday 11 May, 2020

Thanks for yours, as entertaining as ever, and for the beautiful birthday card of Zanzibar with dhow and ngalawa set in an emerald sea. It brought back many happy memories. My birthday was a subdued affair, as you may imagine. I still have a line of ten cards along the back of the desk including one from 'The Chaplaincy Team'. Funny how almost every organisation now forms 'teams' as if they were competing in sports championships. The Chaplaincy deliver birthday cards to all prisoners here, regardless of religious persuasion, but only with permission. The Salvation Army lady has taken on this responsibility, taps timidly on the doors and says, "I hear you have a special day – would you be willing to accept a card from the Chaplaincy?" I wonder if she ever gets rebuffed? (Even Len has kind words for her.) Yours is my only card this year to feature boats, which usually predominate, enough over the years to fill a sizeable marina with yachts. Flowers are 'in' this year, plus one showing a frothing pint of beer – another forbidden pleasure.

I look forward to your updates on the Thursday 'street claps' for the NHS, and your ever more imaginative choice of noise-making utensils. For a couple of weeks we applauded the officers (or 'gave them the clap' as some wag said) during our Thursday evening roll-checks, but this has now subsided into a slightly awkward and sheepish silence. Whether the knowledge that they are 'minting it' in extra pay and £500 bonuses has dampened our enthusiasm I cannot say (but unlikely). However on 30 April we held a 'clapathon' for our new national hero, Capt. Tom (now elevated to Hon-Col. Tom), standing to attention outside our doors to give him a hundred claps on his birthday. To exercise my ailing brain cells I mentally counted in Swahili but only got as far as 79 having forgotten the Swahili for eighty. I don't suppose Capt. Tom would mind shedding 21 years. There was a huge card in the dining hall for us to sign and also a sheet to donate to his fund (deducted from 'spends' account).

Back to my own more modest birthday. Len presented me with a small coaster made entirely from used lollipop sticks arranged endways in an ingenious cross-hatch pattern (he has been gathering them up on ice-lolly days in the dining hall). He really is a meticulous and imaginative craftsman. I had ordered a fruit cake on 'canteen' to share with him (a fruit cake for a 'fruitcake') but it failed to arrive. Shortages are increasingly common and the list of available items has shrunk from 5 pages to 3 ½, with some of these now rationed, e.g. only 4 extra-creamy yoghurts per week, which may be better for my waistline than the 8 I used to order. (They are excellent comfort food, I find.) Butter, cheese, salami and other chilled items disappeared several weeks ago so there are fewer and fewer treats available, especially as I don't care for the flavoured water and extra crisps in our free daily goody-bags. (I've just noticed that regular prison-issue crisps say on the packet 'Made since 1945'. That may explain their stale taste.)

Meanwhile Len and I (and most other residents too) tune in day by day to the teatime Covid briefings from No. 10. What a poker-faced crew our politicians have now become, like tin pot dictators surrounding themselves with flags as they announce the latest 'R' number to justify the next round of restrictions. The lugubrious Matt Hancock is the worst, with his grating voice and wry smile as if he has something up his sleeve that he's not telling us. The whole charade reminds me of those school assemblies when the entire school was punished for some minor misdemeanour by a few. But we must look on the bright side of life – the sun still shines, 'R' is back below one, and as yet we have no Covid cases here, just a lot of disgruntled convicts pissed-off at all the additional curbs on our already limited liberties.

All 48 BUNKABIN 'pods' on the field are now occupied, though not by me, and it is rumoured that a further 24 are on order. (Good to know someone is doing well out of The Emergency!) The criteria for selection remain as elusive as ever but, contrary to expectations, isolating the aged, infirm or vulnerable is not high up the list of priorities. Let us perish! The Rev tells me that the pods may remain on site until next year by when new permanent accommodation blocks should be built to house everyone in single rooms. A frequently-heard gripe by prisoners who have been sent here from C-Cat establishments is that it is a backwards step for them to return to shared cells, single-occupancy being the norm in C-Cat prisons. The opposite was true for me, coming from a B-Cat Local where sharing was standard practice and only 'risky' or 'at risk' individuals enjoyed the luxury of single occupancy. With 48 more beds now available here, at least one of the existing blocks has become all-single rooms, a welcome improvement.

We are told that the NSC 'pods' are officially known as 'Nightingale Units', as reported in the national press (a rare good news story from here – the press are usually only interested in absconders, invariably described as 'dangerous' *). It seems odd to name the new units after a bird or a nurse – surely 'Howard' or 'Fry' would have been more suitable? Or maybe not, lest they become associated with Michael Howard or Stephen Fry.

For the record, there were just 4 absconders from NSC in 2018, 2 in 2019 and 4 in 2021. These numbers are well down on a decade ago – the record was set in 2006 when there were 49 absconders! Almost all are caught and returned within a day or two only to be sent back to the far more restrictive regime of a closed prison. According to the press, police and prison authorities invariably describe our absconders as 'dangerous' despite the fact that D-Cat open prisons are intended only for people judged not (or no longer) to be dangerous. So which is it?

BUT… there has to be a 'but' … Transfer to the new units does not guarantee hours of fresh air, fun and frolics out on the field. Though not physically locked in, occupants are obliged to remain within their own unit at all times except for a statutory hour's exercise period. They may sit just inside their own open doorways, but are banned from speaking to their new neighbours. I don't know if they were allowed a 'Capt. Tom Clapathon'. It is rumoured that certain pod-residents (peas or podcasters?) have been caught escaping to enjoy secret trysts on the farm under cover of darkness and have accordingly been IEP-ed (see previous letters, passim, as *Private Eye* might say). The only permissible reason to leave their pods is – wait for it – to have a smoke! As smoking (real fags or roll-ups) is still allowed at NSC, though not indoors, smokers alone now have the privilege of being allowed to go outside (max six at a time) to designated smoking zones. This is a cause of some resentment to those of us trapped indoors while little knots of sociable smokers gather outside, chatting and puffing on their limp ciggies with ash on their shit-brown fingers and haloes of white smoke hanging round their heads. Smoking has suddenly become a very desirable pastime.

I continue to plod my daily rounds of the field here, usually clocking up nine circuits or so in our permitted hour, about two miles. Last Saturday was Mediterranean hot and many of us gave our shorts an airing and went bare-chested on the field. But not elsewhere on site, where anything even slightly *déshabillé* is classified as 'indecent' and therefore a 'nickable' offence. Today the North Sea designation predominates. There's a bitter nor'-easterly blowing sheets of rain and salty spume across the marshes so I've had to dig out the old sheepskin coat from under my bed. The sheep are truly bedraggled, especially the local long-wool breed who give an ovine impression of 'pulling the wool over the eyes'. They must be due for shearing soon, but not on a cold day like today I hope.

To give me a further break from my room (and room-mate!) the chaplain has very kindly allowed me into the chapel, otherwise out of bounds and locked. I have spent a happy hour or so on the keyboard playing hymns and songs (from my 1930s *News Chronicle Song Book* that S brought in for me on a visit). The instrument has a selection of passable organ sounds, or I can choose piano – concert or honky-tonk - calypso, jazz or other effects. My playing isn't up to any sort of public airing, but it keeps me amused.

Harry thoughtfully enclosed six books of stamps in a letter last week, maybe as a hint that I hadn't been writing frequently enough. In the event, only a dozen stamps were delivered along with a note saying (all in capitals, which I will spare you): 'Please note only a max of 12 stamps to be sent in at a time othe (sic) 5 books sent to reception.' This is quite bizarre. Without any hindrance or restriction, S has sent me a similar number of stamps every couple of months since I first landed in prison. The sequel to this came a couple of days later when I was tannoyed to go to Reception (an experience that always gives me the willies!) The duty officer there seemed as puzzled as I was. He couldn't see any point in retaining the remainder of the stamps, he said, and handed them all over, but asked me not to mention it to the wing officers. (I've kept my counsel, until now. The NSC 'Welcome' booklet says we may receive 'a few', defined in my dictionary as 'not many but more than one'. Perhaps 36 truly was a trifle excessive.)

61. Monday 25 May, 2020

Thanks for your letters and cuttings, especially the tongue in cheek VE Day retrospective from *The Times*. I had missed it, the library now being closed, and I can only afford the 'i' newspaper from my prison non-earnings. The librarian, however, is still very much active and runs an efficient book loan system delivering requests to the different units within a couple of days. He also operates a CD and DVD loan service, something that was never available at my previous establishment. I begin to understand why some of my former fellow prisoners groused about the restrictive regime there and described it as the worst prison they'd experienced. I'm not entirely convinced. At least we didn't have rats – well, not many, and only in the food servery area, so I suppose that was OK really.

Len has been very subdued and uncomplaining these past few days. I think he must be practising his best behaviour ahead of his parole board hearing before a judge next week. This could determine whether he gets released (after 17 years inside) or spends even longer in prison which, given his age, could become a life sentence. I really hope it all goes well for him. Keeping him inside would be both cruel and pointless. Len is also quiet because he's absorbed in making himself a pencil box. It is now almost finished and is truly a thing of beauty, inlaid with his initials and a swirly geometrical pattern in different coloured wood inlays. The box itself is made out of headless matches carefully laid and bonded together with

PVA glue. He has a special matchstick cutter shaped like miniature hippo's jaws and he works with great precision using homemade setsquares, etc. He is (we are) very fortunate to have one of the few larger-sized rooms, big enough for us both to have our own desks and chairs (and lamps!). It would be all but impossible for Len to work (or me to write) perched on the edge of a bed, as most residents have to.

Our creative writing group's collaborative stories are at last finished, or most of them, but not yet circulated. I am on tenterhooks to discover how my beginning and middle sections got finished off but am disappointed that the other offerings are all so very serious! The librarian rashly declared his intention of typing up the finished works but fell at the first hurdle when confronted by the sheer illegibility of some of the scripts. Not to mention the spelling. I know what he means, on both counts. He was kind enough to say that he hadn't had to struggle with mine, which may surprise you. However he has typed up and circulated the reading group members' reviews of *The Beekeeper of Aleppo* and *Normal People*. You are probably aware of this much-praised racy novel from its BBC1 post-watershed serialisation. Understandably, it's been a 'must watch' in prison where smooth and youthful naked female flesh is rarely glimpsed except in the imagination.

At last I have found a fellow-sailor and we meet up (when allowed, which is not often just now) for earnest exchanges about the pros and cons of different rigs, hull configurations, anchor chain scopes and baggywrinkles. Actually not the last. I've never had a yacht with baggywrinkles except the baggy wrinkles on my ageing face. Colin, being some years younger than myself, plans to celebrate his release later this year (virus permitting) by circumnavigating the British Isles with his 28-year-old son. This is not something I will ever persuade my own 28-year-old son to contemplate, so I am quite envious of their bonding as well as the voyage. Colin (who proposes to change his name on release to Saltydog) has sailed in many desirable places, mostly abroad as paid crew aboard gentlemen's large and lavish yachts, but also more modestly in Holland and the Hebrides where his family lived on Mull and Harris at various times in the past, so our courses may once have almost converged when I lived on Skye.

But I fear my sailing days may be over. The current issue of *Yachting Monthly* is the last of the annual subscription you gave me. It has sustained me throughout the year and kept my dreams alive. Thank you! I have passed the back numbers on to the engaging and amiable Nigerian at the end of the corridor, a big meaty guy who's into body-building and is said to be a 'gangsta', though I'm not really familiar with the type. He has been picking my pickled brains for boating tips, though not about baggywrinkles. He plans to buy a yacht on leaving prison, the bigger the better. Money no object, he says. Now if he's looking for crew, there's a couple of people here who might just be interested... Dream on!

We had a very windy week-end here with great gusts swirling dust clouds across the fens, making the window frames rattle like old washboards and bringing down dead wood and leaves round the field. As you comment, the land is totally parched and I feel for the farmer who planted rows of cabbages in the huge field between the prison site and the Boston river. They have lost some of the topsoil that anchored them in place and are already wilting. Our NSC gardens are effectively out of bounds in accordance with Covid semi-lockdown restrictions, but from what I glimpse on the way to the dining hall the wallflowers are fading fast, the soil is dry as dust, and nothing (and nobody) is available for a re-planting scheme. A few of last year's hanging baskets round the windy walkway are blooming again, but someone has attacked the honeysuckle with shears just as it was about to flower. I'd gladly volunteer to do some much-needed weeding, and earn a few extra outdoor hours, but that would probably breach whatever guidelines we are currently in thrall to. Besides, I am probably not qualified for such tasks since the obligatory H&S course was terminated (in mysterious circumstances, as you will recall) and I didn't progress beyond the introductory 'metal guards on machines' stage. I wonder if hoes and hand rakes featured on the syllabus?

I regret to report that you are entirely mistaken to surmise that I am 'fairly svelte' by now. Anything but. For starters, I don't walk far enough, and this week our outdoor time has been cut back further to a measly 40 minutes per day. Nor do I have an exercise routine, unlike Len. When I first moved into this room I was quite perturbed by some of the sounds coming from the other end between about 7.30 and 8 every morning. Wheezing, stretching, sinews cracking, panting and heavy breathing (think *Normal People*) – Len seemed just too old for that sort of thing, and for several days I resisted the temptation to roll over and look. Eventually my curiosity got the better of me. This was Len doing his exercises in bed with the aid of 2-litre drinks bottles strapped together like pairs of dumbbells for weight lifting, up and down, his home made weights first at his side, then raised at an angle, then thrust in the air at full stretch, then his legs... No wonder his arms are so wiry and strong. When he threatened to throw somebody out of the window, he really meant it!

There's no competing with Len, and I have regained an unenviable prisoner's paunch. Now I am cutting back on the unforgiving stodge, donating at least some of our daily 'treats' to the needy, and pleading 'just <u>one</u> scoop please' as emphatically as I can to the man on chips duty at the servery. It's no good, though. I still can't button up my second best jeans.

I was pleased to read that your local VE Day commemoration went ahead, albeit masked and distanced, and would have loved to see Maggie in her Indian finery. I too have a rich silk kurta (from Fab India in Panaji) and wore it with an embroidered waistcoat for my brother's eightieth. I thought I stole the show until he referred to it as my 'fancy dress costume'. VE Day passed largely unnoticed here apart from a small display of photos in the dining hall put together by the librarian. In better times we would probably have had the full works with bunting, speeches and music, perhaps the North Sea Singers rendering patriotic songs. The only live music I heard was my own attempts to play old songs on the chapel instrument (thanks chaplain!). I hope any passers-by were not too shocked to hear strains of *There is a Tavern in the Town* and *Little Brown Jug* coming from the chapel.

Today is Eid el Fitr. Our Muslim brethren are celebrating, back with everyone else in the socially-distanced dining hall having put away their Ramadan food boxes for another year. That's something positive to report. I must say that I have not noticed much overt racism since I've been here, but then I'm not likely to be on the receiving end. So I was quite shocked when someone casually referred to my proto-yotty Nigerian friend as a 'jungle bunny'. I took him to task over that, but he seemed incapable of understanding why the term was offensive. Another training need identified. The term is not the least bit appropriate for someone so enviously lubricated with effortless charm that he is instantly at home in any company.

62. Sunday 7 June, 2020

North Sea Camp Protected Characteristic of the Month: **Age.**

Both your letters arrived ahead of schedule so I am following suit by starting this on Sunday. It has always been a languorous day in prison but is even more so with no choir practice or chapel, but still with the Sunday papers to digest though their delivery is forgivably erratic. What a change, though, from last Sunday when I spent almost the entire day in shorts and T-shirt. Today I'm swaddled in my warmest jersey and comforting dressing gown while Len has filled two big pop bottles with hot water to improvise a foot warmer (he suffers from cold extremities). I guess some HMPS directive bans all heating after the end of May, however bitter the weather, and now our north aspect room is as cold as a tomb. I'm not surprised your garden is stressed by such sudden and extreme changes. So am I!

As for the Covid crisis, we are now at 'Level 4 State of Alert' – that's official. I know this from the latest Residents' Newsletter put out by Ms Quirke, the Governing Governor (so what do the other governors do?) who aims to put out fortnightly updates in future. She's said this before. With ever-increasing degrees of verbal ingenuity she reports that there is almost nothing to report, but still manages to fill a whole page of prison-speak to communicate no hard information. Quite an achievement. But it's a step in the right direction for an organisation that is generally so reluctant or inept at communication.

Notice 1, outside unit office: 'URGENTLY WANTED – Deep cleaners. Pay £15 per week + £5 bonus. Must have cleaning qualifications.' That much is fact. What follows is imaginary and carries a health warning. Qualifications for the above job may include Level 1 basic sweeping, dusting, hoovering, mopping and bin emptying, plus Level 2 in disinfection, wiping and general arse-licking. Variety of positions for imaginative cleaners, all openings must be filled. (Apologies! I'm obviously suffering from over-exposure to prison humour.)

Notice 2, location ditto. 'Recently there has (sic) been incidents of excrement being wiped round the outside of toilet bowls. This practice is to STOP IMMEDIATELY. The situation is being monitored by wing staff.' This brought back memories of 'the phantom crapper' (as he became known) when I was at school. I pitied our scholarly priest-headmaster whose sensibilities were so obviously offended at having to address this issue at school assembly. The matter was eventually cleared up, in both senses, as doubtless it will be here, but it may explain the urgent tone of Notice 1.

Notice 3, ditto. This, with a hint of desperation, comes from Governor G who repeats the appeal for cleaners (above) and notes that cleaners are 'business critical' (prison-speak for 'essential', I presume). Unless volunteers are forthcoming, she will have to 'allocate residents with the appropriate qualifications to these positions.' Forced labour, eh?

The good news is that it is hoped to re-introduce social visits at some point, possibly before the end of the month (my underlinings). 'We will be working to a National Framework which mirrors the state of alert system the Government have introduced,' it rambles on. That would be reassuring if we were confident that our Great Leaders had actually got things under control. Now here's the rub. 'Social distancing' must be maintained during visits, so numbers will be very limited and people will not be allowed to touch. Ouch! I've told S not to bother trekking over here – I'll be home in a month and others' needs are greater. The genuinely good news is that there have still been no cases of the virus here at NSC, probably thanks to our isolated rural location. Conditions in some prisons are ghastly just now with prisoners locked in almost all day long – though even this has a silver lining: incidents of violence are much reduced (for lack of opportunity).

There is still no mention of *exeats* on ROTL here. For obvious reasons these remain suspended. I omitted to tell you that my ROTL Board finally took place back in March when I was, *in absentia,* granted the usual day release entitlement with effect from whenever visits resume. In practice, that means never in my case. Pity. I was looking forward to exploring Boston, despite restrictions on fancy dress and personal services at 'abodes' in the town. By the way, I had mentioned to the officer my idea of putting together a heritage guide for prisoners, but was rebuffed. He felt it would be 'inappropriate'. I wonder what he thought I had in mind?

However, the official countdown to my release has already started with a summons to attend ITTG. This (you'd never guess, and nor could I) stands for **I**ntegrated **T**hrough **T**he **G**ate and involves a range of assessments of preparedness for life after prison with support where needed. Len, needless to say, is very suspicious of all such initiatives. However, I went along as bidden to see a very agreeable chap in Education who asked me what 'resettlement needs' I had. I replied, somewhat bashfully, that I didn't think I had any. To which he said, 'Yes, I could tell that immediately from the way you entered the room', shook me warmly by the hand and wished me the best of luck. Re-reading the NSC induction booklet, the ITTG team really do go above and beyond in helping prisoners transition back to life outside. No chucking us out on the street to get kicked around like an empty can, and no Urban Survival Pack with free blanket, waterproof hat, nutritious biscuit and £5 supermarket voucher! Here they provide support with finding accommodation, contacting health services, benefits applications, employment and so forth. They seem serious about rehabilitation.

According to reports in the press, most prisoners are currently unable to access books because prison libraries (staffed by librarians from outside) have all closed as a Covid precaution. How fortunate we are here that our indefatigable librarian still comes in every day to process requests, though we don't meet him face to face. Not only that, but I can report that I was one of the three winners of his recent 'literary quiz', winning myself a little pile of new books – a mini-Keats, *The Dolly Llama* ('words of wisdom from a spiritual animal') and *How to think like Obama*. I thought it a rather handsome prize and the fourth award on my literary CV. The others, listed by both date and esteem, being a Children's Book of the Year award, a trophy for a *Yachting Monthly* cruising article and the Holocaust memorial prison prize. My literary career is not on an upward trajectory! My latest win was earned mainly, I suspect, by my answer to the question 'What is the hardest book to read? My answer was James Joyce *Ulysses*, or a thumbnail-size miniature Bible. Or, for a real killer, a thumbnail copy of *Ulysses*.

I enjoyed your anecdotes of Josh and Aaron picking strawberries, or rather, removing tendrils. My own love affair with the strawberry is once again unrequited. I must try chatting up one of the pickers here, unless The Emergency dictates leaving them to moulder in the ground. Last week there were just a couple of flaccid pluckers at work, but I think all the produce ended up in the officers' mess. The rotters! With any luck there will still be some locally-grown strawbs around next month. Sampling them will be sweet indeed after my enforced abstinence.

A disadvantage of our current early (8 am) exercise slot is the lack of any activity (apart from lunch) to break up the rest of the day. I envy you your opportunities for masked, disinfected and socially-distanced shopping expeditions, plus short drives and long walks. I try to eke out my lunch break by ambling very very slowly to the dining hall, sniffing on the way at the roses and pungent petunias in low-hanging baskets along the covered walkway. The alternative route, via the ponds and library, is now out of bounds for no discernible reason. The officers who supervise our movements (warm days only!) may begin to suspect from my apparent lethargy that I'm 'on something' – either that or suffering extreme withdrawal symptoms. I've always been a slow eater and am now perfecting the art of making my overloaded plate last as long as possible before heading languidly back to base. Roll on July!

A report from the 'i' newspaper, 4 June, lists five things that have most come to symbolise lockdown. These include 'Finding that being with the same person all day is mostly a pleasure.' Try telling that to prisoners forced to share cells! An unrelated article records a 14% rise during 2019 in incidents of self-harm in English prisons to 63,328. That's almost three times as high as in 2012.

63. Monday 22 June, 2020

I put off replying to your letters until this afternoon in the hope that John's would arrive, which it duly did just as we were tannoyed for our outdoor exercise slot (currently at a sensible afternoon time). So it was an added pleasure to be able to take it with me to read while sitting shirtless under my favourite tree. Also it was an excuse to opt out of my usual perambulations, putting the world to rights with my regular walking companion. I enjoy exercise, especially when performed by others! Today we were entertained by some of the lads playing football at the far end of the field while others sweated over circuit training directed by one of the PE instructors. There is something of a fitness culture amongst certain prisoners who practise with running on the spot, weight-lifting, cycle and rowing machines, striking old tractor tyres with sledgehammers (an exercise peculiar to NSC?) and so on, accompanied by thumping pop music from a portable boom box (which the rest of us could well do without). The gym here is closed because of the pandemic, so fitness has become an exclusively outdoor activity and thus a spectator sport for the unfit rest of us. By the way, you might assume that during these restrictive times everyone would go outside for the all-too-brief exercise periods. Not a bit of it. Even on the warmest of days barely half the lumpen proletariat of North Unit bother to heave themselves off their beds in pursuit of H & E. No wonder we have so many corpulent convicts!

I enjoyed your lockdown tales of socially-distanced outdoor coffee mornings, canal-side walks (with dragonflies – here they hover above the drainage dyke that marks our boundary with open farmland). I hope we'll all live long enough to reminisce about these restrictive times and remember the unexpected pleasures we found in small things – and big things too, like clear night skies, birdsong and the hush of traffic-free roads. You and your friends all seem to be following the government's often opaque instructions to the letter rather than copying the example of Johnson's side-kick Dominic Cummings. Mind you, just now I'd jump at the chance to test my eyesight with a drive up to beautiful Barnard Castle had I not recently had an eye test here (with peripatetic optician) and a new pair of free specs.

Lockdown regulations cannot be set in stone, especially within an organisation as diverse as the Prison Service. The Rev tells me that the obvious caution here re. lifting of restrictions comes from Head Office (MoJ). He believes that it is driven by fear of deaths and potential claims against HMPS if inadequate precautions or lack of shielding could be demonstrated by rapacious compensation lawyers. As previously mentioned, in enclosed prisons every cell is a designated household. But here the nature of the accommodation means I am in a household of <u>ninety</u> people, i.e. all North Unit residents. In theory we are banned from entering other people's rooms, but we cannot possibly maintain any sort of 'distance' (social or otherwise) in the corridors, washrooms and showers, or even the dining hall. Going over there for lunch feels like a little adventure, though not always in the culinary sense despite the best efforts of the kitchen workers whose wings have been clipped by cutbacks.

I have had a couple more solitary sessions in the chapel since my last letter and my musical sight-reading is improving. I have even attempted a couple of hymn tunes with four flats or sharps, two more than when I last wrote. I've also taken a break from playing the instrument to check through some of the messages written in the Book of Remembrance. They make sobering and poignant reading and really bring home the pain of separation from family and loved ones. Examples (with corrected spelling):

- 'RIP DAD. I will miss you like mad. U have gone to Heaven. RIP'
- 'Mum, six years have passed since I saw you last. You are never out of my thoughts. I love you more every day that you are gone. Thank you for your life. Thank you always for saving this young lad. X'
- 'RIP Dad. I'm sorry that I couldn't be there for you. I know you're not suffering now but me and the kids are going to be lost without you. We will meet again, but until then sleep tight. All my love X'
- 'In loving memory of my daughter… Loving you is easy, I say it every day. Missing you is heartache that never goes away. All my love, Daddy XXX'

My room mate has been on tenterhooks for almost four weeks waiting to hear the outcome of his parole hearing. (As an IPP prisoner he does not have an automatic release date.) Well finally the decision has come and after seventeen years in prison he is to be released, though it could be a couple of months yet before he actually walks out of the door. I came into the room on Friday to find him in high dudgeon and a picture of abject misery, so I assumed the worst. "Did you not get it?" I asked, as solicitously as I could. "Yes, I've got it," he said, "But I don't agree with the things they say about me!" It would be unfair to quote the example he read out, but they certainly have the measure of the man.

As previously described, every day at lunchtime we are presented with a 'grab bag' of little treats as a way of ameliorating the restrictions of the current regime. Instead of just throwing things at us (not literally) there is now a bin provided for us to place any items that we don't actually want (e.g. hand-cut but flavourless crisps, in my case). Also, instead of giving us two packs of cereal for the following day's breakfast, we are now invited to choose which one we want, if we do. These initiatives must represent such an obvious if small saving that it's hard to understand why it wasn't done this way from the start. The dustbins in the unit used to be swamped with surplus cereal packs. Even so, despite our 'extras' now coming net rather than gross, so to speak, their effect may be measured in the expanding waistlines of the already overweight or obese. I can no longer squeeze into two of my favourite shirts without popping the buttons, so I know what I'm talking about.

There are other beneficiaries of this HMPS profligacy that I have not mentioned before – foxes and badgers, pigeons and (especially) seagulls, plus the ever-present and obscenely bloated grey rats who inhabit the underworld of our pre-fab units and scratch around noisily beneath the floorboards. I have yet to catch sight of the foxes, but badger-watching has become an unlikely late-night pastime. The badgers come from their sett which is in a woody bank just behind the OMU offices where they won't be disturbed – it was never a hive of activity at the best of times and especially not now. Badgers are regular visitors, up to three of them coming over after about 10.30 p.m. to snuffle round the gravel just outside our windows looking for tit-bits and morsels such as bread buns and popcorn. Honey-coated peanut bars (a daily offering in our grab-bags) are especially popular with the badger family, though I can't imagine they are good for their digestion (or their teeth – which equally applies to prisoners). It's a rare privilege to see badgers so tame and so close up and, through our open windows, hear their little grunts of satisfaction as another sugary morsel slips down. Last week quite a crowd gathered to watch and I heard one young man (not a country lad) ask, "Are badgers mammals or reptiles?" I read recently that a new GCSE in Natural History is to be introduced. It's obviously long overdue.

This morning I was tannoyed to attend Healthcare for a pre-release check-up. The good news is that I am, on most counts, 'normal' (though not as in *Normal People*, for which I am now sadly much too old). This may surprise you. The blood pressure has stabilised, peak-flow is now average, and my lung function is spot on with a 'lung age' of 70 rather than 90 (!) as it was back in February before my hospital visit. Even my weight is borderline between healthy and overweight but well below clinically obese, so my determined efforts to resist second scoops of chips and more than one chocolate bar a day may be paying off. I expect to leave bearing something of a prisoner's paunch, but that is a family trait so I can't entirely blame it on HMPS. S is lining up lashings of strawberries and cream for my first home meal, so it's anyone's guess which way the waistline will go from then on.

I enjoyed your anecdotes on the paucity these days of public lavatories, one of the glories of UK holidays in the grand old days of Baedeker Guides, and also of 'she-wees'. Of course I'm only familiar with these from museum displays. I highly recommend the International Museum of Toilets in Delhi, well worth a bumpy rickshaw ride through the suburbs to find it. They have on display many examples of she-wees, from patterned porcelain receptacles for discreet use by Georgian gentlewomen on long coach journeys to modern wax-card disposables. There is nothing new under the sun, as the old adage says. As for public loo use, NSC does not come off well. Currently there is no liquid soap available for the dispensers (a victim of the pandemic, apparently) and paper hand-towels usually run out by mid-morning so the roaring blow-drier or a quick wipe on the trousers are the only drying options. I'm pleased to say the 'phantom crapper' has not struck again, though illustrations in indelible pen of naked ladies (and I don't mean those beautiful pink nerines that flower in winter) have started appearing on the backs of doors. They owe more to a fevered imagination than anatomical accuracy. Idle hands are indeed the devil's playground.

Good news – I have also secured a pre-release haircut, albeit a covert operation in a discreet corner and paid for in chocolate. The unofficial barber has made a splendidly neat and comfortable job of it so I can face the outside world with confidence, no longer looking like a shaggy cross between Albert Einstein and the Wild Man of the Woods.

Dulce Domum

64. Monday 6 July, 2020

Dear John and Maggie,

My thanks for your recent letters and for all the preceding weekly cards and letters too, a total of over 120 according to my tally. What a magnificent record that is and a monument to your love and lasting friendship. They have truly helped to entertain and sustain me, keeping my sights trained beyond the prison walls, a necessary corrective to what could become a very inward-looking existence. I'm not sure that others, such as my current pad-mate here, have fully understand my wish to maintain such a voluminous correspondence. Len doesn't envy it in the least – he has said so. We have compared notes. In seventeen years he has received only two personal letters. True, he has had rather more official and legal correspondence, but that is a matter of regret on his part as it has rarely borne good news. Life with Len has been an illuminating experience and I hope he will find happiness in his final years. I really wish him well. I shall bequeath him my can opener and bedside rug to remember me by.

Only three days to go! At prep school we used to sing
    "Three more days of pain,
    Three more days of sorrow,
    Three more days in this old dump
    And I'll be home tomorrow!"
Funny, I'd quite forgotten that little ditty but now find myself humming it again as I go round the unit with a frisky spring in my stride. Harry has been working in the south of France but flies back today just in time for a brief quarantine before driving up to Boston to collect me on Friday. He will then whisk me home for a celebratory late lunch (with Prosecco and strawberries). You can imagine my excitement – even more than as a small boy heading home for the hols – not least because I haven't seen either Sara or Harry in four months thanks to the pandemic.

I've no idea what the post-lockdown 'new normal' will look like when I get home, especially as I never got to know the 'old abnormal'. S tells me that the town is perking up with many shops now re-opened. Several 'Welcome Home' cards have already been hand-delivered to our house and I suspect I may be called upon for prison anecdotes for some time to come. If virtue is its own reward, this may also be true of notoriety.

Now I have a few busy days ahead. I must bag or box up all my possessions for Thursday morning to be checked in advance of Friday's release. I mustn't be caught nicking prison-issue clothing and thus will return my cellophane-wrapped long johns unopened. Conversely, I must not give away or dispose of any items of value (e.g. radio and headphones) listed on my 'prop card' without going through a convoluted official process to prove that I have not sold them or been bullied into parting with them. It's not worth the hassle. I have accumulated quite a library of 73 books (61 more than Mrs May would have allowed!) but can't physically take all home. I'll offer some of the hardbacks to the library and put out a few paperbacks on the windowsills for anyone to take. Harry is driving up to collect me and I shall walk out with £46 in cash – my bountiful release grant.

The collaborative story-writing venture, in the end, produced a very mixed bag. What everyone knows, but of course no one would ever say, is that the vastly different literacy levels, personal and educational experiences of the participants made the results very uneven. Most of the little 'hooks' that I worked into my sections for other writers to pick up on were either not understood or ignored, so that the story endings bore no relation whatever to the earlier sections. Never mind. It was a worthwhile experiment and I am indebted to our amazing librarian for his dedication and patience.

Let's finish on a positive note. You may remember that one of the lads I first shared a dormitory with here was 'Please-Don't-Speak-To-Me William' or Wilting Willie, as I we called him. Well last week he came to say a sort of good-bye. He is being moved out to the Jubilee Houses so he can learn to shop and cater for himself prior to release later in the year. Willie is a new man – full of smiles, laughing and joking, relaxed and self-confident. He is even getting more adventurous with food (benefiting from a spell working in the kitchens, perhaps) and now sometimes eats chicken-flavour noodles as an alternative to tomato. He is very obviously looking forward to the second half of his life after spending 20 of his first 42 years in prison. I have seen how prison can wreck lives, and often does far more harm than good not only to individuals, but to wider society too. But, whatever certain curmudgeons may think, there are some whose lives are turned round and given a fresh start by their time in prison. I doubt if our handwritten correspondence will continue post-release, but it will be strange to be able to write whatever I want, knowing it will not be checked by other eyes. Not that I would ever knowingly write anything false, slanderous or even risqué, but a certain restraint has been required, especially when describing the sometimes weird, Kafkaesque and inscrutable official workings of Her Majesty's Prison Service, not to mention the failings and foibles of its inmates and officials.

For the last time from prison, very best wishes as ever,

Tom

ABOUT THE AUTHOR

Tom Thoresby lives in Norfolk and has been happily married to journalist and writer Sara for thirty-five years. They have one grown-up son. Tom was born in Lincolnshire and educated at Catholic boarding schools before reading History at Cambridge. After a few years teaching, he worked in museum education and consultancy in East Anglia and briefly in East Africa. He has always enjoyed writing with over twenty children's history books published as well as museum and church guides and articles in the yachting press. In 2020 he won second prize in a prison writing competition judged by the Governor. Little did she know... Tom's principal passions include sailing, photography, church architecture and travel – none of which found much outlet in prison.

Printed in Great Britain
by Amazon

47565369R10155